ASOKA'S PILLAR AT LAURIYÂ-NANDANGARH

ASOKA

THE BUDDHIST EMPEROR OF INDIA

ASOKA

THE BUDDHIST EMPEROR OF INDIA

VINCENT ARTHUR SMITH

THIRD EDITION
REVISED AND ENLARGED

ISBN : 978-93-5324-525-2 (HB)

First Published, Oxford, 1920

Published, 2020

Published by

Facsimile Publisher
12 Pragati Market
Ashok Vihar, Ph-2
Delhi-110052
E-mail: books@facsimilepublisher.com

Printed at: G. Print Process, Delhi.

Asoka

The Buddhist Emperor of India

Author: Vincent Arthur Smith

ASOKA

THE BUDDHIST EMPEROR OF INDIA

BY

VINCENT A. SMITH, C.I.E.

M.A. (DUBL. ET OXON), HON. LITT D. (DUBLIN)
INDIAN CIVIL SERVICE RETIRED, M.R.A.S.
Author of *The Early History of India*, &c.

THIRD EDITION, REVISED AND ENLARGED

OXFORD
AT THE CLARENDON PRESS
M CM XX

PREFACE TO THIRD EDITION

During the ten years elapsed since the publication of the second edition of this book knowledge of the subject has made material advances. I have read everything printed that could be of use and am in a position to offer considerable improvements in the versions of the inscriptions, which are now fully understood, with small exceptions. Chapters IV and V have been rewritten, continuous comments on each document or group of documents being substituted for footnotes. The Maski Minor Rock Edict, the latest addition to the collection of edicts, which alone gives Asoka's name, is duly noticed, and the Gorathagiri labels on the Barâbar rocks have not been overlooked.

The corrections in Chapters I to III are mostly consequential on the revised interpretation of the inscriptions, but some are required by archaeological discoveries, while others merely set right sundry minor slips or errors, or effect necessary changes in references. I do not see any reason to change my scheme of chronology, although it may be open to slight revision at some future time. The Bibliographical Note has been enlarged. The alterations in Chapters VI and VII are few and unimportant.

The war has delayed the completion and publication of the long expected critical edition of the inscriptions by Professor E. Hultzsch. The loss arising from the delay has been neutralized to a large extent because the learned professor published his principal emendations in the *Journal of the Royal Asiatic Society* from time to time.

V. A. S.

November, 1919.

EXTRACT FROM PREFACE TO FIRST EDITION

A VOLUME on Asoka Maurya by Professor Rhys Davids was intended to be the first of the 'Rulers of India' series, but unfortunately circumstances prevented the fulfilment of that intention, and the series was closed leaving vacant the niche destined for the great Buddhist emperor. With the approval of Professor Rhys Davids I have undertaken the preparation of a supplementary volume giving in a popular form the substance of what is known concerning the Maurya empire. . . .

The chapter entitled 'The History of Asoka' will be found to differ widely from all other publications, such as Cunningham's *Bhilsa Topes*, which treat of that topic. I have tried to follow the example of the best modern historians, and to keep the legends separate from what seems to me to be authentic history. Among the legends I have placed the stories of the conversion of Ceylon and of the deliberations of the so-called Third Council. All the forms of those stories which have reached us are crowded with absurdities and contradictions from which legitimate criticism cannot extract trustworthy history.

In dealing with the vexed question of transliteration I have shunned the pedantic atrocities of international systems, which do not shrink from presenting Krishna in the guise of Kṛṣṇa, Champâ as *K*ampâ, and so on. The consonants in the Indian words and names in this book are to be pronounced as in English, and the vowels usually as in Italian. The short unaccented *a* has an indistinct sound as in the word 'woman.' Long vowels are marked when necessary; other diacritical marks have not been used in the text.

CONTENTS

ILLUSTRATIONS

If it be true, as seems probable, that the Parkham statue is a contemporary portrait of King Ajâtasatru, the patron of Buddha in the sixth century B.C., and that the Patna statues are similar portraits of his successors, Kings of Magadha in the fifth century B.C., our ideas concerning the evolution of Indian sculpture require reconstruction. See Jayaswal, Green, Arim Sen, M. M. Haraparshad Sastri, and others in *J. B. O. Res. Soc.*, vol. v., part iv, December, 1919.

V. A. S.

Feb. 1, 1920.

CHAPTER I

THE HISTORY OF ASOKA

WHEN Alexander, invincible before all enemies save death, passed away at Babylon in June, B. C. 323, and his generals assembled in council to divide the empire which no arm but his could control, they were compelled perforce to decide that the distant Indian provinces should remain in the hands of the officers and princes to whom they had been entrusted by the king. Two years later, when an amended partition was effected at Triparadeisos in Syria, Sibyrtios was confirmed as governor of Arachosia (Kandahâr) and Gedrosia (Makrân), the provinces of Aria (Herat) and Drangiana (Sistân) being assigned to Stasander the Cyprian, while Bactriana and Sogdiana to the north of the Hindû Kush were bestowed on Stasanor of Soli, another Cyprian. Oxyartes, father of Alexander's consort, Roxana, obtained the satrapy of the Paropanisadai, or Kâbul territory, the neighbouring Indian districts to the west of the Indus being placed in charge of Peithon, son of Agênor, whom Alexander had appointed ruler of Sind below the confluence of the rivers. Probably Peithon was not in a position to hold Sind after his master's death. Antipater, who arranged the partition, admitting that he possessed no force adequate to remove the Râjâs to the east of the Indus, was obliged to recognize Omphis or Âmbhi, king of Taxila, and Pôros, Alexander's honoured opponent, as lords of the Panjâb, subject to a merely nominal dependence on the Macedonian power[1]. Philippos, whom Alexander had made satrap of that province, was murdered by his mercenary troops early in B. C. 324, and Alexander, who heard the news in Karmania, was unable to do more than appoint an officer named Eudêmos to act as the colleague of King Âmbhi. Eudêmos managed to hold his ground for some time, but in or about B. C. 317 treacherously slew his Indian colleague, seized a hundred and twenty elephants, and with them and a considerable body of troops, marched off to help Eumenes in his struggle with Antipater[2]. The departure of Eudêmos marks the final collapse of the Macedonian attempt to establish a Greek empire in India.

But several years before that event a new Indian

[1] 'For it was impossible to remove (μετακινῆσαι) these kings without royal troops under the command of some distinguished general' (Diodorus Sic. xviii. 39).

[2] The partition of Triparadeisos is detailed in Diodorus Siculus, xviii. 39. His statement that the country along the Indus was assigned to Pôros, and that along the Hydaspes to Taxiles (*scil.* Âmbhi) cannot be correct, and the names of the kings seem to have been transposed.

The departure of Eudêmos is related, ibid. xix. 14. He is said to have seized the elephants after the death of Alexander, 'having treacherously slain Pôros the king.' But there is a various reading πρῶτον ('first') for Πῶρον ('Pôros').

power had arisen which could not brook the presence of foreign garrisons, and probably had destroyed most of them prior to the withdrawal of Eudêmos. The death of Alexander in June, B. C. 323, must have been known in India early in the autumn, and it is reasonable to suppose that risings of the natives occurred as soon as the season for campaigning opened in October, if not earlier. The leader of the movement for the liberation of his country which then began was a young man named Chandragupta Maurya, who seems to have been a scion of the Nanda dynasty of Magadha, or South Bihâr, then the premier state in the interior. With the help of an astute Brahman counsellor named Chânakya, who became his minister, Chandragupta dethroned and slew the Nanda king, exterminating his family. He then ascended the vacant throne at Pâtaliputra the capital, the modern Patna, and for twenty-four years ruled the realm with an iron hand. If Justin may be believed, the usurper turned into slavery the semblance of liberty which he had won for the Indians by his expulsion of the Macedonians, and oppressed the people with a cruel tyranny. Employing the fierce and more than half-foreign clans of the north-western frontier to execute his ambitious plans, he quickly extended his sway over the whole of Northern India, probably as far as the Narbadâ. Whether he first made himself master of Magadha and thence advanced northwards against the Macedonian garrisons, or first headed the risings in the Panjâb, and then with the forces collected there swooped down upon the Gangetic Kingdom, does not clearly appear [1]. There is, however, no doubt about the result of his action. Chandragupta became the first strictly historical emperor of India and ruled the land from sea to sea.

Seleukos, surnamed Nikator, or the Conqueror, by reason of his many victories, had established himself as Satrap of Babylon after the partition of Triparadeisos in B. C. 321, but six years later was driven out by his rival Antigonos and compelled to flee to Egypt. After three years' exile he recovered Babylon in B. C. 312, and devoted himself to the consolidation and extension of his power. He attacked and subjugated the Bactrians, and in B. C. 306 assumed the royal title. He is known to historians as King of Syria, although that province formed only a small part of his wide dominions, which included all western Asia.

About the same time (B. C. 305) he crossed the Indus, and directed his victorious arms against India in the hope of regaining the provinces which had been held

[1] 'Auctor libertatis Sandrocottus fuerat: sed titulum libertatis post victoriam in servitutem verterat. Siquidem occupato regno, populum, quem ab externa dominatione vindicaverat, ipse servitio premebat. Fuit hic quidem humili genere natus . . . contractis latronibus, Indos ad novitatem regni sollicitavit. Molienti deinde bellum adversus praefectos Alexandri . . . . Sic acquisito regno, Sandrocottus ea tempestate, qua Seleucus futurae magnitudinis fundamenta iaciebat, Indiam possidebat: cum quo facta pactione Seleucus.' The miracles are omitted from the quotation. The word *deinde* seems to indicate that the war with Alexander's officers followed the usurpation (Justin, xv. 4).

by his late master for a brief space, and of surpassing his achievement by subduing the central kingdoms. But the vast hosts of teeming India led by Chandragupta were more than a match for the power of the Macedonian, who was compelled to withdraw from the country and renounce his ambition to eclipse the glory of Alexander. No record of the conflict has survived, and we are ignorant of the place of battle and everything save the result. Terms of peace, including a matrimonial alliance between the two royal houses, were arranged, and the Indian monarch obtained from his opponent the cession of four satrapies, Aria, Arachosia, Gedrosia, and the Paropanisadai, giving in exchange the comparatively small recompense of five hundred elephants. This memorable treaty extended Chandragupta's frontier to the Hindû Kush mountains, and brought under his sway nearly the whole of the present Kingdom of Afghanistan, besides Balûchistan and Makrân [1].

A German writer has evolved from his inner consciousness a theory that Chandragupta recognized the suzerainty of Seleukos, but the plain facts are that the Syrian monarch failed and was obliged to surrender four valuable provinces for very inadequate consideration. Five hundred elephants at a high

[1] The current assertion that the Syrian King 'gave his daughter in marriage' to Chandragupta is not warranted by the evidence, which testifies merely to a 'matrimonial alliance' (κῆδος, ἐπιγαμία). The authorities for the extent of the cession of territory by Seleukos are textually quoted and discussed in *Early History of India*, 3rd ed., App. F.

valuation would not be worth more than about two millions of rupees, say £200,000 sterling. Seleukos never attempted to assert any superiority over his successful Indian rival, but, on the contrary, having failed in attack, made friends with the power which had proved to be too strong for him, and treated Chandragupta as an equal.

In pursuance of this policy, soon after his defeat, in or about B. C. 305, Seleukos dispatched Megasthenes, an officer of Sibyrtios, the satrap of Arachosia, as his ambassador to the court of Chandragupta at Pâtaliputra on the Sôn, near the confluence of that river with the Ganges, which in those days was situated below the city. The modern city of Patna, the civil station of Bankipore, and adjoining villages have been proved by partial excavations to occupy the site of the ancient capital, the remains of which now lie buried at a depth of from ten to twenty feet below the existing surface. Megasthenes resided there for a considerable time, and fortunately for posterity, took the trouble to record carefully what he saw and heard. The ambassador found the government of the Indian king strong and well organized, established in a magnificent fortified city, worthy to be the capital of a great kingdom. The royal camp at the capital was estimated to contain 400,000 souls, and an efficient standing army numbering 600,000 infantry, 30,000 cavalry, 9,000 elephants, and a multitude of chariots, was maintained at the king's expense. On active service the army is said to have mustered the huge total of 600,000 men of all arms, a number not incredible in the light of our knowledge of the unwieldy size of the hosts employed by Indian princes in later ages. With this overwhelming and well-equipped force Chandragupta, as Plutarch tells us, 'overran and subdued the whole of India,' that is to say, at least all the country to the north of the Narbadâ. His empire, therefore, extended from that river to the Himalaya and Hindû Kush[1].

[1] The chief authority for the history of Chandragupta is Megasthenes. His work has been lost, but the pith of it is preserved in extracts or allusions by Arrian, *Anabasis*, Bk. v. ch. 6; *Indika*, various passages; Q. Curtius, Bk. viii. ch. 9; Plutarch, *Life of Alexander*, ch. 62; Justin, Bk. xv. ch. 4; Appian, *Syriakê*, ch. 55; Strabo, i. 53, 57; ii. 1. 9; xv. i. 36; Athenaios, *Deipnosophists*, ch. 18 *d*; and Pliny, *Hist. Nat.* vi. 19, &c. The testimony of Megasthenes concerning all matters which came under his personal observation is trustworthy, and Arrian rightly described him as 'a worthy man' (δόκιμος). Strabo and some other ancient writers censure him unjustly on account of the 'travellers' tales' which he repeated. The passages above cited and most of the other references in Greek and Roman authors to India have been carefully translated in Mr. McCrindle's works (*Ancient India as described by Megasthenes and Arrian*, Trübner, 1877; *Invasion of India by Alexander the Great*, 2nd ed., 1896; and *Ancient India as described in Classical Literature*, 1901). Interesting traditional details are given in the *Mudrâ-Râkshasa* drama, which is now believed by some scholars to date from the fifth or sixth century A.D. But Mr. Keith places it in either the seventh or the ninth century (*J. R. A. S.*, 1909, p. 149). The *Arthaśâstra* of Kautilya or Chânakya, discovered in 1904, and completely translated in 1915 by R. Shamasastry (Bangalore Government Press) is the best commentary on the Asoka inscriptions and on his institutions. The Purâṇas and the chronicles of Ceylon also give

After twenty-four years of stern and vigorous rule, Chandragupta died or abdicated, and transmitted the empire which he had won to his son Bindusâra Amitraghâta, who reigned for twenty-five or, according to other authorities, twenty-eight years[1]. The only recorded public event of his reign, which may be assumed to have begun in either B.C. 298 or 301, according to the chronology adopted, is the dispatch to his court by the King of Syria of an ambassador named Deïmachos. The information is of interest as proving that the official intercourse with the Hellenic world begun by Chandragupta was continued by his successor. In the year B.C. 280 Seleukos Nikator, then in the seventy-eighth year of his age, was murdered, and was succeeded on the Syrian throne by his son Antiochos Soter.

Greek writers have preserved curious anecdotes of private friendly correspondence between Seleukos and Chandragupta and between Antiochos and Bindusâra, of value only as indications that the Indian monarchs

valuable information, and a few particulars are obtainable from other sources. Solinus (McCrindle, *Megasthenes*, p. 156) gives the infantry force as 60,000 only, and the elephants as 8,000.

[1] The name Bindusâra is attested by the Hindu *Vishṇu Purâṇa*, the Buddhist *Mahâvaṁśa* and *Dîpavaṁśa*, and the Jain *Pariśishṭaparvan*. The variants in other *Purâṇas* seem to be mere clerical errors. The name or title Amitraghâta ('slayer of foes') is a restoration in Sanskrit of the Amitrochades or Amitrochates of Greek writers, who is stated to have been the son of Chandragupta (Sandrakoptos, &c.). Târanâth indicates that Bindusâra extended the empire towards the south. See S. K. Aiyangar, *The Beginnings of Indian History*, chap. ii. (Madras, 1918.)

communicated with their European allies on terms of perfect equality. The mission of Dionysios, who was sent to India, and no doubt to the Maurya court, by Ptolemy Philadelphos, King of Egypt (B. C. 285–247), must have arrived in the reign of either Bindusâra or his son Asoka. Patrokles, an officer who served under both Seleukos and his son, sailed in the Indian seas and collected much geographical information which Strabo and Pliny were glad to utilize.

About seven years after the death of Seleukos, Asoka-vardhana, commonly called Asoka, a son of Bindusâra, and the third sovereign of the Maurya dynasty, ascended the throne of Pâtaliputra (B. C. 273), and undertook the government of the Indian empire, which he held for about forty years. According to the silly fictions which disfigure the Ceylonese chronicles and disguise their solid merits, Asoka waded to the throne through a sea of blood, securing his position by the massacre of ninety-nine brothers, one brother only, the youngest, being saved alive. These fictions, an extract from which will be found in a later chapter, do not deserve serious criticism, and are sufficiently refuted by the testimony of the inscriptions which proves that the brothers and sisters of the king were still living in the middle of the reign, and that they and all the members of the royal family were the objects of the sovereign's anxious solicitude[1].

[1] Asoka's 'brothers and sisters' are mentioned specifically in Rock Edict V. See also Rock Edicts IV and VI, Pillar Edict VII, and the Queen's Edict.

The tradition that Asoka, previous to his accession, served his apprenticeship to the art of government as Viceroy first of Taxila, and afterwards of Ujjain, may be accepted, for we know that both viceroyalties were held by princes of the royal family.

It seems to be true that the solemn consecration, or coronation, of Asoka was delayed for about four years after his accession in B. C. 273, and it is possible that the long delay may have been due to a disputed succession involving much bloodshed, but there is no independent evidence of such a struggle. The empire won by Chandragupta had passed intact to his son Bindusâra, and when, after the lapse of a quarter of a century, the sceptre was again transmitted from the hands of Bindusâra to those of his son Asoka, it seems unlikely that a prolonged struggle was needed to ensure the succession to a throne so well established and a dominion so firmly consolidated. The authentic records give no hint that Asoka's tranquillity was disturbed by internal commotion but on the contrary exhibit him as fully master in his empire, giving orders for execution in the most distant provinces with perfect confidence that they would be obeyed.

The numerous inscriptions recorded by Asoka are the leading authority for the events of his reign. All the inscriptions, except the latest discovered, that at Maski in the Nizam's Dominions, are anonymous, describing their author by titles only. The Maski record, beginning with *Devânaṁpiyasa Asokasa*, supersedes much argument concerning the identity of

Devânaṁpiya and Piyadasi with Asoka. The titles Devânaṁpiya and Piyadasi are frequently combined, although also used separately. The name of Asoka next occurs in Rudradâman's inscription, c. A. D. 152. A few other inscriptions and traditions preserved in various literary forms help to fill up the outline derived from the primary authority, and by utilizing the available materials of all kinds, we are in a position to compile a tolerably full account of the reign, considering the remoteness of the period discussed, and the well-known deficiency of Hindu literature in purely historical works. The interest of the story is mainly psychological and religious, that is to say, as we read it we watch the development of a commanding personality and the effect of its action in transforming a local Indian sect into one of the leading religions of the world. That interest is permanent, and no student of the history of religion can ignore Asoka, who stands beside St. Paul, Constantine, and the Khalîf Omar in the small group of men who have raised to dominant positions religions founded by others.

The dates which follow may be open to slight correction, for various reasons which we need not stop to examine, but the error in any case cannot exceed three years, and the chronology of the reign may be regarded as practically settled in its main outlines. Bearing in mind this liability to immaterial error, we may affirm that Asoka succeeded his father in 273, and four years later, in B. C. 269, was solemnly consecrated to the sacred office of Kingship by the rite of aspersion (*abhisheka*), equivalent to the coronation of European monarchs[1]. Like his fathers before him, Asoka assumed the title of *devânam piya*, which literally means 'dear to the gods,' but is better treated as a formal title, suitably rendered by the phrase current in Stuart times, 'His Sacred Majesty.' He also liked to describe himself as *piyadasi*, literally 'of gracious mien,' another formal royal title, which may be rendered as 'His Grace' or 'His Gracious Majesty.' Asoka's grandfather, Chandragupta, assumed the closely related style of *piyadasana*, 'dear to the sight,' which one of the Ceylonese chronicles applies to Asoka. Thus, when the above two titles were combined with the word *rājā*, or 'king,' Asoka's full royal style was 'His Sacred and Gracious Majesty the King.' The complete formula is often used in the inscriptions, but in many cases it is abbreviated[2].

Nothing authentic is on record concerning the early

[1] Dr. Fleet prefers the term 'anointing,' and states that the liquid poured over the king included 'ghee' or clarified butter (*J. R. A. S.*, 1909, p. 30 note).

[2] The reasons for rendering the royal style as in the text are explained in 'The Meaning of Piyadasi' (*Ind. Ant.*, xxxii (1903), p. 265). Chandragupta is called *piadaṁsana* in the *Mudrâ-Râkshasa* (Act vi), which used to be dated in the eighth century, but is now ascribed by some scholars to the Gupta period, in the fifth or sixth century (Hillebrandt, *Über das Kauṭilîyaśāstra*, Breslau, 1908, pp. 26, 30); *contra*, Keith, in *J. R. A. S.*, 1909, p. 149. I do not deny that the chroniclers of Ceylon used Piyadasi and Piyadassana as quasi proper names, but I affirm that in the inscriptions the titles are not so used.

years of the reign of His Sacred and Gracious Majesty King Asoka. The monkish chroniclers of India and Ceylon, eager to enhance the glory of Buddhism, represent the young king as having been a monster of cruelty before his conversion, and then known as Asoka the Wicked, in contradistinction to Asoka the Pious, his designation after conversion. But such tales, specimens of which will be found in Chapters VI and VII, are of no historical value, and should be treated simply as edifying romances. Tradition probably is right in stating that Asoka followed the religion of the Brahmans in his early days, with a special devotion to Siva, and we may assume that he led the life of an ordinary Hindu Râjâ of his time. We know, because he has told us so himself, that he then had no objection to sharing in the pleasures of the chase, or in the free use of animal food, while he permitted his subjects at the capital to indulge in merry-makings accompanied by feasting, wine, and song[1]. Whether or not he waged any wars in those years we do not know. There is no reason to suppose that his dominions were less than those of his grandfather and father, and equally little reason for supposing that he made additions to them. In his inscriptions he counts his 'regnal years' from the date of his consecration, which may be taken as B.C. 269[2], and

[1] Rock Edicts I, VIII.

[2] The earliest dated inscriptions are of the thirteenth, and the latest (Pillar Edict VII) of the twenty-eighth 'regnal year,' corresponding respectively with B.C. 257 and 242. The Minor

he always observed the anniversary of the ceremony by a jail delivery of prisoners condemned to death.

The earliest recorded events belong to the ninth 'regnal year,' B.C. 261, the thirteenth from the accession of Asoka. In that year he sought to round off his dominions by the conquest of the Kingdom of the Three Kalingas, or Kalinga, on the coast of the Bay of Bengal between the Mahânadî and Godâvarî rivers. His arms were successful and the kingdom was annexed to the empire. But the horrors which must accompany war, even successful war, made a deep impression on the heart of the victorious monarch, who has recorded on the rocks in imperishable words the sufferings of the vanquished and the remorse of the victor. The record is instinct with personal feeling, and still carries across the ages the moan of a human soul. The words clearly are those of the king himself, for no Secretary of State would dare to express in such a language 'the profound sorrow and regret' felt by His Sacred Majesty. The rocks tell the tale as follows:—

'The Kalingas were conquered by His Sacred and Gracious Majesty the King when he had been consecrated eight years. One hundred and fifty thousand persons were thence carried away captive, one hundred thousand were there slain, and many times that number died.

Directly after the Kalingas had been annexed began His Sacred Majesty's zealous protection of the Law of Piety; his

Pillar Edicts, which are not dated, appear to be certainly later than 242. The Queen's Edict is the latest of all.

love of that Law, and his inculcation of that Law. Thence arises the remorse of His Sacred Majesty for having conquered the Kalingas, because the conquest of a country previously unconquered involves the slaughter, death, and carrying away captive of the people. That is a matter of profound sorrow and regret to His Sacred Majesty. . . . So that of all the people who were then slain, done to death, or carried away captive in Kalinga, if the hundredth part or the thousandth part were now to suffer the same fate, it would be matter of regret to His Sacred Majesty.'

The royal preacher proceeds to prove in detail the horrors of war, and to draw the lesson that the true conquest is that of piety [1].

After the triumphant conclusion of the war and the annexation of the kingdom Asoka issued two long special edicts prescribing the principles on which both the settled inhabitants and the wild jungle tribes of the conquered provinces should be treated. These two edicts, in substitution for three documents published in other localities, were issued in Kalinga only, where they are preserved at two sites, now called Jaugada and Dhauli [2]. The conquered territory, no doubt, formed a separate unit of administration, and seems to have been constituted a viceroyalty under a Prince of the royal family stationed at Tosali, a town situated in the Purî District of Orissa, and apparently identical with Dhauli [3]. There is no

[1] Rock Edict XIII.

[2] The Kalinga Edicts, formerly called Detached, replacing Nos. XI–XIII of the series published elsewhere.

[3] Dhauli version of the Borderers' Edict.

reason to believe that after the subjugation of the Kalingas Asoka ever again waged an aggressive war. His officers, the Wardens of the Marches mentioned in the edicts, may or may not have been compelled at times to defend portions of his extended frontiers against the incursions of enemies, but all that we know of his life indicates that once he had begun to devote himself to the love, protection, and teaching of the Law of Piety, or *dharma*, he never again allowed himself to be tempted by ambition into an unprovoked war. It is possible that the Kalinga conflict may not have been his first, but certainly it was his last war undertaken voluntarily.

The full meaning of the statement that the king's love for and protection of the Law of Piety and his teaching of that Law began directly after the annexation of Kalinga is brought out by comparison with another document (Minor Rock Edict I) published a few months earlier than the edict describing the annexation. In the earlier document, three copies of which are addressed to officers in the South through the Prince at Suvarnagiri, who apparently was the Southern Viceroy, and four to other officials, Asoka explains that for more than two years and a half he had been a lay disciple, without exerting himself strenuously, but that for more than a year prior to the publication of the edict he had become a member of the Buddhist Order of monks (*saṁgha*) and had devoted himself with the utmost energy to the winning of immense heavenly bliss for his people by his teaching. The total period referred to is consequently somewhere about four years. The conquest of the Kalingas took place in the ninth 'regnal year' (B.C. 261), while the Rock Edict describing that operation was issued four years later in the thirteenth 'regnal year' (B.C. 257). When that edict, which expressly ascribes Asoka's conversion to his remorse for the sufferings caused by the war in the ninth 'regnal year,' is read together with the Minor Rock Edict which traces his progress in virtue for four years, from the condition of a comparatively careless lay disciple to that of a zealous monk, it seems to be a necessary inference that Asoka became a lay disciple under the Buddhist system in his ninth 'regnal year,' immediately after the conquest of Kalinga, that he began to be zealous about two and a half years later, when he had been consecrated for about eleven years, and that he attained to a high standard of zeal more than a year subsequently when he began to issue his religious edicts in his thirteenth 'regnal year,' B.C. 257. He expressly informs us that his earliest inscriptions date from that year[1]. The Minor Rock Edict I, of which seven copies are known, appears to be the first fruits of the epigraphic zeal of the convert, who longed to make everybody as energetic as himself, and resolved that the imperishable record of his 'purpose must be written on the rocks, both afar off and here, and on a stone pillar, wherever a stone pillar exists.' These orders were largely executed and resulted in the

[1] Pillar Edict VI.

considerable number of rock and pillar inscriptions now extant and known. Many more probably remain to be discovered, and at least two inscribed pillars are known to have been deliberately destroyed[1]. The period consisting of more than a year, say fifteen or sixteen months of strenuous exertion, must have been spent in preparations for his propaganda work, both in his own territories and in foreign countries, but no details are on record.

Asoka's conversion to Buddhism, therefore, may be dated in B.C. 261–260. It is impossible to be more precise because we do not know the exact value of the expressions 'more than two years and a half' and 'more than a year.' The transition from the easy-going attitude of the lay disciple to the fervent zeal of the monk was effected when His Majesty, in his eleventh 'regnal year' (B.C. 259) entered the Order, abolished the Royal Hunt, and substituted pious tours, enlivened only by sermons and religious discussions, for the tours of pleasure which he had enjoyed in his unregenerate days[2].

[1] Namely, Lâṭ Bhairo at Benares, smashed during a riot in 1809, and one at Pâṭaliputra, numerous fragments of which were found by the late Bâbû Purna Chandra Mukharjî, as described in an unpublished report. See the author's paper identifying Lâṭ Bhairo with a pillar described by Hiuen Tsang published in *Z. D. M. G.*, 1909, pp. 337–49.

[2] This argument was lucidly stated by M. Senart in 1886 (*Les Inscriptions de Piyadasi*, tome II, pp. 222–45). When the first edition of this book was published I was misled by interpretations of Minor Rock Edict I now proved to be erroneous.

Before proceeding farther in tracing the story of Asoka's religious development, which is the history of his life and reign, it will be convenient to pause and explain the nature of the *dharma*, or Law of Piety, which he loved, protected, and promulgated with all the energy of his temperament and all his power as a mighty sovereign. We must also consider how he managed to reconcile the apparently inconsistent positions of monk and monarch.

Dharma, or *Dhaṁma*, means to a Hindu the rule of life for each man as determined by his caste and station, or, in other words, the whole duty, religious, moral, and social, of a man born to occupy a certain position in the world. For many ages past this conception of *dharma* has been inseparably associated with the notions of caste. Each caste has its own *dharma*, and conduct most proper for the member of one caste is reprehensible in the highest degree for a member of another. In Asoka's time caste, although in some respects less rigid than it has been since the shock of the Muhammadan invasions, which did so much to solidify the institution, was well developed, and the now current Hindu notion of *dharma* does not seem to diverge widely from that then entertained by the followers of the Brahmanical law. The *dhaṁma* of the Edicts is that Hindu *dharma* with a difference, due to a Buddhist tinge, nay, rather due

The position adopted in this edition, which has the support of Mr. F. W. Thomas as well as of M. Senart, was opposed by Fleet, whose latest article appeared in *J. R. A. S.*, 1913, p. 655.

to saturation with the ethical thought which lies at the basis of Buddhism, but occupies a subordinate place in Hinduism. The association of the idea of duty with caste is dropped by Asoka, and two virtues, namely, respect for the sanctity of animal life and reverence to parents, superiors, and elders, are given a place far more prominent than that assigned to them in Hindu teaching. In short, the ethics of the Edicts are Buddhist rather than Brahmanical. This proposition, of course, does not involve contradiction of the equally true statement that Buddhism is a development of Hinduism. The marked prominence given to the two specially Buddhist virtues above mentioned suggests so strongly the connotation of the Latin word *pietas* that the phrase 'the Law of Piety,' or sometimes simply 'piety,' or 'the Law' seems to me the best ordinary rendering of *dhaṁma* in the Edicts, and preferable to 'righteousness,' 'religion,' 'the moral law,' or other renderings favoured by various authors [1]. 'The Law of Duty' is an alternative.

Many summaries of the *dhaṁma*, or Law of Piety, are to be found in the Edicts, the most concise being that in Minor Rock Edict II:— [2]

'Thus saith His Sacred Majesty:—Father and mother must be hearkened to; similarly, respect for living creatures

[1] In the Bhâbrû Edict the Good Law (*sadhaṁme*) means the collective sayings of Buddha, the recorded expression of the Law of Piety in its highest form.

[2] Other summaries are given in Rock Edicts III, IV, IX, XI, and Pillar Edict VII, sec. 7.

must be firmly established; truth must be spoken. These are the virtues of the Law of Piety which must be practised. Similarly, the teacher must be reverenced by the pupil, and towards relations proper courtesy should be shown.

This is the ancient nature of piety—this leads to length of days, and according to this men should act.'

No part of the royal teaching is inconsistent with that pithy abstract, but other documents lay stress on the duties of almsgiving, toleration of all denominations, abstention from evil-speaking, and sundry other virtues. One of them defines the Law of Piety as comprising the duties of 'compassion, almsgiving, truth, purity, gentleness, and saintliness [1].' Excellent moral doctrine of such a kind is inculcated over and over again, and men are invited to win both the royal favour and heavenly bliss by acting up to the precepts of the Law.

No student of the edicts can fail to be struck by the purely human and severely practical character of the teaching. The object avowedly aimed at, as in modern Burma, is the happiness of living creatures, man and beast [2]. The teacher assumes that filial piety and the other virtues commended open the path to happiness here and hereafter, but no attempt is made to prove any proposition by reasoning, nor is any value attached to merely intellectual cognition.

[1] Pillar Edict VII.

[2] 'His religion says to him [the Burmese], "the aim of every man should be happiness," and happiness only to be found by renouncing the whole world' (Fielding Hall, *The Soul of a People*, p. 113).

No foundation of either theology or metaphysics is laid, the ethical precepts inculcated being ordinarily set forth as rules required for practical guidance and self-evidently true. One edict only, that of Bhâbrû, probably early in date, expressly alleges the authority of the Venerable Buddha as the basis of the king's moral doctrine, and that authority undoubtedly is the one foundation of Asoka's ethical system [1]. The king was an earnest student of the Buddhist sacred books, several of which he cites by name, and the edicts throughout are full of words and turns of phrase characteristic of, even if not peculiar to Buddhist literature [2]. So long as he felt assured that his teaching was in accordance with that of his Master he needed not to allege any other justification.

The authority expressly cited in the Bhâbrâ Edict is understood throughout the whole series, and the only non-Buddhist inscriptions of Asoka are the Barâbar cave dedications in favour of the Âjîvika ascetics, who were more akin to the Jains than to the Buddhists.

[1] Having adopted the opinion of M. Senart and Mr. F. W. Thomas that Minor Rock Edict I is the earliest of the series, I am inclined to assign the Bhâbrû Edict to the same time. That Edict and a version of Minor Rock Edict I were recorded close together near Bairât in Râjputâna.

[2] All the seven passages cited in the Bhâbrû Edict have been identified in the *Nikâya* portion of the Canon. The quoted sayings, 'The Good Law will long endure' (Bhâbrû Edict), and 'All men are my children' (Borderers' Edict), also are canonical. M. Senart has noted many specially Buddhist words and phrases throughout the inscriptions.

The blessings offered by the Law of Piety, that is to say, the ethical teaching of Buddha, are not to be won by indolent acquiescence in a dogma or formal acceptance of a creed. Asoka's favourite maxim, apparently composed by himself, was the text 'Let small and great exert themselves[1].' He never tires of urging the necessity of exertion and effort, explaining that he himself had set a good example of hard work.

'Whatever exertions,' he observes, 'His Sacred and Gracious Majesty the King makes, all are for the sake of the life hereafter, so that every one may be freed from peril, which peril is vice. Difficult, however, it is to attain such freedom, whether by people of low or of high degree, save by the utmost exertion and giving up all other aims. That, however, for him of high degree is difficult[2].' But 'even by the small man who chooses to exert himself, immense heavenly bliss may be won[3].'

This doctrine of the need for continual self-sustained exertion in order to attain the highest moral level is fully in accordance with numerous passages in the *Dhammapada* and other early Buddhist scriptures. The saying about the difficulties of the man of high degree, recalls, as do many other Buddhist aphorisms, familiar Biblical texts, but the spirit of the Bible is totally different from that of Asoka's teaching. The Bible, whether in the Old Testament or the New, insists upon the relation of man with God, and upon

[1] Minor Rock Edict I.

[2] Rock Edict X.

[3] Minor Rock Edict I (Brahmagiri text).

man's dependence on the grace of God. Asoka, on the contrary, in accordance with the practice of his Master, ignores, without denying, the existence of a Supreme Deity, and insists that man should by his own exertions free himself from vice, and by his own virtue win happiness here and hereafter. As it is said in the *Dhammapada*:

By ourselves is evil done,
By ourselves we pain endure,
By ourselves we cease from wrong,
By ourselves become we pure.

No one saves us but ourselves,
No one can and no one may,
We ourselves must tread the Path:
Buddhas only show the way.

The same self-reliant doctrine is taught at this day in Burma, where 'each man is responsible for himself, each man is the maker of himself. Only he can do himself good by good thoughts, by good acts; only he can hurt himself by evil intentions and deeds[1].' The Buddhist attitude is akin to the Stoic, Zoroastrian, and Jain, but directly opposed to the Christian.

So much exposition may suffice to enable the reader to understand the general nature of the Buddhist *dhamma*, or Law of Piety, as taught by Asoka. Special topics of the doctrine will be discussed later, as occasion arises.

[1] Fielding Hall, *The Soul of a People*, p. 226. Contrast the teaching of the Church Catechism:—'My good Child, know this, that thou art not able to do these things of thyself, nor to

The fact is undoubted that Asoka was both monk and monarch at the same time. The belief held by some learned writers that he had abdicated before he assumed the monastic robe is untenable, being opposed to the plain testimony of the edicts. We have seen that the earliest of them, unquestionably issued by Asoka as sovereign, expressly states that at the time of issue (B.C. 257) he had been for more than a year exerting himself strenuously as a member of the Buddhist *Saṁgha*, or Order of Monks, the organized monastic Church, of which the sovereign had assumed the headship. Throughout his reign he retained the position of Head of the Church and Defender of the Faith. His latest proclamations, the Minor Pillar Edicts, issued at some time during the last ten years of the reign, exhibit him as actively engaged in protecting the Church against the dangers of schism and issuing his orders for the disciplinary punishment of schismatics. In the Bhâbrû Edict, seemingly of early date, we find him describing himself as 'King of Magadha,' and using his royal authority in order to recommend to his subjects seven favourite passages selected by himself from the sacred books [1]. That edict was recorded on a boulder within the precincts of a monastery on the top of a hill in Râjputâna, and the presumption is that the sovereign was residing in

walk in the Commandments of God, and to serve him, without his special grace.'

[1] The correct reading is *Mâgadhe*, agreeing with *lâjâ*, and not *Mâgadhaṁ*, agreeing with *Saṁghaṁ* (Bloch).

the monastery when he issued the orders, which are on record there only. A copy of the Minor Rock Edict I in which he gives a summary of his early religious history is engraved on a rock at the foot of another hill close by. The inscriptions give no support to the late legends which represent the great emperor as a dotard in his old age, and suggest that he abdicated his sovereign functions. His authentic records show him to have been the same man throughout his career from 257 to the end, a zealous Buddhist, and at the same time a watchful, vigorous, autocratic ruler of Church and State.

How did he manage to reconcile the vows and practices of a Buddhist monk with the duties and responsibilities of the sovereign of an enormous empire? It is not possible to give a complete answer, but fairly satisfactory explanations can be presented. The pilgrim I-tsing in the seventh century notes that the statue of Asoka represented him as wearing a monk's robe of a particular pattern[1]. He does not seem to have been offended by any incongruity in the situation, and his attitude may be explained by the fact that he knew a Chinese Emperor to have done the same thing. It is recorded that Kao-tsu Wu-ti (alias Hsiao-Yen), the first emperor of the Liang dynasty, who reigned from A. D. 502 to 549, was 'a devout Buddhist, living upon priestly fare and taking only one meal a day; and on two occasions, in

[1] Takakusu, translation of I-tsing, *A Record of Buddhist Practices*, p. 73.

527 and 529, he actually adopted the priestly garb[1].' Du Halde relates of this emperor that—

'He was not without eminent qualities, being active, laborious, and vigilant; he managed all his affairs himself, and dispatched them with wonderful readiness; he was skilled in almost all the sciences, particularly the military art, and was so severe upon himself, and so thrifty, as 'tis said, that the same cap served him three years; his fondness at last for the whimsical conceits of the bonzes carried him so far as to neglect intirely the concerns of the State, and to become in effect a bonze himself; he put out an edict forbidding to kill oxen or sheep even for the sacrifices, and appointed ground corn to be offered instead of beasts[2].'

A large part of Du Halde's description applies accurately to Asoka, but I see no reason to believe that the Indian monarch resembled his Chinese imitator in entirely neglecting affairs of State during his later years.

However exact or inexact the parallel may be in detail, it holds good for the main fact that both Asoka and Wu-ti succeeded somehow in combining the duties of monk and monarch.

A slightly less exact parallel to Asoka's action is offered by the case of the Jain Kumârapâla, King of Gujarât in the twelfth century, who assumed the title of 'Lord of the Order,' and at various periods of his reign took vows of continence, temperance, abstention from animal food, and refraining from confiscation of

[1] Giles, *Chinese Literature* (1901), p. 133.

[2] Du Halde, *History of China*, Engl. transl., 3rd. ed. (London, 1741), vol. i, p. 381.

the property of the faithful. Indeed, the whole story of Kumârapâla's proceedings after his conversion to Jainism offers the best possible commentary on the history of Asoka [1].

The legend of Vîtâsoka, the hermit brother of Asoka according to one form of the story, who was permitted to beg his alms within the palace precincts, is good evidence to show that people were accustomed to arrangements making asceticism easy for princes [2].

We must further remember that the Buddhist ceremony (*upasampadâ*) of full admission to the Order, commonly, but inaccurately, called 'ordination,' does not convey indelible 'orders' or involve a lifelong vow. In both Burma and Ceylon men commonly enter the Order temporarily, and after a time, long or short, resume civil life. Asoka could have done the same, as Wu-ti afterwards did in China, and a proceeding easy for an ordinary man is doubly easy for an emperor. In short, although we do not know the details of the arrangements by which Asoka reconciled his monastic obligations with his duties as sovereign, we know as a fact that he arranged the

[1] Bühler, *Ueber das Leben des Jaina Mönches Hemachandra* (Wien, 1889), pp. 29-42.

[2] 'Il se mit à parcourir en mendiant les appartements intérieurs, mais il recevait de très bons aliments. Le roi dit aux femmes des appartements intérieurs: Donnez-lui des aliments semblables à ceux que ramassent les Religieux qui mendient.' (Burnouf, *Introduction à l'Histoire du Buddhisme Indien*, 2e éd., p. 375, with Burnouf's necessary emendation.) See *post*, chap. vii.

difficulty somehow, and the parallel cases enable us to understand how the business could be settled in more ways than one[1].

Having now defined the nature of the *dhaṁma*, or Law of Piety, which Asoka made it the business of his life to preach and propagate, and having shown how the apparently inconsistent rôles of monk and monarch could be reconciled in practice, we may resume his life story. We have seen that his ninth 'regnal year' (B. C. 261) was the turning-point of his career, that he then began to love, protect, and preach the Buddhist Law of Piety as a lay disciple, and that two and a half years later he assumed the monastic robe, abolished the Royal Hunt, and instituted 'pious tours.'

The memory of such a 'pious tour' in his twenty-first 'regnal year' (B. C. 249) is preserved by the commemorative records on the Rummindeî and Niglîva pillars in the Nepalese Tarâi, where there is reason to believe that other similar pillars exist. Those records prove that Asoka visited the 'Lumbini garden,' the traditional scene of the birth of Gautama Buddha, and also paid reverence to the *stûpa* of Konâkamana, or Kanakamuni, the 'former Buddha,' which he had already enlarged six years earlier. It is interesting

[1] Bodoahprâ, the ferocious king of Burma, who reigned from 1781 to 1819, and claimed descent from Asoka (Phayre, *History of Burma*, 1884, p. 235), proclaimed himself to be a Buddha, and dwelt for some time in a monastery, but tired of it, resumed power, and reverted to his evil ways (*Calc. Rev.*, 1872, p. 136).

to learn that the cult of the 'former Buddhas,' a subject imperfectly understood, was already well established in Asoka's days, but no one can tell how or when it originated.

The memory of the same pilgrimage was preserved also by literary tradition, as recorded in the Sanskrit romance called the *Asokâvadâna*. According to the story, which will be found in a later chapter, the king, under the guidance of his preceptor, a saint named Upagupta, visited in succession the Lumbini garden, Kapilavastu, the scene of Buddha's childhood, the Bodhi tree at Bodh Gayâ, Rishipattana, or Sârnâth, near Benares, Kusinagara, where Buddha died, the Jetavana monastery at Srâvastî, where he long resided, the *stûpa* of Vakkula, and the *stûpa* of Ânanda. The words graven on the Rummindeî pillar, 'Here the Venerable One was born,' are those ascribed by the tradition to Upagupta as spoken when he guided his royal master to the holy spot. Asoka bestowed great largess at every place except the *stûpa* of Vakkula, where he gave only a single copper coin, because that saint had met with few obstacles to surmount, and had consequently done little good to his fellow creatures. The explanation accords well with the severely practical character of Asoka's piety[1].

[1] Rummindeî on the Tilâr river certainly is the site of the Lumbini garden (see Plate II). The Kapilavastu visited by Hiuen Tsang is represented by Tilaurâ Kôṭ (Mukherjî and V. A. Smith, *Antiquities in the Tarâi, Nepâl; Archaeol. S. Rep. Imp. S.*, vol. xxvi, 1901). Bodh Gayâ, six miles south of Gayâ, is

The preceptor Upagupta, who probably converted Asoka, as Hemachandra converted Kumârapâla in a later age, seems to have been a real historical personage. The famous monastery at Mathurâ which bore his name appears to have been situated at the Kankâlî Tîla, a Buddhist as well as a Jain site, and his memory was also associated with various localities in Sind. He is said to have been the son of Gupta the perfumer. In the traditions of Ceylon his place is taken by Tissa, the son of Mogali, who should be regarded as a fictitious person made up from the names of Buddha's two principal disciples, as ingeniously argued by Colonel Waddell [1].

The eleventh 'regnal year' (B. C. 259), memorable

well known. The discoveries made at Sârnâth in 1904 and subsequent years include an edict of Asoka. The site of Kusinagara has not been finally determined. I believe it to have been near Tribenî Ghât, where the Little Râptî joins the Gandak (*E. Hist. India*, 3rd ed., p. 159 *n.*). See also the author's work, *The Remains near Kasia, the reputed Site of Kuçanagara* (Allahabad, 1896); 'Kusinârâ or Kuśinagara,' *J. R. A. S.*, 1902; *Archaeol. S., Annual Rep.*, 1904–5. The site of Srâvastî seems to be at Sahât-Mahât on the south bank of the Râptî in Oudh. I once believed it to be in Nepal on the upper course of the Râptî; but *contra*, Vogel, *J. R. A. S.*, 1908, p. 971. The legend of Bakkula or Vakkula is told in the *Bakkula-sutta* (*J. R. A. S.*, 1903, p. 373). There were two *stûpas* of Ananda, one on each side of the Ganges (Legge, *Travels of Fa-hien*, ch. xxvi; Hiuen Tsang). For the *Asokâradâna* see Burnouf, *Introduction à l'Histoire du Buddhisme*, or Râjendralâl Mitra, *Sanskrit Nepalese Literature*.

[1] Growse placed the Upagupta monastery at the Kankâlî mound (*Mathurâ*, 3rd ed., p. 122). For references to other books and papers see 'Asoka's Father-Confessor' in *Ind. Ant.*, 1903, p. 365.

as the date from which Asoka began to exert himself strenuously as Head of the Church and prophet of the *dhamma*, was marked, not only by the abolition of the Royal Hunt and the substitution of tours devoted to works of piety for the pleasure excursions of other days, but by a much more important measure, the most important ever taken by Asoka, and one which to this day bears much fruit. In or about the year mentioned he took the momentous resolution of organizing a network of preaching missions to spread the teaching of his Master, not only throughout and on the borders of his own wide empire, but in the distant regions of Western Asia, Eastern Europe, and Northern Africa. Rock Edict XIII, published with the rest of the Fourteen Rock Edicts in the fourteenth 'regnal year' (B.C. 256), gives a detailed list of the countries to which the imperial missionaries of the Law of Piety had been dispatched. We are told that His Majesty sought the conversion of even the wild forest tribes, and that missions were sent to the nations on the borders of his empire, who are enumerated as the Yonas, Kâmbojas, Nâbhapamtis of Nâbhaka, Bhojas, Pitenikas, Ândhras, and Pulindas, that is to say, various more or less civilized tribes occupying the slopes of the Himalaya, the regions beyond the Indus, and parts of the Deccan and Central India, which were under imperial control, although not included in the settled provinces administered by the emperor or his viceroys. Envoys were also sent, as far as the Tâmraparni river, to the Chola and

Pândya kingdoms of the extreme south of the peninsula, which were independent. But these operations, extensive though they were, did not satisfy the zeal of Asoka, who ventured to send his proselytizing agents far beyond the limits of India, into the dominions of Antiochos Theos, King of Syria and Western Asia (B. C. 261–246); Ptolemy Philadelphos, King of Egypt (B. C. 285–247); Magas, King of Cyrene in Northern Africa, half-brother of Ptolemy (about B. C. 285–258), Antigonos Gonatas, King of Macedonia (B. C. 277–239), and Alexander, King of Epirus (acc. B. C. 272). Rock Edict V adds to the list of border nations given above the names of the Râshtrikas of the Marâthâ country, and the Gândhâras of the Peshâwar frontier, noting that there were yet others unnamed; while Rock Edict II, which again names Antiochos, with a reference to his Hellenistic neighbours, as well as the Cholas, and Pândyas, as far as the Tâmraparni river, adds the Satiyaputra and Keralaputra kingdoms of the Western coast to the list of countries in which healing arrangements for man and beast were carried out. The date of the missions is fixed approximately by the fact that the year B. C. 258 is the latest in which all the Greek sovereigns named were alive together. The statements in the two edicts quoted constitute almost the whole of the primary and absolutely trustworthy evidence concerning Asoka's missionary organization.

The Ceylonese chronicles, the earliest of which was composed by Buddhist monks about six centuries after the Edicts, give a different list of countries and add the names of the missionaries as follows:—

	Country.	*Missionaries.*
1.	Kashmîr and Gandhâra (Peshâwar, &c.)	Majjhantika.
2.	Mahîshamaṇḍala (Mysore)	Mahâdeva.
3.	Vanavâsi (North Kannara)	Rakkhita.
4.	Aparântaka (coast north of Bombay)	Yona-Dharmarakkhita.
5.	Mahâraṭṭha (West Central India)	Mahâ-Dharmarakkhita.
6.	Yona region (N.W. frontier provinces)	Mahârakkhita.
7.	Himavanta (the Himalayan region)	Majjhima, Kassapa, &c.
8.	Suvaṇṇabhûmi (Pegu and Moulmein)	Soṇa and Uttara.
9.	Lankâ (Ceylon)	Mahinda (Mahendra), &c.

All the names of countries in this list, except Nos. 8 and 9, can be reconciled with the differently worded enumeration in the inscriptions. The inclusion of No. 8, Suvaṇṇabhûmi, which is identified by most authorities with the Pegu and Moulmein territories, is, I believe, at the best, a half-truth; that is to say, that the mission, if really sent, produced little effect. Burma, as a halfway house between India and China, seems to have first received Buddhism effectively early in the Christian era in two streams converging from China on one side and northern India on the other. The close connexion between the Churches of Ceylon and Burma is of much later date[1].

The exclusion of the Hellenistic kingdoms from the Ceylon list is easily explained when we remember that those kingdoms had ceased to exist centuries before that list was compiled. The omission of the Tamil

[1] The argument is worked out at length in the author's essay, 'Asoka's alleged Mission to Pegu (Suvaṇṇabhûmi),' *Ind. Ant.*, xxxiv (1905), pp. 180–6), and is carried further in Mr. Taw Sein Ko's *Progress Report of the Archaeol. S. Burma* for 1905–6.

countries of Southern India may be ascribed to the secular hostility between the Sinhalese and the Tamils of the mainland, which naturally would indispose the oppressed Sinhalese to recognize the ancestors of their oppressors as having been brothers in the faith. The island monks were eager to establish the derivation of their religion direct from Magadha through the agency of Mahinda and his supposed sister, and had no desire to recall the bygone days of friendly intercourse with the hated Tamils. Sound principles of historical criticism require that when the evidence of the inscriptions differs from that of later literary traditions, the epigraphic authority should be preferred without hesitation, and there is no reason to doubt the reality of the missions to the Tamil kingdoms of the south.

The Ceylon tradition as to the names of the missionaries is partially confirmed by Cunningham's discoveries at the Bhilsâ topes or *stûpas* near Sânchî, which included relic caskets bearing the name of 'Kâsapa Gota, missionary (*âchariya*) of the whole Hemavanta,' or Himalayan region. Other caskets bore the name of Majjhima[1]. But when the chronicler ascribes to the monk Tissa, son of Mogali, all the credit for the organization of the missions, and ignores Asoka, we are clearly bound to apply the principle of preferring the authority of the contemporary inscriptions, and to allow Asoka the honour of having personally organized,

[1] *Bhilsa Topes*, pp. 287, 289, 317, pl. xx. The finding of a casket inscribed *Mogaliputasa* does not establish the real existence of the Ceylonese Tissa, son of Mogali, as distinct from Upagupta.

with the aid of his enormous imperial power, the most comprehensive scheme of religious missionary enterprise recorded in the history of the world. The scheme was not only comprehensive but successful. It resulted in Buddhism quickly becoming the dominant religion throughout India and Ceylon, and in its ultimate extension over Burma, Siam, Cambodia, the Indian Archipelago, China, Korea, Japan, Mongolia, Tibet, and other countries of Asia. In some of these countries Buddhism did not effect its entry until centuries after the time of Asoka, but the diffusion of the religion in them all was due to the impetus given by the great Buddhist emperor of India, who transformed the creed of a local Indian sect into a world-religion, the most important of all the religions, perhaps, if the numbers of its adherents be taken as the test.

The obvious comparison of Asoka with Constantine suggests the thought that the action of the Indian monarch was far more influential than that of the Roman emperor, whose official patronage of Christianity was rather an act of tardy and politic submission to a force already irresistible than the willing devotion of an enthusiastic believer[1]. If Constantine had not

[1] 'When Constantine, partly perhaps from a genuine moral sympathy, yet doubtless far more in the well-grounded belief that he had more to gain from the zealous sympathy of its professors than he could lose by the aversion of those who still cultivated a languid paganism, took Christianity to be the religion of the empire, it was already a great political force, able, and not more able than willing, to repay him by aid and submission' (Bryce, *Holy Roman Empire* (1892), p. 10).

adopted the Christian creed himself, his successors would have been compelled to do so, but if Asoka had withheld his heartfelt adherence to the teaching of Buddha there is no reason to suppose that the doctrine had strength enough to impose itself upon the faith of India and half of the civilized world. Gautama Buddha lived, moved, and died within a small territory in and near Magadha, and there is no indication that during the interval of three centuries which elapsed between his death and the dispatch of missions by Asoka the Buddhist teaching had made any great noise in the world or was known beyond very narrow limits, nor is there any reason to believe that Asoka was constrained by political reasons to make a virtue of necessity and yield to the demands of an imperious priesthood. We watch in the personal records drafted by himself the gradual growth of his sincere convictions and the orderly development of the policy which consecrated his immense autocratic power and diplomatic influence as the sovereign of one of the greatest empires in the world to the service of the religion which had captured his heart and intellect.

An abstract of the monastic legends of Ceylon and India which purport to describe the conversion of Ceylon will be found in Chapters VI and VII. They cannot be accepted as history, and, in reality, the conversion of the island must have been a process much slower then it is represented to have been. But we do not possess any authoritative account of what actually happened. The Edicts, as now interpreted, are silent about Ceylon, and cannot be cited in support of the local monastic traditions which, although resting upon a basis of fact, are wholly untrustworthy for details. We must be content to admit our ignorance, which is likely to continue. I am sceptical about the tale of Sanghamitrâ, the supposed daughter of Asoka. Her name, which means 'Friend of the Order,' is extremely suspicious, and the inscriptions give no indication of her existence. Professor Oldenberg has much justification for his opinion that the story of Mahinda and his sister seems to have been—

> 'invented for the purpose of possessing a history of the Buddhist institutions in the island, and to connect it with the most distinguished person conceivable—the great Asoka. The historical legend is fond of poetically exalting ordinary occurrences into great and brilliant actions; we may assume that, in reality, things were accomplished in a more gradual and less striking manner than such legends make them appear[1].'

The naturalization in Ceylon of the immense mass of Buddhist literature now existing in Pâli and, I believe, also in Sinhalese, must necessarily have been a work of time, and would seem to be the fruit of long and continuous intercourse between Ceylon and the adjacent parts of India, rather than the sudden result of direct communication with Magadha. The statements of the Chinese pilgrims in the fifth and seventh centuries prove that Asoka's

[1] *Introduction to the Vinayapitakam*, p. 4 (ii).

efforts to propagate Buddhism in the far South were not in vain, and that monastic institutions existed in the Tamil countries which were in a position to influence the faith of the island. Hiuen Tsang mentions one *stûpa* in the Chola country, and another in the Drâvida or Pallava kingdom as being ascribed to Asoka. Still more significant is his description of the state of religion in A. D. 640 in the Malakotta Pândya country to the south of the Kâviri (Cauvery), where he found that—

'Some follow the true doctrine, others are given to heresy. They do not esteem learning much, but are wholly given to commercial gain. There are the ruins of many old convents, but only the walls are preserved, and there are few religious followers. There are many hundred Deva [Brahmanical] temples, and a multitude of heretics, mostly belonging to the Nirgranthas [Jains].

Not far to the east of this city [the unnamed capital, ? Madura] is an old *sanghârâma* [monastery] of which the vestibule and court are covered with wild shrubs; the foundation walls only survive. This was built by Mahendra, the younger brother of Asoka-râja.

To the east of this is a *stûpa*, the lofty walls of which are buried in the earth, and only the crowning part of the cupola remains. This was built by Asoka-râja[1].'

This interesting passage, which shows how vivid the traditions of Asoka and his brother continued

[1] Beal, *Records of the Western World*, ii. 231; instead of 'only the walls are preserved,' Watters renders 'very few monasteries were in preservation,' which agrees with the context and seems to be correct (*On Yuan Chwang*, ii. 228).

to be in the south after the lapse of nine centuries, and locates Mahendra in a monastery to the south of the Kâviri, within easy reach of Ceylon, goes a long way to support the hypothesis that Mahendra really passed over to the island from a southern port on the mainland. That hypothesis is certainly much more probable than the Ceylonese story that he came flying through the air, 'as flies the king of swans.' Nor is it likely that his first discourse converted the king and forty thousand of his subjects.

But, notwithstanding the mythology which has gathered round his name, Mahendra or Mahinda, the younger brother of Asoka, was a real, historical personage, and there can be no doubt that he was a pioneer in the diffusion of Buddhism in Ceylon. The concurrence of Indian and Ceylonese traditions, and the existence of monuments bearing his name both in the island and on the mainland do not permit of scepticism as to his reality. But the Ceylonese version of the story which represents him as an illegitimate son of Asoka is unsupported, and is opposed to the Indian tradition as current in both Northern and Southern India, at Pâtaliputra and at Kânchî (Conjeeveram), and reported by Fa-hien at the beginning of the fifth century, as well as by Hiuen Tsang in A.D. 640. Even the monks of Ceylon, who met the later pilgrim at Kânchî, and told him the accepted legend of the conversion of their country, knew Mahendra as the younger brother, not the son of Asoka[1]. It is obvious that the true form of the tradition was more likely to survive at Pâtaliputra, the ancient capital, than anywhere else, and Fa-hien when there about A. D. 400 heard anecdotes concerning Asoka's hermit brother[2], who is named Mahendra by Hiuen Tsang. Other forms of the legend call him Vîtâsoka or Vigatâsoka, but the evidence of the monuments in India and Ceylon fixes his name as Mahendra or Mahinda.

The assumption of the monastic robe by the emperor's younger brother, or rather half-brother on the mother's side, was quite in accordance with precedent and rule. 'According to the laws of India,' says a Chinese historian, 'when a king dies, he is succeeded by his eldest son (*Kumârarâja*); the others leave the family and embrace a religious life, and they are no longer allowed to reside in their native kingdom[3].' In Tibet the rule was varied in the case of the famous king Ral-pa-chan (died A. D. 838), who allowed his *elder* brother, Gtsang-ma, to enter the Order, and was succeeded by his *younger* brother[4]. Other parallel cases might be cited to justify the assertion of Prof. Jacobi that 'the spiritual career in India, just as the Church in Roman Catholic countries, seems to have offered a field for the ambition of younger sons[5].' We may

[1] Beal, *Life of Hiuen Tsiang*, p. 144.

[2] Legge, *Travels of Fa-hien*, p. 77, chap. xxvii.

[3] Ma-twan-lin in *Ind. Ant.*, ix. 22.

[4] Rockhill, *Life of the Buddha*, p. 225. [5] *S. B. E.*, xxii, p. 15.

feel assured that Mahendra or Mahinda, the apostle of Ceylon, was the brother, not the son of Asoka. As to the conversion of the king and people of the island, I hold that it was only begun by Mahendra, that the existence of his sister Sanghamitrâ is doubtful, and that the chroniclers' accounts of Mahendra's proceedings should be treated as edifying romances resting on a basis of fact, the extent of which cannot be determined precisely.

The thirteenth and fourteenth 'regnal years' (B. C. 257, 256) were busy ones for Asoka, marking great advance in his spiritual development and religious policy. Two (Nos. III and IV) of the Fourteen Rock Edicts are expressly dated in the thirteenth, while No. V mentions the fourteenth, 'regnal year.' In the localities where all the fourteen edicts occur it is clear that the whole set was engraved at once. The publication, therefore, may be dated in B. C. 256. The two special Kalinga Edicts, which were substituted in the newly conquered province for Nos. XI–XIII of the series, may be assigned to the same period, which also witnessed the dedication of costly caves in the Barâbar Hills near Gayâ to the use of the non-Buddhist Âjîvika ascetics and the institution of quinquennial official transfers for the purpose of public instruction in the Law of Piety [1]. Officers of all ranks, when serving in their several jurisdictions, were directed to undertake the business of propaganda in addition to their ordinary duties.

[1] Rock Edict III.

The Kalinga Provincials' Edict, by a supplementary clause, modified the general orders and instructed the Princes of Ujjain and Taxila to have the transfers carried out at intervals of three years only. Elaborate arrangements were made for ensuring full publicity to the royal commands.

Another important administrative measure was taken in the fourteenth 'regnal year' (B.C. 256) by the appointment for the first time of special officers of high rank, entitled *Dharma-mahâmâtras*, that is to say, *mahâmâtras*, or superior officials, exclusively engaged in the enforcement of the edicts concerning *dharma*, or the Law of Piety, and additional to the ordinary civil *mahâmâtras*. These officers may be described conveniently as Censors, and similar appointments have been made under the name of *Dharmâdhikârîs* in Kashmîr and other Hindu states in modern times[1]. Asoka attached high importance to the organization of the body of Censors, who received very comprehensive instructions to enforce the Law of Piety among all religious denominations, among the Yonas and other border tribes, and even in the households of the sovereign's brothers, sisters, and other relatives[2]. They were assisted by subordinate officials termed *Dharmayuktas*[3].

In the following year (fifteenth 'regnal,' B.C. 255)

[1] *Ind. Ant.*, xxxii (1903), p. 365. The word 'minister' would be a good rendering of *mahâmâtra*, in some cases at all events.

[2] Rock Edict V, Pillar Edict VII.

[3] The subordinate civil officials were known simply as *yuktas*, *upayuktas*, or *âyuktas*.

Asoka enlarged for the second time the *stûpa* of the 'former Buddha' Konâkamana, or Kanakamuni, which he visited personally six years later. The relation of the cult of the 'former Buddhas' to the religion of Gautama, as already observed, is a subject concerning which very little is known.

In the twentieth 'regnal year,' B.C. 250, the sovereign presented a third costly rock-dwelling to the Âjîvikas; and in the year following, B.C. 249, made the pilgrimage to the holy places of Buddhism already noticed. The dated record is then interrupted until the twenty-seventh 'regnal year,' B.C. 243, when Pillar Edict VI, dealing with the necessity that every man should have a definite creed, was composed. The dated series of inscriptions as discovered up to the present terminates in B.C. 242 with Pillar Edict VII, comprising ten distinct sections or separate edicts, and giving a comprehensive review of the measures taken during the reign for the propagation of the Law of Piety within the empire.

The Minor Pillar Edicts of Sârnâth, Allahabad-Kausâmbî, and Sânchî must be later in date because the position and mode of engraving the Queen's and Kausâmbî Edicts on the Allahabad pillar, which evidently was removed from Kausâmbî, indicate clearly that the short records are supplementary and posterior to the main series of Pillar Edicts on the same monument. The Kausâmbî and Sânchî documents are merely variants of the Sârnâth Edict. The Queen's Edict treats of another subject.

Inasmuch as the Sârnâth Edict and its variants deal with the disciplinary punishment to be inflicted on schismatic persons and emphatically declare the imperial resolve that no rending in twain of the Church should be permitted, it is reasonable to connect those orders with the Buddhist Council which tradition affirms to have been convened by Asoka at his capital for the purpose of suppressing heresy. The Ceylonese books date the Council either sixteen or eighteen years after the consecration of Asoka, but those dates must be erroneous, because, if the Council had been convened before the twenty-eighth 'regnal year,' it would surely have been mentioned in the seventh Pillar Edict, which reviews all the internal measures taken up to that date by the sovereign for the promotion of the Law of Piety. The Council, however, may well have taken place in any one of the ten or eleven years intervening between the last dated edict and the close of the reign. It is said in various traditions to have been concerned with the overthrow of heresy, and if there be any truth in that story, the Sârnâth Edict and its variants may be regarded as embodying the resolution of the Council, and may be dated in one or other of the years near the end of the reign [1].

[1] The value of the traditions of the Councils is discussed at length in the author's essay 'The Identity of Piyadasi (Priyadarśin) with Aśoka Maurya and some connected Problems,' *J. R. A. S.*, 1901, pp. 842–58; and also by M. Poussin in *Ind. Ant.*, 1908, and by Professor R. Otto Franke (transl. Mrs. Rhys

Having thus traced Asoka's religious history in chronological order as far as positive dates are available, we shall now proceed to discuss certain features of his policy which cannot be treated with equal chronological accuracy. Several edicts record the successive steps taken by the king to give effect to the principle of the sanctity of animal life, which was one of his cardinal doctrines. In the early years of his reign Asoka was not troubled by any scruples on the subject, and he confesses in the first Rock Edict, it is to be hoped with some exaggeration, that 'formerly in the kitchen of his Sacred and Gracious Majesty each day many hundred thousand of living creatures were slaughtered to make curries.' Afterwards, presumably from the time when he became a lay disciple, or, perhaps, from the eleventh 'regnal year,' the slaughter was reduced to 'two peacocks and one antelope—the antelope, however, not invariably.' From the thirteenth 'regnal year' all killing for the royal table was stopped. The same edict prohibits at the capital the celebration of animal sacrifices and merry-makings involving the use of meat, but in the provinces such practices apparently continued to be lawful. The suppression of the Royal Hunt some two years later than his conversion marked an intermediate stage in the monarch's growing devotion to his favourite doctrine. The final development of his

Davids) in *J. Pāli Text Soc.*, 1908. Any attempt to reconstruct a narrative of the actual proceedings of the Council from the conflicting traditions is hopeless.

policy in this matter is defined by Pillar Edict V, dated B. C. 243, which lays down an elaborate code of regulations restricting the slaughter and mutilation of animals throughout the empire. Those regulations were imposed on all classes of the population without distinction of creed, social customs, or religious sentiment. A long list was published of animals the slaughter of which was absolutely prohibited, and other rules prescribed restrictions on the slaughter of animals permitted to be killed, and prohibited or limited the practice of different kinds of mutilation. Asoka could not venture to absolutely forbid the castration of bulls, he-goats, rams and boars, but he regarded the practice as unholy, and prohibited it on all holy days, amounting to about a quarter of the year. The branding of horses and cattle was treated in the same spirit. On fifty-six days the capture or sale of fish was prohibited, and on the same days, even in game preserves, animals might not be destroyed. The caponing of cocks was declared to be absolutely unlawful at all times.

The practical working of such minutely detailed rules must have been almost intolerably vexatious, and they cannot fail to have pressed with painful harshness upon people who believed sacrifice on certain days to be necessary to salvation and on many classes of the working population. The insistence on the display of energy by the Censors and all classes of officials in carrying out the imperial commands must have produced a crowd of informers and an immense amount of tyranny. Regard for the sanctity of animal life, even that of the meanest vermin, is not peculiar to Buddhism, being practised even more strictly by the Jains, and esteemed more or less highly by most Brahmanical Hindus. It rests on the theory of re-birth, which underlies nearly all forms of Indian religion, and binds together in one chain all classes of living creatures, whether gods or demi-gods, angels or demons, men or animals. But, although that doctrine had been familiar to the mind of India for ages, its strict enforcement to a certain extent as part of the civic duty of every loyal subject, irrespective of his personal religious belief, was a new thing, and imposed a novel burden on the lieges. The regulations must have had permanent influence in obtaining the general acceptance of ideas formerly restricted to sections of the population. It is noteworthy that Asoka's rules do not forbid the slaughter of cows, which, apparently, continued to be lawful. The problem of the origin of the intense feeling of reverence for the cow, now felt by all Hindus, is a very curious one, imperfectly solved. The early Brahmans did not share the sentiment.

The doctrine of the duty of reverence to parents, seniors, and teachers seems to have held in Asoka's eyes a place second only to that of the sanctity of animal life. It is reiterated over and over again in the Edicts, but no development of the principle is traceable.

The sanctity attaching to the life of the most insignificant insect was not extended to the life of man. The monkish legend that Asoka abolished the death penalty is not true. His legislation proves that the idea of such abolition never entered his thoughts, and that like other Buddhist monarchs, he regarded the extreme penalty of the law as an unavoidable necessity, which might be made less horrible than it had been, but could not be dispensed with. Late in his reign, in B.C. 243, he published an ordinance that every prisoner condemned to death should invariably be granted before execution a respite of three days in which to prepare himself for the next world. This slight mitigation of the usual practice of Indian despots, whose sentence was commonly followed by instant or almost instant execution, is all that Asoka claims credit for. The inferior value attaching to human as compared with animal life presumably is due to the fact that men are responsible for their deeds while animals are not. In later times Hindu Râjâs have not hesitated to execute a man for killing a beast, and it is unlikely that Asoka was less severe.

One of the most noticeable features in the teaching of Asoka is the enlightened religious toleration which is so frequently and emphatically recommended. The *Dharma*, or Law of Piety, which he preached and propagated unceasingly with amazing faith in the power of sermonizing, had few, if any, distinctive features. The doctrine was essentially common to all Indian religions, although one sect or denomination might lay particular stress on one factor in it rather than on another. The zeal of Asoka for Buddhism is proved, not by his presentation of *Dharma*, but by his references to the canon, by the cast of his language, by his pilgrimages to Buddhist holy places, and by his active control of the Church. His personal devotion to the teaching of Gautama did not cool his goodwill to other sects. The edicts repeatedly enjoin the duty of almsgiving to Brahman as well as Buddhist ascetics: the king, using his Master's words, declares all men to be his children, announces his impartial consideration for all denominations, including Jains and Âjîvikas, and implores people to abstain from speaking ill of their neighbours' faith. He sees good in all creeds, and is persuaded that men of all faiths perform, at any rate, a part of the commandment. So much may be gathered from the Fourteen Rock Edicts of B.C. 257 and 256. The sixth Pillar Edict of B.C. 243 goes a little further and insists on the necessity for every person having a definite creed. 'I devote my attention,' Asoka observes, 'to all communities, for all denominations are reverenced by me with various forms of reverence. Nevertheless, personal adherence to one's own creed is the chief thing in my opinion.' These latitudinarian views did not, as we have seen, prevent him from imposing very stringent rules of conduct on persons of all ranks and classes, irrespective of their religious denomination. Men might believe what they liked but must do as they were told.

When we apply to Asoka's policy the word toleration with its modern connotation and justly applaud the liberality of his sentiments, another qualification is needed, and we must remember that in his days no really diverse religions existed in India. The creeds of Jesus, Zoroaster, and Muhammad were unknown. The only organized religion other than Buddhism or Jainism was Hinduism, and that complex phenomenon at all times is more accurately described as a social system than by the name of either a religion or a creed. When Asoka speaks of the toleration of other men's creeds, he is not thinking of exclusive, militant religions like Christianity and Islam, but of Hindu sects all connected by many links of common sentiment. The dominant theory of rebirth, for instance, was held by nearly all. Buddhism and Jainism both were originally mere sects of Hinduism—or rather schools of philosophy founded by Hindu reformers—which in course of time gathered an accretion of mythology around the original speculative nucleus, and developed into religions.

Asoka, therefore, was in a position which enabled him to realize the idea that all Indian denominations were fundamentally in agreement about what he, from the practical point of view, calls 'the essence of the matter,' all of them alike aiming at self-control and purity of life; and he thus felt fully justified in doing honour in various ways to Jains and Brahmanical Hindus as well as to Buddhists. While lavishing his treasure chiefly on Buddhist shrines and monasteries, he did not hesitate to spend large sums in hewing out of hard gneiss spacious cave-dwellings for the Âjîvika naked ascetics, not even grudging the expense of polishing the interiors like a mirror; and there can be no doubt that liberal benefactions were bestowed likewise on the Jains and Brahmans. Indeed, Kashmîr tradition has preserved the names of Brahmanical temples built or restored by Asoka[1]. Similar toleration, evidenced in practice by concurrent endowment of various creeds, was practised by later princes. Khâravela of Orissa, for instance, used language almost identical with that of Asoka, and avowed that he did reverence to all creeds[2]. In much more recent times the cases of Harsha and many other Râjâs who acted on the same principle are familiar to students of Indian History[3].

The sentiment which dictated the tolerant conduct of the old kings is still accepted, and has been expressed by a lady who has penetrated deeply below the surface of Indian character:

'It is natural enough to the Hindu intellect,' she observes, 'that around each such forth-shining of the divine should grow up a new religious system. But each of them is only a special way of expressing the one fundamental doctrine of Mâyâ [*scil.* illusion], a new mode of endearing God to man. At the same time it is thought that every one, while recognizing

[1] Stein, transl. *Râjatar.*, Bk. I, vv. 101–7.

[2] *Journal, Bihar and Orissa Research Society*, vol. iii (1917), pp. 460, 467.

[3] *E. Hist. India*, 3rd edition, pp. 178, 179, 265, 303, 331, 346. But religious persecutions occurred occasionally (ibid., pp. 202, 203, 347, 455).

this perfect sympathy of various faiths for one another, should know how to choose one among them for his own, and persist in it, till by its means he has reached the point where the formulae of sects are meaningless to him . . . . "A man has a right to hold his own belief, but never to force it upon another" is the dictum that has made of India a perfect university of religious culture, including every stage of thought and practice.'

A modern Hindu writer, following the same line of thought, lays down the rule:

'Let every man, so far as in him lieth, help the reading of the scriptures, whether those of his own Church or those of another[1].'

Asoka presumably did not believe in the Vedântist doctrine of Mâyâ, which forms a bond of union between so many Hindu sects, but, nevertheless, his theory of the relation which one sect or denomination should bear to another, as expressed in Rock Edict XII and Pillar Edict VI, agrees exactly with the principles formulated by Miss Noble and Pratâpa Siṁha[2].

Although Asoka unquestionably was familiar with a body of sacred Buddhist literature substantially identical with a large part of the Pâli canonical scriptures, the teaching of the edicts gives the impression of being different from that of most Buddhist works. We find no distinct reference to the doctrine of *karma*, or transmitted merit and demerit, nor is any allusion made to *nirvâṇa*, as the goal to be obtained

[1] Miss Noble, *The Web of Indian Life*, pp. 224, 281.

[2] Pratâpa Siṁha, *Bhakta Kalpadruma* (1866), transl. Grierson (*J. R. A. S.*, 1908, p. 359).

by the good man. No doubt the emperor believed in *karma*, although he does not plainly say so, and very probably he may have looked forward to *nirvâṇa*, although he does not express the hope. His precepts, as already observed, are purely practical and intended to lead men into the right way of living, not into correct philosophical positions. Many passages in the edicts indicate that he believed firmly in the 'other world' or 'future life.' He tells us, for instance (Rock Edict VIII), that all his exertions were directed to the end that he might discharge his debt to animate beings, make some of them happy in this world, and also enable them in the other world to gain heaven[1]. Again (Rock Edict IX), making the same contrast, he warns his people that ordinary ritual may be of only temporal effect, good for this world alone, while the ritual of the Law of Piety produces endless merit (*puṇyam*) in the other world. The next following edict offers the same promise to those who practise the true kind of almsgiving. Still more emphatic is the declaration near the close of Rock Edict XIII that only the things concerning the other world are regarded by His Majesty as bearing much fruit, and he concludes by adjuring his descendants to place all their joy in efforts which avail for both this world and the next. The warning given in the Provincials' Edict to negligent officials in Kalinga is couched in the following remarkable terms:—

[1] 'In this world,' literally 'here'; 'in the other world,' literally 'on the other side'; 'heaven,' *svarga*.

'See to my commands; such and such are the instructions of His Sacred Majesty. Fulfilment of these bears great fruit, non-fulfilment brings great calamity. By those who fail neither heaven (*svarga*) nor the royal favour can be won. Ill performance of this duty can never win my regard, whereas by fulfilling my instructions you will gain heaven and also pay your debt to me.'

The inducements thus held out seem hardly consistent with the Buddhist philosophy of most books, but the reference to heavenly bliss is supported by the words of the Buddha in the *Kûtadanta Sutta*:—'Then the Blessed One discoursed to Kûtadanta the Brahman in due order; that is to say, he spake to him of generosity, of right conduct, of *heaven*, of the danger, the vanity, and the defilement of lusts, of the advantages of renunciation [1].'

While Asoka took infinite pains to issue and enforce 'pious regulations,' he put his trust in the 'superior effect of reflection' as the chief agent in the promotion of 'the growth of piety among men and the more complete abstention from killing animate beings, and from sacrificial slaughter of living creatures [2].' Nor did he rely solely upon the combined effect of reflection and pious regulations for the success of his propaganda. He continually extolled the merit of almsgiving, and attached much importance to practical works of benevolence, in the execution of which he set a good example. Within his own dominions he provided for the comfort of man and

[1] Rhys Davids, *Dialogues of the Buddha*, p. 184.

[2] Pillar Edict VII, sec. 9.

beast by the plantation of shade-giving and fruit-bearing trees, the digging of wells, and the erection of rest-houses and watering-places at convenient intervals along the highroads. He devoted special attention to elaborate arrangements for the care and healing of the sick, and for the cultivation and dissemination of medicinal herbs and roots in the territories of foreign allied sovereigns as well as within the limits of the empire. Although the word hospitals does not occur in the edicts, such institutions must have been included in his arrangements, and the remarkable free hospital which the Chinese pilgrim found working at Pâtaliputra six and a half centuries later doubtless was a continuation of Asoka's foundation. The curious animal hospitals which still exist at Surat and certain other cities in Western India also may be regarded as survivals of Asoka's institutions [1].

The greater part of Asoka's moral teaching is in agreement with, and may be fairly summed up in the familiar words of the Church Catechism:

> 'To love, honour, and succour my father and mother . . . to submit myself to all my governours, teachers, spiritual pastors and masters: to order myself lowly and reverently to all my betters: to hurt no body by word nor deed: to be true and just in all my dealing: to bear no malice nor hatred in my heart: to keep my hands from picking and stealing, and my tongue from evil-speaking, lying, and slandering . . . and to do my duty in that state of life, unto which it shall please God to call me.'

[1] Rock Edict II, Pillar Edict VII; Fa-hien, *Travels*, ch. xxvii; *E. Hist. India*, 3rd ed., pp. 183, 296.

Although Asoka probably had no clear faith in a living, personal God, his teaching certainly attained to a level of practical morality little inferior to that of the Church of England in many respects, and superior in one point, by the inclusion of animals within the circle of neighbours to whom duty is due. Until very recent times Christian moralists and divines have been slow to recognize the obligation to treat animals with kindness, or even to abstain from inflicting wanton cruelty upon them, while Asoka brackets together the 'sparing of living creatures' and the 'kind treatment of slaves and servants.' These remarks, of course, apply only to the documents as they stand. The question as to how far the admirable sentiments of the edicts were acted on by either teacher or taught is incapable of solution, but there can be little doubt that on the whole Buddhism produced a valuable and permanent improvement in Indian notions of morality, and that its beneficent action was largely promoted by Asoka's official propaganda. Brahmanical Hinduism always has shown a tendency either to exalt unduly the purely intellectual apprehension of transcendental propositions or to attach excessive value to the performance of ceremonies, which, as Asoka observed, 'bear little fruit,' and, consequently, to undervalue moral duty. Buddhism put moral obligation in the front.

The last glimpse obtained of the historical Asoka is that afforded by the Minor Pillar Edicts, which exhibit him as the watchful guardian of the unity and discipline of the Church which he loved. How, when, or where he died we know not, and no monument exists to mark the spot where his ashes rest. The Hindu Purânas assign him a reign of either thirty-six or thirty-seven years, in substantial agreement with the chronicles of Ceylon, which also give the duration of the reign as thirty-seven years. By adding the interval of about four years between his accession and coronation, the total duration of the reign may be taken as either forty or forty-one years. The materials available do not permit of the chronology being adjusted with more minute accuracy, but in assigning the period B.C. 273–242 to the reign of Asoka we cannot be far wrong. The initial date is fixed within narrow limits of possible error by two independent calculations, one starting from the death of Alexander in B.C. 323 and the nearly contemporaneous accession of Chandragupta, the other working backwards from B.C. 258, the date of the death of Magas of Cyrene, who is mentioned in the thirteenth Rock Edict, published presumably in the fourteenth 'regnal year' reckoned from Asoka's consecration. Some uncertainty is introduced into the first calculation by doubts as to the exact time of Chandragupta's accession and by the discrepancy of authorities concerning the length of the reign of Bindusâra, whether twenty-five or twenty-eight years. The second calculation, based upon the year B.C. 258, leaves very little room for doubt, and all authorities are agreed that Chandragupta reigned for twenty-four years [1]. On the

[1] Rhys Davids' note in *Anc. Coins and Measures of Ceylon*,

whole, I think it best to assign B. C. 325 for the accession of Chandragupta, 301 for that of Bindusâra, and 273 for that of Asoka, whose coronation followed in 269.

Several eminent scholars have held and defended the opinion that the figures 256 at the end of Minor Rock Edict I must be interpreted as a date expressing the number of years elapsed since the death of Buddha, and in the first edition of this work that opinion was treated as probable. But further examination of the problem has convinced me that M. Senart and Mr. F. W. Thomas are right in rejecting the date theory, according to which, if the death of Buddha be assumed to have taken place in 487, the edict would be dated in B. C. 231, at the close of Asoka's life. I now accept the view that the edict in question is the earliest of the whole collection, and dates from *cir.* B. C. 257. This divergence of opinion as to the interpretation of that document seriously affects the treatment of the life history of Asoka[1]. As already observed, I reject the theory that he abdicated, and am of opinion that the connected theory of his conversion late in life is opposed to the clear testimony of the inscriptions.

p. 41, corrects the copyist's error which makes the *Mahâvaṁsa* assign thirty-four years to the reign.

[1] Bühler maintained the date theory to the last (*Ind. Ant.*, xxii. 302), and has been followed by Dr. Fleet in several articles in the *J. R. A. S.*, of which the latest is in the volume for 1913, p. 655. For date of death of Buddha see *E. Hist. India*, 3rd ed., pp. 46, 47. If B. C. 487 be correct, the Ceylonese date 218 A. B. for the consecration of Asoka also will be right (487−218 = 269). But I now incline to 544 or 543 B. C.

Nothing of importance is known about the successors of Asoka. His grandson, Dasaratha, mentioned in the Purânas, is shown to have been a real personage by his inscriptions in the Nâgârjuni Hills near Gayâ, where he dedicated caves to the use of the Âjîvikas, as his grandfather had done in the neighbouring Barâbar Hills. The Jain literary tradition of Western India has much to tell about a grandson named Samprati, who is represented as having been an eminent patron of Jainism—in fact, a Jain Asoka, but these traditions are not supported by inscriptions or other independent evidence. The hypothesis that the great emperor left two grandsons, of whom one succeeded him in his eastern and the other in his western dominions, is little more than a guess; but it appears to be nearly certain that in the east he was followed directly by Dasaratha. The pathetic story of the blinded son, Kunâla, briefly related in Chapter VII of this book, is mere folk-lore, and the account in the Kashmîr chronicle of Jalauka, another son, is little more, although fortified by some prosaic details. He is represented as an ardent worshipper of Siva, while his queen was devoted to the service of the Mother-goddesses, or Saktis[1]. The edicts, which indicate that Asoka had many sons and grandsons, give the name of only one son, Tîvara, whose mother was the second queen, the Kâruvâkî, and nothing is known about his fate[2].

[1] Stein, transl. *Rājatar.*, Bk. i. vv. 108-52.

[2] Queen's Edict.

The names of the successors of Asoka after Dasaratha as stated in different books vary, but the Purânas agree that the dynasty came to an end after a duration of either 133 or 137 years. Taking the accession of Chandragupta to have occurred in B. C. 325, the extinction of the Maurya line may be dated in B. C. 188. It seems plain that the later Mauryas were comparatively insignificant princes ruling a restricted territory, and that the empire governed for about ninety years with such distinction by Chandragupta, Bindusâra, and Asoka, crumbled to pieces when the strong arm of the third sovereign dropped the sceptre. The end is said to have come when Brihadratha, the last of the Maurya dynasty, was put to death by Pushyamitra Sunga, his commander-in-chief, who usurped the throne. But, although the imperial dynasty became extinct within half a century after the death of Asoka, his descendants seem to have continued to be local chieftains in Magadha for some eight centuries, because Hiuen Tsang, the Chinese pilgrim, tells us that shortly before his arrival, Pûrnavarman, Râjâ of Magadha, and the last descendant of Asoka, had piously restored the sacred Bodhi tree at Gayâ, which Sasânka, King of Bengal, had destroyed. These events happened soon after A. D. 600.

CHRONOLOGY OF THE MAURYA PERIOD

(Indian dates merely approximate)

B. C.	Regnal year of Asoka.	Event.	Remarks.
327-25	—	Indian campaigns of Alexander the Great; Chandragupta in his youth met Alexander.	
325-22	—	Revolt of Indian provinces.	
325	—	**Accession of Chandragupta Maurya** as king of Magadha and emperor of India.	
cir. 324	—	Murder of Satrap Philippos; Indian provinces placed in charge of Eudêmos and King Âmbhi (Omphis) of Taxila.	
323, June	—	Death of Alexander at Babylon.	
321	—	Partition of Triparadeisos; kings Âmbhi and Pôros in charge of the Panjâb.	
cir. 317	—	Withdrawal of Eudêmos.	
315	—	Seleukos Nikator driven out of Babylon.	
312	—	Recovery of Babylon by Seleukos; Seleukidan era, 1st October.	
306	—	Seleukos assumed title of king.	
cir. 305	—	War between Seleukos and Chandragupta; cession of four satrapies west of Indus by Seleukos; mission of Megasthenes to Pâṭaliputra.	
301	—	Battle of Ipsos. **Accession of Bindusâra Amitraghâta Maurya.**	
cir. 300	—	Mission of Deïmachos.	
285	—	Accession of Ptolemy Philadelphos, king of Egypt.	
280	—	Death of Seleukos Nikator; accession of Antiochos Soter, his son.	
278 or 277	—	Accession of Antigonos Gonatas, king of Macedonia.	

B. C.	Regnal year of Asoka.	Event.	Remarks.
273	—	**Accession of Asoka-vardhana Maurya.**	
272	—	Accession of Alexander, king of Epirus.	
269	1	**Consecration** (*abhisheka* = coronation) **of Asoka.**	
261	9	Conquest of Kalinga by Asoka, who became a Buddhist lay disciple (*upâsaka*); accession of Antiochos Theos, king of Syria.	Rock E. XIII; Minor Rock E. I.
259	11	Asoka entered the Buddhist Order as a monk, abolished Royal Hunt, established 'pious tours,' and dispatched missionaries.	Rock E. II, VIII, XIII; Minor Rock E. I; Pillar E. VII.
258	12	Death of Magas, king of Cyrene, half-brother of Ptolemy Philadelphos; (?) death of Alexander, king of Epirus.	
257	13	Asoka composed Minor Rock Edict I and Rock Edicts III and IV, dedicated Barâbar Caves 1 and 2 to the Âjîvikas, and instituted quinquennial transfers of officials.	Minor Rock E. I; Rock E. III, IV; Minor Rock E. II may be a little later. Barâbar Cave dedications.
256	14	Completion of Fourteen Rock Edicts; Kalinga Borderers' Edict; appointment of Censors; (?) Bhâbrû Edict.	Rock E. V, XIV; Borderers' E.; Bhâbrû E.
255	15	(?) Kalinga Provincials' Edict; enlargement for second time of *stûpa* of Konâkamana Buddha near Kapilavastu.	Provincials' E.; Niglîva Pillar inscription.
250	20	Dedication of Barâbar Cave No. 3 to the Âjîvikas.	Barâbar Cave dedication.
249	21	Pilgrimage to Buddhist holy places.	Rummindeî and Niglîva Pillar inscriptions.

B. C.	Regnal year of Asoka.	Event.	Remarks.
248–46	22 to 24	Declaration of independence by Bactria and Parthia.	
247	23	Death of Ptolemy Philadelphos, king of Egypt.	
247 or 246	23 or 24	Death of Antiochos Theos, king of Syria.	
243	27	Composition of Pillar Edict VI.	Pillar E. VI.
242	28	Completion of Seven Pillar Edicts; (?) death of Antigonos Gonatas, king of Macedonia.	Pillar E. VII.
cir. 240	30	Buddhist Council at Pâṭaliputra.	
240–32	30 to 37	Minor Pillar Edicts.	Minor Pillar E.
232		Death of Asoka; accession of Dasaratha, and (?) of Samprati; dedication of Nâgârjuni Caves to the Âjîvikas.	*Dîpavaṁśa*, *Mahâvaṁśa*, *Purâṇas*, Nâgârjuni Cave dedications.
188		Murder of Bṛihadratha Maurya by Pushyamitra Śunga; extinction of Maurya imperial dynasty.	

CHAPTER II

EXTENT AND ADMINISTRATION OF THE EMPIRE

THE limits of the vast empire governed successfully by Asoka for so many years can be determined with sufficient accuracy by the testimony of the Greek and Roman authors concerning the dominions of his grandfather, by the internal evidence of the edicts, and by the distribution of the monuments and inscriptions, with some aid from tradition.

The Indian conquests of Alexander to the east of the Indus, which extended across the Panjâb as far as the Hyphasis or Biâs river, quickly passed, as we have seen, soon after the death of Alexander, into the hands of Chandragupta Maurya, and the four satrapies of Aria, Arachosia, Gedrosia, and the Paropanisadai were ceded to him by Seleukos Nikator about B.C. 305. The Maurya frontier was thus extended as far as the Hindû Kush Mountains, and the greater part of the countries now called Afghanistan, Balûchistan and Makrân, with the North-Western Frontier Province, became incorporated in the Indian Empire. That empire included the famous strongholds of Kâbul, Zâbul[1], Kandahar, and Herat, and so possessed the

[1] Not Ghaznî (also spelt Ghaznîn and Ghazna), which was not founded until near the close of the ninth century. Zâbul,

'scientific frontier' for which Anglo-Indian statesmen have long sighed in vain. There is no reason to suppose that the trans-Indus provinces were lost by Bindusâra, and it is reasonable to assume that they continued under the sway of Asoka, who refers to Antiochos, King of Syria, in terms which suggest that the Syrian and Indian empires were conterminous. Costly buildings ascribed to Asoka were seen by Hiuen Tsang in different parts of Afghanistan. Among others he mentions a stone *stûpa*, a hundred feet high, at the town of Kapisa, somewhere in Kâfiristân, and a remarkable building of the same kind, three hundred feet in height and richly decorated, at Nangrahâr, near Jalâlâbâd, on the Kâbul river. The Swât valley also contained evidences of Asoka's passion for building[1].

Abundant testimony proves the inclusion of the vale of Kashmîr within the limits of the empire. The city which preceded the existing town of Srînagar or Pravarapura as the seat of government was founded by Asoka, and is generally believed to be represented by the ancient site called Pândrethan, two or three miles to the south-east of the present capital. But the Muhammadan chroniclers locate Asoka's city at

the ancient capital of Arachosia, stood on or near the Mihtar-i-Sulaimân range to the east of Ghaznî and the south of Kâbul. The ruins, although known to exist, have not been visited by any European (Raverty, *Notes on Afghanistan*, pp. 457, 506–10).

[1] Beal, *Buddhist Records*, i. 57, 92, 125; Watters *On Yuan Chwang*, i. 129, 183, 237. For the name Nangrahâr or Nangnahâr see Raverty, *Notes on Afghanistan*, p. 49.

Sîr on the Lidar river, not far from Islâmâbâd and Mârtânda and more than thirty miles distant from Srînagar. Legend credited Asoka with having built five hundred Buddhist monasteries in Kashmîr, and it is certain that his zeál was responsible for many important edifices, including some dedicated to the Brahmanical faith[1].

The inclusion in the empire of the Nepalese Tarâi, or lowlands, is proved conclusively by the inscriptions on the Rummindeî and Niglîva pillars which commemorate the pilgrimage of the sovereign to the Buddhist holy places in B. C. 249.

Genuine local tradition—not mere literary legend—confirmed by the existence of well-preserved monuments, attests Asoka's effective possession of the secluded valley of Nepâl. The pilgrimage under the guidance of Upagupta, described in the last chapter, or another of the same kind, was continued, through either the Churiâ Ghâtî or the Goramasân Pass, into the valley, the capital of which, then known by the name of Manju Pâtan, occupied the same site as the modern city of Kâthmându. Asoka resolved to commemorate his visit by the foundation of a city and the erection of massive monuments. The site selected for the new capital was some rising ground about two miles to the south-east of Kâthmându, and there the city now known as Lalita Pâtan or Pâtan was laid out. Exactly in its centre Asoka erected a

[1] Stein, transl. *Râjatar.*, Bk. i. vv. 101–7 and notes.

temple which still stands near the southern side of the palace or 'Darbar,' and at each of the four sides of the city, facing the cardinal points, he built four great hemispherical *stûpas*, which likewise remain to this day. Certain minor structures at Pâtan also bear his name. Asoka was accompanied in his pilgrimage by his daughter Chârumatî, the wife of a Kshatriya named Devapâla. Both husband and wife settled in Nepâl near the holy shrine of Pasupati, where they founded and peopled Deva Pâtan. They were there blessed with a numerous family, and becoming aged determined to pass the remainder of their lives in religious retirement, vowing that each would build a retreat for members of the Order. Chârumatî had the good fortune to fulfil her vow, and in due course died in the nunnery which she had erected. The building still exists at the village of Chabâhil, north of and close to Deva Pâtan. Devapâla is said to have died in great distress because he was unable to complete before his death the monastery which he had vowed to found. These things are believed to have happened while the Kirâtas, or hill-men from the east, ruled Nepâl and Sthunko was the local Râjâ [1].

In Asoka's days, and for many centuries later, Tâmralipti, the capital of a small dependent kingdom

[1] Oldfield, *Sketches from Nipâl*, ii. 246-8; Wright, *History of Nepâl*, p. 110; Sylvain Lévi, *Le Nepâl*, i. 67; ii. 82. The photograph on p. 263 of tome i is a good representation of the southern Asoka *stûpa* at Pâtan, the antiquity of which is guaranteed by its form. See also *Ind. Ant.*, xiii. 412.

named Suhmâ, was the principal port for the embarkation and landing of passengers and goods conveyed to or from Ceylon, Burma, China, and the islands of the Indian Ocean. There is no doubt that this important mart was under the jurisdiction of Asoka, who built a *stûpa* there, which was still in existence nine centuries later. The port was destroyed long since by the accumulation of silt and changes of the land level. Its modern representative, the small town of Tamlûk, stands fully sixty miles distant from the sea. The old city lies buried under the deposits made by the rivers, the remains of masonry walls and houses being met with at a depth of from eighteen to twenty-one feet[1]. Another *stûpa* of Asoka stood in the capital of Samatata or the Brahmaputra Delta[2], and others in various parts of Bengal[3] and Bihâr.

It is thus manifest that the whole of Bengal must have been subject to the Maurya suzerainty. The conquest in B.C. 261 of the neighbouring kingdom of Kalinga between the Mahânadî and Godâvarî rivers, narrated in the preceding chapter, completed the circle of Asoka's sovereignty over India to the north of the

[1] Tamlûk is in the Midnapore District on the Rûpnarâyan river in lat. 22° 18′ N., long. 87° 56′ E. See *Imp. Gaz.* (1908), *s.v.* Tamlûk; Fa-hien, *Travels*, transl. Legge, ch. xxxvii, p. 100; Hiuen Tsang, in Beal, *Records*, ii. 200; Watters, *On Yuan Chwang*, ii. 190. In Fa-hien's time (A.D. 410) there were twenty-two Buddhist monasteries at Tâmralipti, which were reduced to about half the number in the seventh century.

[2] Beal, ii. 199; Watters, ii. 187.

[3] Beal, ii. 195; Watters, ii. 184.

Narbadâ. We do not know for certain in whose reign the southern provinces were annexed, but it is probable that they were incorporated in the empire during the reign of Bindusâra, whose son is known from the Girnâr inscription of Rudradâman to have been master of Surâshtra, the peninsula of Kathiâwâr, in the far west [1].

The approximate southern boundary of the empire is easily defined by the existence of three copies of the Minor Rock Edicts in Northern Mysore (N. lat. 14° 50′, E. long. 76° 48′) [2] and by the references in the Fourteen Rock Edicts to the Tamil states as independent powers. The frontier line may be drawn with practical accuracy from Nellore (14° 27′ N.) on the east coast at the mouth of the Pennâr or Penner river to the mouth of the Kalyânapuri river (13° 15′ N.) on the west coast. That river formed the northern boundary of the Tuluva country, which was separated from Kerala or Malabar by the Chandragiri or Kangarote river (12° 27′ N.), which still forms an ethnic frontier which no Nâyar woman can venture to cross [3].

Asoka's empire, therefore, comprised the countries now known as Afghanistan, as far as the Hindû Kush,

[1] *Ep. Ind.*, viii. 36.

[2] This is the position of the Jaṭinga-Râmeśvara hill. The Siddâpura and Brahmagiri recensions are close by.

[3] Balfour, *Cyclopaedia*, *s.v.* Tuluva and Malabar; *Imp. Gaz.* (1908), *s.v.* Chandragiri. Formerly I guessed that Tuluva might represent the Satiyaputra kingdom of R.E. II, which I now identify with the Satyamangalam Tâlûk of Coimbatore.

Balûchistan, Makrân, Sind, Kachh (Cutch), the Swât valley, with the adjoining regions, Kashmîr, Nepâl, and the whole of India proper, except the extreme south, Tamilakam or Tamil Land. His dominions were far more extensive than British India of to-day, excluding Burma. The kingdom of Kâmarûpa, or Assam, in the north-east, seems to have been independent, and certainly remained outside the sphere of Asoka's religious propaganda. Hiuen Tsang, who visited the country in the seventh century, expressly affirms that Buddhism had failed to obtain a footing, and that not a single monastery had ever been built within its limits.

The legends of Tibet, recorded in more forms than one, assert that the city and kingdom of Khotan, to the north of the Himalayan range, were founded during the reign of Asoka by the co-operation of Indians and Chinese who divided the country between them; and one form of the story distinctly states that 'all the lands above the river Shal-chhu Gong-ma were given to Yaksha, which thenceforth belonged to Âryâvarta [*scil.* India].' It is also alleged that 'Asoka, the King of Âryâvarta,' visited Khotan in the year 250 after the death of Buddha, and that he was the contemporary of Shi-hwang-ti, the famous Chinese emperor who built the Great Wall. The chronology certainly is approximately correct, because Shi-hwang-ti reigned from 246 to 210, becoming 'universal emperor' in 221 [1], and Asoka's reign, as we have seen, extended from 273 to 232. The date of the alleged

[1] Tchang, *Synchronismes Chinois* (Chang-hai, 1905), pp. 112–16.

visit would fall in B. C. 237, on the assumption, sometimes made on plausible grounds, that Buddha died in B. C. 487. It is very remarkable that the Tibetan books alone have preserved an approximately accurate tradition of the dates of both Asoka and the death of Buddha. But, while duly noting that fact and admitting the probability of extensive intercourse between Asoka's dominions and Khotan, the evidence is hardly sufficient to justify the belief that the trans-Himalayan kingdom was subject to the political authority of the Indian monarch [1]. It is admitted that Buddhism was not introduced into Khotan until a date considerably later. Asoka's propaganda in the Himalayan region seems to have been confined to the southern side of the main range.

The materials available for a description of the organization and administration of the enormous empire defined in the preceding pages are surprisingly copious. Megasthenes has recorded with the pen of an intelligent foreign observer a detailed account of the institutions of Chandragupta, and the assumption is warranted that the system of government developed by the genius of the first emperor of India was maintained as a whole by his grandson, although

[1] Sarat Chandra Das, *J. A. S. B.*, Part i (1896), pp. 195–7; Rockhill, *Life of the Buddha*, pp. 233–7. The works used by Rockhill place the foundation of Khotan in 234 A. B. [487 − 234 = B. C. 253], and the accession of Asoka apparently 48 or 49 (30th year + 19, age of Kustana) years earlier, in B.C. 301 or 302, assigning fifty-four years to his reign. The legends are discussed by Stein, *Ancient Khotan* (1907), pp. 156–66.

supplemented by some novel arrangements and slightly modified by certain reforms. The systematic and invaluable treatise on the Art of Government ascribed to Kautalya, Kautilya, or Chânakya, the capable, although unscrupulous, minister of the first Maurya sovereign [1], and undoubtedly of early date, throws much welcome light on the principles of government as practised by ancient Indian kings, confirming and explaining in many respects the Greek accounts which previously stood alone. Numerous particulars of the civil and ecclesiastical organization of the empire are revealed by close examination of the Asoka inscriptions, and careful comparison of all the data of various kinds enables the historian to say with truth

[1] The minister's name is given as Kauṭalya, Kauṭilya, Châṇakya, or Vishṇugupta. Mr. R. Shamasastry is entitled to the credit of bringing to public notice for the first time a manuscript of the *Arthaśâstra* and an imperfect manuscript of a commentary by Bhaṭṭasvâmi on the same, which have been deposited by a pundit in the Mysore Government Oriental Library. Two more MSS. of the work have been lent by Professor Jolly to the Münich State Library, and another appears to exist in the collection of the Sanskrit College at Calcutta (Hillebrandt, *Ueber das Kauṭilîyaśâstra und Verwandtes*, Breslau, 1908). Mr. Shamasastry has printed the text, which was discovered in 1904, as vol. xxxvii of the Bibliotheca Sanskrita of Mysore (1909). The same learned scholar, having published translations of parts of the book in various forms, produced a complete version in 1915 (Bangalore Government Press). That version, although obviously needing revision, is a most creditable performance, and has been of the utmost value to me. The difficulties confronting the translator of the work are formidable. A considerable literature is growing up round the subject, and years must elapse before a perfect version can be expected.

that more is known about the internal polity of India as it was in the Maurya age than can be affirmed on the subject concerning any period intervening between that age and the reign of Akbar eighteen centuries later.

Pâtaliputra, the capital of the kingdom of Magadha and the head quarters of the imperial government, stood on the northern bank of the Sôn, a few miles above the confluence of that river with the Ganges. The Sôn changed its course long ago and now unites with the larger stream near the cantonment of Dinapore (Dhânapur) above Bankipore, but the old bed of the river can be readily traced and vestiges of the *ghâts* or steps which lined its bank can still be discerned. The capital, thus protected by two great rivers against hostile approach, occupied a strong, defensible position such as was much favoured by the founders of Indian towns. The site is now covered by the large native city of Patna, the English civil station of Bankipore, the East Indian Railway, and sundry adjacent villages. The belief at one time current that a large part of the ancient city has been cut away by the rivers is erroneous. Diluvial action seems to have been slight, and the remains of the early buildings still exist, but lie buried for the most part under a deep layer of silt.

The ancient city, like its modern successor, was a long, narrow parallelogram, about nine miles in length and a mile and a half in breadth. When Megasthenes lived there in the days of Chandragupta, it was defended by a massive timber palisade, pierced by sixty-four gates, crowned by five hundred and seventy towers, and protected externally by a broad, deep moat filled from the waters of the Sôn. Fragments of the palisade have been found at several places in the course of casual excavations. Asoka improved the defences by building an outer masonry wall, and beautified the city with so many richly decorated stone buildings that they seemed to after ages to be the work of the genii and beyond the power of human skill. I have myself seen two magnificent sandstone capitals dug up, one close to the railway and the other in a potato-field, which must have belonged to stately edifices of large size. Unfortunately, the depth of the overlying silt, often reaching twenty feet, and the existence of numerous modern buildings make excavation exceptionally difficult.

The royal palace, or one of the palaces, seems to have occupied the site now covered by the village and fields of Kumrâhâr, to the south of the railway, and the partial excavations carried out there by Dr. Spooner are sufficient to prove that remains exist suggestive of extremely puzzling problems. Further systematic exploration may reveal startling discoveries. I believe that it would be possible to identify many of the sites of the monuments at and near Pâtaliputra mentioned by the Chinese pilgrims, if a thorough survey were made by an adequate staff working with suitable appliances under skilled supervision, but the results of the praiseworthy efforts hitherto made excite rather than satisfy curiosity[1]. The Kumrâhâr palace apparently was that of Asoka's grandfather. Chandragupta's abode, although probably constructed mostly of timber like the palaces of the modern kings of Burma, is described as excelling in magnificence the royal pleasaunces of Susa and Ekbatana. The pillars, we are told, were clasped all round with vines embossed in gold, and adorned with silver figures of the most attractive birds. The gardens were replete with the choicest plants and furnished with artificial ponds of great beauty. Those splendours have all gone beyond recall, but extensive and costly excavation, no doubt, would disclose something of the magnitude at least of the masonry foundations of the earlier buildings and possibly might reveal more characteristic remains of Asoka's stone edifices and inscriptions.

The administration of the metropolis was organized with much elaboration, and was confided to a commission of thirty members divided into six Boards of five members each—a development, perhaps, of

[1] For changes in the rivers, see Cunningham, *Archaeol. S. Rep.*, vol. viii, p. 6; vol. xi, p. 154. Many identifications, more or less convincing, will be found in Lieut.-Col. Waddell's tract entitled *Discovery of the Exact Site of Asoka's Classic Capital of Pâtaliputra, &c.*, Calcutta, 1892; 2nd ed., 1903. This interesting work, although open to criticism, has added much to knowledge. A good deal of information is buried in an unpublished and rather crude report, of which I possess a proof, by the late Bâbû P. C. Mukharjî, whose drawings must be in the Calcutta Secretariat. The Greek and Roman notices will be found in Mr. McCrindle's works already cited.

the ordinary Hindu *panchâyat.* The first Board was charged with the superintendence of the industrial arts, and of artisans, who were regarded as servants of the State. The second was entrusted with the duty of supervising foreigners, and attending to their wants, being responsible for medical aid to the strangers in case of sickness, for their decent burial in case of death, and for the administration of the estates of the deceased. The officials were also required to provide foreign visitors with suitable lodgings and to furnish them with adequate escort when returning home. The duties of this Board closely resembled those imposed upon the *proxenoi* of Greek cities, but in India the persons performing such duties were officials of the Indian king, whereas in Greece the *proxenos*, like a modern consul, was appointed by the state whose subjects he protected [1].

The third Board was charged with the duty of maintaining a register of births and deaths, which was kept up for the information of the Government as well as for revenue purposes.

The fourth Board may be called the Board of Trade, because it exercised a general superintendence over the trade and commerce of the capital, and regulated weights and measures. The tax on sales being one of the principal sources of the royal revenue, everything for sale had to be marked with

[1] 'Consular Officers in India and Greece,' *Ind. Ant.*, xxxiv (1905), p. 200; Newton, *Essays on Art and Archaeology*, pp. 104, 121.

the official stamp[1]. The rules about weights and measures were laid down in minute detail. The fifth Board had similar duties in respect of manufactured goods. Traders were required to keep old and new goods separate, and careful distinctions were drawn between merchandise from foreign parts, that from the country, and that produced or made inside the city. The sixth Board collected the tax on sales, which is said by Megasthenes to have been one-tenth *ad valorem*, but, as a matter of fact, was levied at various rates. Evasion of this tax was punishable with death, according to Megasthenes as reported by Strabo. Chânakya lays down that 'those who utter a lie shall be punished as thieves[2],' that is to say, by mutilation or death.

The documents do not supply similar details concerning the municipal government of the other cities of the empire, but the edicts refer more than once to the officers in charge of particular towns, and it is probable that the greater cities were administered on the same lines as the capital.

The court was characterized by semi-barbaric magnificence which Quintus Curtius considered to be carried to 'a vicious excess without a parallel in the world.' The stories about the king's golden palanquin and other articles of ostentatious luxury

[1] ἀπὸ συσσήμου in Megasthenes, Fragm. xxxiv, mistranslated by McCrindle (*Megasthenes*, p. 87) as 'by public notice.' Σύσσημον is the *abhijñânamudrâ* of Chânakya, Bk. ii, ch. 21.

[2] *Arthaśâstra*, Bk. ii, ch. 21, 22.

may be accepted as true, because such extravagances have always been a weakness of Indian Râjâs, and it would not be difficult to find parallels even in Europe. The Roman author was especially scandalized by the information that the sovereign used to be 'accompanied by a long train of courtesans carried in golden palanquins, which takes a place in the procession separate from that of the queen's retinue, and is as sumptuously appointed.' The statement quoted is supported by Chânakya, who speaks of such women 'holding the royal umbrella, golden pitcher, and fan, and attending upon the king when seated on his royal litter, throne, or chariot [1].' Everybody acquainted with modern India is aware that similar customs still survive.

The close attendance of female guards, not of the courtesan class, on the royal person is an extremely ancient Indian custom, which was observed by Ranjit Singh less than a century ago, and may, perhaps, still be practised in out-of-the-way States. Chânakya lays down the rule that the sovereign on getting up from bed in the morning should be received first by the female archers, whose appearance seems to have been considered of good omen [2]. These Amazonian guards attended the king when he went out hunting in state, and prevented intrusion on the road of the procession, which was marked out by ropes. Death was the penalty of him who passed the barrier. Asoka, like his ancestors, indulged

[1] Bk. ii. ch. 27. [2] Bk. i. ch. 21.

without scruple in such formal hunting expeditions during his earlier years, but when he began to 'exert himself strenuously' in the cause of the Law of Piety about B.C. 259, he suppressed the establishment of the Royal Hunt and substituted for the pleasures of the chase the less exciting exercises of interviewing holy men, giving alms, and holding disputations on religious subjects during 'pious tours' similar to the pilgrimage which he undertook in B.C. 249.

Before the introduction of Buddhist puritanism the Maurya court used to amuse itself, not only with hunting, but with racing, animal fights, and gladiatorial contests. A curious form of racing, not now in vogue, was practised with a special breed of oxen, which are said to have equalled horses in speed. The car was harnessed to a mixed team with horses in the centre and an ox on each side. The course was about a mile and three quarters in length, and the king and his nobles betted keenly in gold and silver on the result. Animal fights were much enjoyed, elephants, rhinoceroses, bulls, rams, and other beasts being pitted against one another. Elephant fights continued to be a favourite diversion at Muhammadan courts up to recent times, and the unpleasant spectacle of a ram fight may still be witnessed at the palaces of many Râjâs. Such entertainments, of course, are abhorrent to the spirit of Buddhism, and all came to an end when Asoka resolved that there should be no more 'cakes and ale [1].' His courtiers must have had

[1] For the Maurya court see Q. Curtius, *History of Alexander*

a terribly dull time and often have sighed for the good old days of worldly-minded Chandragupta.

Communication between the capital and the provinces was maintained by the river waterways and a system of roads, the principal of which was the royal highway leading from Pâtaliputra to the Indus through Taxila, the forerunner of Lord Dalhousie's Grand Trunk Road. Distances were marked by pillars erected at intervals of ten *stadia*, or half a *kôs*, about an English mile and a quarter. Asoka added a well beside each pillar, and further consulted the comfort of travellers by planting trees for shade and fruit, and by providing rest-houses and sheds supplied with drinking-water. The communications must have been good to make possible the control of the whole empire from a capital situated so far to the east as Pâtaliputra [1].

the Great, Bk. viii, ch. 9, transl. McCrindle (*Invasion of India by Alexander the Great*, p. 188); and Aelian, *On the Peculiarities of Animals*, Bk. xiii, ch. 18, 22; Bk. xv, ch. 15, transl. McCrindle (*Ancient India*, pp. 141–5). Trotting oxen are used largely to this day, especially in Western and Southern India, but I have never heard of the racing breed except in Ceylon and in the pages of Megasthenes. I fully believe his statement.

[1] Strabo (Bk. xv, ch. 11; McCrindle, *Anc. India*, p. 16) gives the length of the royal road as 10,000 *stadia*, or about 1150 English miles, on the authority of Megasthenes and Eratosthenes, who obtained the figures from an official record, and as 9,000 according to another authority. 1 *stadium* = $202\frac{1}{4}$ yards; 10 *stadia* = $2022\frac{1}{2}$ yards. The mean length of the Mughal *kôs* as measured between the existing pillars (*mînârs*) is 4558 yards, but a shorter *kôs* is used in the Panjâb. I do not think it possible to accept the proposed interpretation of *aḍhakosikya* in

The imperial government was an absolute autocracy in which the king's will was supreme. From about B.C. 259 Asoka applied his autocratic power to the Buddhist Church, which he ruled as its Head. In the Bhâbrû Edict 'His Grace the King of Magadha addresses the Church with greetings and bids its members prosperity and good health,' and after this exordium proceeds to recommend to the faithful, lay and clerical, the passages from the holy books which he desires them to study with special care. Many years later, in the Sârnâth Edict and its variants, we find His Sacred Majesty declaring that 'the Church may not be rent in twain by any person,' and prescribing the canonical penalties to be inflicted upon schismatics. Asoka's position finds a close parallel in that of Charlemagne, whose 'unwearied and comprehensive activity made him throughout his reign an ecclesiastical no less than a civil ruler, summoning and sitting in councils, examining and appointing bishops, settling by capitularies the smallest points of Church discipline and polity[1].'

The imperial orders, whether in purely civil or in ecclesiastical matters, between which nice distinctions were not drawn, were communicated through an organized body of officials, the superior grades of

Pillar Edict VII, sec. 5, as meaning 'at intervals of eight *kôs*.' *Aḍha* in the language of the edicts does not apparently mean 'eight.' The direct distance between Pâṭaliputra and Taxila as measured on the map is about 950 miles.

[1] Bryce, *The Holy Roman Empire* (1892), p. 64.

whom were called *mahâmâtras*, and the lower ranks were known as *yuktas*[1]. When a *mahâmâtra* or *yukta* was assigned to a special department, his sphere of duty was indicated by a prefix to the generic title. The less civilized tribes on the frontiers and in the jungles were governed by their own chiefs subject to the general control of the paramount power, and we may be assured that large portions of the empire were administered by local hereditary Râjâs, who would have been left very much to their own devices as long as they supplied the men and money demanded by their suzerain. But the inscriptions, with one exception, do not mention such Râjâs in the settled provinces, and the view concerning them expressed above is based on the general course of Indian history[2].

The authorities, that is to say, Megasthenes, Chânakya, and the edicts, rather seem to imply that all the work of administration was done by Crown officials. The princely Viceroys stood at the head of the bureaucracy. Four of them—the Princes of Taxila, Ujjain, Tosali, and Suvarnagiri—are mentioned in the edicts[3], and there may have been others. The Viceroyalties of Taxila and Ujjain are known also from

[1] The word *yukta* in this sense occurs several times in the edicts, and frequently in the *Arthaśâstra*.

[2] The Yavana Râjâ Tushâspha in the Girnâr inscription of Rudradâman (*Ep. Ind.*, viii. 36).

[3] Taxila and Ujjain in Kalinga Provincials' Edict; Tosali in Kalinga Borderers' Edict, Dhauli version; Suvarṇagiri in Minor Rock Edict I, Brahmagiri version.

literary tradition, which represents Asoka as having governed both those distant provinces previous to his accession. The Prince of Taxila may be presumed to have controlled at least the Panjâb and Kashmîr. The country now called Afghanistan may have been in charge of another Viceroy, who does not happen to have been mentioned. The Prince of Ujjain would have been responsible for Mâlvâ, Gujarât, and Surâshtra. The Prince of Tosali presumably was Governor of the annexed province of Kalinga, and the Prince of Suvarnagiri seems to have been Viceroy of the South[1].

The more central regions of the empire apparently were administered by officials appointed directly from the capital, without the intervention of any Prince. The distribution of the Pillar inscriptions gives a rough indication of the extent of the home provinces, while the Rock inscriptions occur only in outlying regions.

The Râjûkas, 'set over hundreds of thousands of souls,' probably came next in rank to the Viceroys. The modern term Governor may serve as a rough equivalent. Below them came the Prâdesikas, or District Officers, and both classes seem to have been

[1] Tosali must have been at or near Dhauli in the Purî District, Orissa, and, perhaps, was the Dosara of Ptolemy. The position of Suvarṇagiri is not known. The name means Golden Hill, and the fact that the inscription discovered in 1915 at Maski in the Nizam's Dominions was incised on a rock close to ancient goldmines suggests that Suvarṇagiri was in the Raichûr District, not very far from Maski. It is possible that the site of Suvarṇagiri may be found.

comprised under the general name of *mahâmâtras*. A host of petty officials, *yuktas* and *upayuktas*, clerks and underlings of sorts, carried out the orders of their superiors. The king and his great officers, of course, had their secretariat establishments, worked by secretaries, or *lekhakas*[1]. All the evidence goes to show that the civil administration was highly organized for purposes of both record and executive action.

Departments were numerous. Megasthenes was impressed by the working of the Irrigation Department, which performed functions similar to those of the corresponding institution in Egypt, regulating the sluices so as to distribute the water fairly among the farmers. The Rudradâman inscription at Girnâr gives us a glimpse of the actual working of the Department, which had embanked the lake at Girnâr in the time of Chandragupta Maurya, and under Asoka's Persian (Yavana) Râjâ, Tushâspha, had equipped it with the needful watercourses. This instance shows the care that was taken to promote agricultural improvement and so to develop the land revenue, even in a remote province distant more than a thousand miles from the capital. The farmers did not get the water for nothing. It was supplied on strictly business principles, and paid for by heavy water rates (*udakabhâgam*) varying from one-fourth to one-third of the produce, according to the mode of irrigation[2].

The land revenue, or Crown rent, as always in India,

[1] Defined in *Arthaśâstra*, Bk. ii, ch. 10.

[2] *Arthaśâstra*, Bk. ii, ch. 24.

was the mainstay of the Treasury. All agricultural land was regarded as Crown property, and the normal theoretical share of the State was either one-fourth or one-sixth of the produce, in addition to water rate, if any, and a host of other dues and cesses. People who grumble at modern assessments will find if they study history that their ancestors often were much more severely fleeced. Chânakya, without the slightest regard for moral principles, explains the methods of more than Machiavellian wickedness by which needy kings may replenish their coffers [1], and many instances of the lesson being well learned are on record. Official misdoings were as common in ancient as in modern times. The textbook writer, with the characteristic Hindu love for categories, explains that 'there are about forty ways of embezzlement,' which he enumerates with painstaking exactness. He sagely observes that 'just as it is impossible not to taste the honey or the poison that finds itself at the tip of the tongue, so it is impossible for a Government servant not to eat up at least a bit of the king's revenue [2].' The Kalinga Provincials' Edict shows how Asoka was worried by negligent or disobedient officers, and expresses in singularly vivid language, evidently the actual words of the sovereign, his displeasure at the neglect of his commands. 'You must,' he declares, 'see to your duty and be told to remember:—"See to my commands, such and such are the instructions of his Sacred

[1] *Ind. Ant.*, xxxiv. 115-19.
[2] *Arthaśâstra*, Bk. ii, ch. 8, 9.

Majesty." Fulfilment of these bears great fruit; non-fulfilment brings great calamity. By those who fail neither heaven nor the royal favour can be won;' and so forth.

He essayed the impossible task of supervising personally the affairs of his wide dominions. 'I never feel satisfaction,' he exclaims, 'in my exertions and dispatch of business. For work I must for the welfare of all the folk; and of that, again, the root is energy, and the dispatch of business; for nothing is more essential than the welfare of all the folk.' Thus he toiled through a long life, priding himself especially on his accessibility to suitors at all hours and in all places, even the most inconvenient[1]. Such accessibility, although inconsistent with really efficient government, is always highly popular in India, where the people never can be persuaded that a ruler may arrange his time more profitably than by exposing himself to incessant interruption. The European critic feels that if Asoka had worked less hard he would have done better work, but must admit that in spite of his defects of method he was wonderfully successful in holding together for forty years an empire rarely exceeded in magnitude. Asoka's procedure was in accordance with the practice of his grandfather, who heard cases even while he was being massaged by his attendants, and with Chânakya's rule, which reads like an extract from the edicts:

'The King, therefore, shall personally attend to the business

[1] Rock Edict VI.

of gods, heretics, Brahmans learned in the Vedas, cattle, sacred places, minors, the aged, the afflicted, the helpless, and women:—all this either in the order of enumeration or according to the urgent necessity of each such business [1].'

The emperor, like most Oriental sovereigns, relied much upon espionage and the reports of news-writers and special agents employed by the Crown for the purpose of watching the executive officers, and reporting to head quarters everything that came to their knowledge. Even the courtesans were employed in this secret service, the nature of which is largely explained in Chânakya's treatise. Kings in those days had reason to be suspicious. It is recorded of Chandragupta that he dared not sleep in the daytime, and was obliged, like a modern king of Burma, to change his bedroom every night [2].

Asoka, in his fourteenth 'regnal year' (B.C. 256), added to the normal establishment a body of officers especially appointed to the duty of teaching and enforcing the Buddhist Law of Piety, or rules of *dharma*. The superior officials of this kind were termed *Dharma-mahâmâtras*, which may be rendered

[1] *Arthaśâstra*, Bk. i. ch. 19, 'The Duties of a King.'

[2] Strabo, I, 53–56 in McCrindle, *Megasthenes*, p. 71; *Arthaśâstra*, Bk. i, ch. 11, &c.; the King's Agents (*pulisâni*) in Pillar Edict III, with whom compare the *missi dominici* of Charlemagne; *Mudrâ-râkshasa*, Act ii. Charlemagne's *missi* were 'officials commissioned to traverse each some part of his dominions, reporting on and redressing the evils they found' (Bryce, *Holy Roman Empire* (1892), p. 68). Their functions must have been similar to those of Asoka's 'men' or Agents.

Censors, and the inferior were called *Dharma-yuktas* or Assistant Censors. The duties of the Censors, as defined in general terms in Rock Edicts V, XII, and Pillar Edict VII, must have included jurisdiction in cases of injury inflicted on animals contrary to the regulations, exhibitions of gross filial disrespect, and other breaches of the moral rules prescribed by authority. They were also instructed to redress cases of wrongful confinement or corporal punishment, and were empowered to grant remission of sentence when the offender was entitled to consideration by reason of advanced years, sudden calamity, or the burden of a large family. They shared with the Inspectors of Women the delicate duty of supervising female morals, the households of the royal family both at the capital and in the provincial towns being subject to their inspection. The practical working of these institutions must have presented many difficulties, and been open to much abuse.

The general severity of the government of Chandragupta is testified to by Justin, who declares that that prince, after his victory over the Macedonian garrisons, 'forfeited by his tyranny all title to the name of liberator, for he oppressed with servitude the very people whom he had emancipated from foreign thraldom.' The Roman historian's impression seems to be justified by the few details on record concerning the ferocity of the penal law. We have seen that evasion of taxes in certain cases was punishable with death, and that an intruder on the king's procession during a hunting expedition was liable to the same punishment. We are also told that the offence of causing the loss of a hand or an eye to an artisan was capital, the reason apparently being that skilled workmen were regarded as being specially devoted to the king's service. Perjury and theft were ordinarily punishable by mutilation. Other instances of severity may be collected from Chânakya's treatise. In certain unspecified cases the eccentric penalty of shaving the offender's hair was inflicted. This punishment apparently was borrowed from Persia, and is one of several indications that the example of the court of the Great King influenced the customs of the Maurya sovereigns[1]. Asoka, as already observed, seems to have maintained the stern methods of his predecessors, the only mitigation for which he claims credit being the grant of three days' respite between a capital sentence and execution. His practice of releasing convicts on the anniversary of his consecration was in accordance with precedent[2]. Megasthenes, from personal experience, was able to testify that the sternness of the government kept crime in check, and that in Chandragupta's capital, with a population of 400,000, the total of the thefts reported in any one day did not exceed two hundred *drachmai*, or about eight pounds sterling.

The two Kalinga Edicts deserve special study as authoritative statements of Asoka's personal ideal of good government, a benevolent paternal despotism.

[1] *Ind. Ant.* xxxiv (1905), p. 202.

[2] *Arthaśâstra*, Bk. ii, ch. 36 (*Ind. Ant.*, xxxiv. 52).

He instructs his officers that they must induce the wilder tribes 'to trust me and grasp the truth that—"the King is to us even as a father; he loves us even as he loves himself; we are to the King even as his children."' The companion edict inculcates similar principles to be applied to the government of the more settled population.

The army, comprising, according to established rule, the four arms of infantry, cavalry, elephants, and chariots, was not a militia, but a permanent force, maintained at the royal cost, liberally paid, and equipped from the Government arsenals. The edicts, as might be expected, throw no light upon its organization in the reign of Asoka, and the information on record chiefly derived from Megasthenes, refers to the time of Chandragupta. The navy, as in Europe until recent times, was regarded as a branch of the army. No evidence as to the extent of the naval force maintained by the Mauryas is available, but it is known that the ancient Hindus did not shun the 'black water' as their descendants do, and that the States of Southern India maintained powerful navies for centuries. It is, therefore, probable that the Maurya ships were not restricted to the rivers, but ventured out to sea. Chânakya, indeed, expressly states that the head of the naval department should look after sea-going ships as well as those concerned with inland navigation[1].

The War Office, like the capital, was controlled by

[1] *Samudra-samyâna*, *Arthaśâstra*, Bk. ii, ch. 28.

a commission of thirty members, divided into six Boards each containing five members, to which departments were assigned as follows:—

Board I: Admiralty, in co-operation with the Admiral;

Board II: Transport, commissariat, and army service, including the provision of drummers, grooms, mechanics, and grass-cutters;

Board III: Infantry;

Board IV: Cavalry;

Board V: War-chariots;

Board VI: Elephants.

The strength of the force maintained by Chandragupta has been stated in Chapter I. Asoka's peaceful policy probably required a smaller military establishment, but nothing on the subject is recorded. The heaviness of the enemy's casualties in the Kalinga war indicates that Asoka must have employed a large force to reduce the country.

The arms, when not in use, were stored in arsenals, and ranges of stables were provided for the horses and elephants. Chariots, when on the march, were drawn by oxen in order to spare the horses. Each war-chariot, which had a team of either two or four horses harnessed abreast, carried two fighting-men, besides the driver. The chariot when used as a state conveyance was drawn by four horses. 'The victory of kings,' it was said, 'depends mainly upon elephants [1],'

[1] *Arthaśâstra*, Bk. ii, ch. 2. The author lays down that 'whoever kills an elephant shall be put to death.'

which, consequently, were kept in vast hosts, numbering many thousands. Each war-elephant carried three fighting-men in addition to the driver.

The interesting details given by Arrian concerning the equipment of the infantry and cavalry may be quoted in full :--

'I proceed now,' he says, 'to describe the mode in which the Indians equip themselves for war, premising that it is not to be regarded as the only one in vogue. The foot-soldiers carry a bow of equal length with the man who bears it. This they rest upon the ground, and pressing against it with their left foot thus discharge the arrow, having drawn the string far backwards; for the shaft they use is little short of being three yards long, and there is nothing which can resist an Indian archer's shot—neither shield nor breastplate, nor any stronger defence if such there be. In their left hand they carry bucklers of undressed ox-hide, which are not so broad as those who carry them, but are about as long. Some are equipped with javelins instead of bows, but all wear a sword, which is broad in the blade, but not longer than three cubits; and this, when they engage in close fight (which they do with reluctance), they wield with both hands, to fetch down a lustier blow.

The horsemen are equipped with two lances like the lances called *saunia*, and with a shorter buckler than that carried by the foot-soldiers. But they do not put saddles on their horses, nor do they curb them with bits like the bits in use among the Greeks or Kelts, but they fit on round the extremity of the horse's mouth a circular piece of stitched raw ox-hide studded with pricks of iron or brass pointing inwards, but not very sharp; if a man is rich he uses pricks made of ivory. Within the horse's mouth is put an iron prong like a skewer, to which the reins are attached. When the rider, then, pulls the reins, the prong controls the horse, and the pricks which are attached to this prong goad the mouth, so that it cannot but obey the reins[1].'

The development during the ninety years of Maurya rule of a system of civil, military, and church government so complex and highly organized is matter for legitimate astonishment. The records of Alexander's invasion disclose the existence of a multitude of independent states governed either by Râjâs or tribal oligarchies, constantly at war with one another and free from all control by a superior power. It is true that, even in those days, Magadha occupied the premier position, but the Nanda king of that state made no claim to be the Lord Paramount of India. The conception of an Indian Empire, extending from sea to sea, and embracing almost the whole of India and Afghanistan, was formed and carried into effect by Chandragupta and his minister in the brief space of twenty-four years. History can show few greater political achievements. Not only was the empire formed, but it was so thoroughly organized that the

[1] Arrian, *Indika*, ch. xvi, transl. McCrindle (*Megasthenes*, p. 220). A nearly life-sized figure of an infantry soldier armed as described by Megasthenes is reproduced by Cunningham, *Stûpa of Bharhut*, Pl. xxxii, 1. For shapes of Indian arms at the beginning of the Christian era, see Cunningham, *Bhilsa Topes*, p. 217, Pl. xxxiii; Maisey, *Sânchi*, Pl. xxxv, xxxvi. A long list of weapons and military engines is given in *Arthaśâstra*, Bk. ii, ch. 18. Tennent (*Ceylon*, 2nd ed., i. 499) compares the Veddah mode of holding the bow with the foot, but it is quite different, the bow not being rested on the ground.

sovereign's commands emanating from Pâtaliputra were obeyed without demur on the banks of the Indus and the shores of the Arabian sea. The immense heritage thus created by the genius of the first emperor of India was transmitted intact to his son and grandson, and all three monarchs were in a position to assert their equality with the leading Hellenistic princes of the age. The figure of Bindusâra, hidden in the darkness, eludes our view, and we can only assume that his capacity must have been equal to the task imposed upon him by his birth, because otherwise it would have been impossible for him to enlarge and pass on to his famous son the splendid dominion which Asoka ruled with so much distinction.

Dim though the picture be in many of its details, the figure of Asoka takes an honourable place in the gallery of the greatest kings known to history. In a sense we know him better than we know any other ancient monarch, because he speaks to us in his own words. It is impossible, I think, for any student to read the edicts with care, and not to hear the voice of the king himself. The abrupt transitions from the third to the first person, from *oratio obliqua* to *oratio directa*, which embarrass the translator, and produced on early interpreters the erroneous impression of clumsy composition, are of the deepest interest when regarded as devices for inserting in official proclamations the very words of the sovereign. We can discern a man of strong will, unwearied application, and high aims, who spared no labour in the pursuit of his ideals, possessed the mental grasp capable of forming the vast conception of missionary enterprise in three continents, and was at the same time able to control the intricate affairs of Church and State in an empire which the most powerful sovereign might envy. His plan of committing to the faithful keeping of the rocks his code of moral duty was equally original and bold, and his intense desire that his measures should result in the 'long endurance' of the Good Law as taught in his ordinances has been fulfilled in no small measure by the preservation of some thirty-five separate documents to this day.

His government—a theocracy without a God—concerned itself, like that of Charlemagne, equally with Church and State, and, so far as we can judge, attained no small success. The number, costliness, and magnitude of his buildings and monuments are enough in themselves to prove that the empire in which the erection of such works was possible must have been rich and tranquil.

We need not be surprised that the fabric collapsed after his death; the wonder rather is that it held together so long.

CHAPTER III

THE MONUMENTS

THE extravagant legend which ascribes to Asoka the erection of eighty-four thousand *stûpas*, 'topes,' or sacred cupolas, within the space of three years, proves the depth of the impression made upon the popular imagination by the number, magnitude, and magnificence of the great Maurya's architectural achievements[1]. So imposing were his works that they were universally believed to have been wrought by supernatural agency.

'The royal palace and halls in the midst of the city (*scil.* Pâtaliputra), which exist now as of old, were all made by spirits which he employed, and which piled up the stones, reared the walls and gates, and executed the elegant carving and inlaid sculpture-work in a way which no human hands of this world could accomplish[2].'

[1] 84,000 *dharmarâjikâs* built by Asoka Dharmarâja, as stated by *Divyâvadâna* (ed. Cowell & Neil, p. 379, quoted by Foucher, *Icon. Bouddhique*, p. 55 n.). In the MS. miniature the words *Râdhya-Dharmarâjikâ-chaityah* denote the *stûpa* and one-story monastery beside the Râdhya Pillar (ibid., p. 195).

[2] Fa-hien, *Travels*, ch. xxvii, transl. Legge. Giles's version differs somewhat:—'The king's palace and courts were all constructed by spirits whom he employed to pile stones, build walls and gates, carve ornamental designs and engrave—truly

Thus wrote the simple-minded Fa-hien at the beginning of the fifth century. More than two hundred years later, when Hiuen Tsang travelled, the ancient imperial city was deserted and in ruins, the effect of the departure of the court and the ravages of the White Huns. Now,

> 'The cloud-capped towers, the gorgeous palaces,
> The solemn temples,'

lie buried deep below the silt of the Sôn and Ganges rivers, serving as a foundation for the city of Patna, the civil station of Bankipore, sundry villages, and the East Indian Railway.

No example of the secular architecture of Asoka's reign has survived in a condition such as would permit of its plan and style being studied. Local tradition indicates the extensive buried ruins at and near the village of Kumrâhâr, to the south of the railway line connecting Bankipore and Patna, as the site of the palace of the ancient kings, and the tradition probably embodies the truth. Mr. Mukharji discovered innumerable fragments of an Asoka pillar between the Kallu and Chaman tanks to the north of the village. The pillar, which was of polished sandstone as usual, was about 3 feet in diameter, and evidently had been broken up by heaping round it a mass of inflammable material which was then set on fire. The similar pillar, to the north-east of

not the work of mortals. These still exist.' Beal, like Legge, places the palace 'in the city,' and according to him 'the ruins still exist.'

Benares City, the stump of which is now known as Lât Bhairo, was destroyed in that way by the local Muhammadans during the great riot of 1809. Various sculptures and other remains at Kumrâhâr indicate the importance of the site. But another palace must have been situated somewhere inside the city walls and a second Asoka pillar is said to exist buried in Patna City [1]. Many of the remains at and near Patna are practically inaccessible, and the incomplete excavations carried out on several occasions have not sufficed to establish great results of definite value. If the scientific exploration of the site begun by Dr. Spooner is carried further, it will need to be done carefully and will be a long and costly business.

The numerous and stately monasteries which Asoka erected at many places in the empire have shared the fate of his palaces, not even one surviving in a recognizable state. Such structures were extremely numerous. Hiuen Tsang mentions more than eighty *stûpas* and monasteries ascribed to Asoka, without counting the legendary five hundred convents in Kashmîr and other large indefinite groups in other countries. The Asokârâma, or Kukkutarâma, the 'Cock Monastery,' which was the first-fruits of the emperor's zeal as a convert, and accommodated a thousand

[1] At Kallu Khan's Bâgh, in the zenâna of Maulavis Muhammad Kabîr and Amîr, buried several feet below the courtyard, and so thick that two men joining their arms could not encircle it (Mukharji's unpubl. *Report*, p. 17). For Lât Bhairo see the author's paper in *Z. D. M. G.* for 1909.

monks, stood on the south-eastern side of the capital, but has not been identified, which is not surprising, as it had been already long in ruins at the time of Hiuen Tsang's visit in the seventh century. According to Târanâth, the great monastic establishment at Nâlandâ near Râjagriha, which became the head quarters of Indian Buddhism, was founded by Asoka, who erected splendid buildings there. It seems likely that excavation on the site of Nâlandâ, which is well defined and easily accessible, will almost certainly yield results far richer than can be hoped for at Patna. The explorations at Nâlandâ started by Dr. Spooner in 1915–16 are most promising.

The *stûpas*, or cupolas, on which the emperor lavished so much treasure, have been more fortunate than the palaces and monasteries in that one group of buildings of this class, thanks to its situation in an out-of-the-way locality, survived destruction, and would now be tolerably perfect but for the ravages of English amateur archaeologists in the early part of the nineteenth century. The group alluded to is that at and near Sânchî in the Bhopâl State, Central India (lat. 23° 29′ N., long. 77° 45′ E.), which included ten *stûpas*, besides the remains of other buildings, as late as the year 1818[1].

A *stûpa*, it should be explained, was usually destined either to enshrine a casket containing the relics of a Buddha or other saint, or simply to mark

[1] These buildings are not mentioned by the Chinese pilgrims.

permanently the reputed scene of some incident famous in the history of the Buddhist Church; but occasionally one was erected merely in honour of a Buddha. The form, apparently of high antiquity, seems to be derived from that of a hut with a curved bamboo roof, not from an earthen tumulus. In Asoka's age a *stûpa* was a nearly hemispherical mass of solid masonry, either brick or stone, resting upon a plinth which formed a perambulation path for worshippers, and flattened at the top to carry a square altar-shaped structure, which was surmounted by a series of stone umbrellas one above the other. The base was frequently surrounded by a stone railing, the pillars, bars, and coping-stones of which might be either quite plain or adorned by all the resources of sculpture in relief. Sometimes the entrances through the railings were equipped with elaborate gateways (*toraṇas*), resembling in style those still common in China, and covered with the most elaborate carvings.

The principal *stûpa* at Sânchî, which stands on the top of a hill and is a conspicuous object as seen from the Indian Midland Railway, is a segment of a sphere, built of red sandstone blocks, with a diameter of 110 feet at the base of the dome. The diameter of the plinth or berm is 121½ feet, and the total height of the monument when perfect is believed to have been about 77½ feet. It is enclosed by a massive plain stone railing with monolithic pillars 11 feet high, entrance being effected through four highly ornate gateways, 34 feet in height, covered with a profusion of relief sculptures illustrating the Buddhist scriptures. Casts of the eastern gateway now at South Kensington and in several other museums can be examined conveniently at leisure. The existing stone *stûpa* and contemporary plain railing are about a century later than Asoka, whose original brick *stûpa* was enclosed in the enlarged building. The sculptured gateways date from about 50 B. C. to the Christian era. No trace has been found of any structure prior to the reign of Asoka, and the details of the succession of the various ancient floors permit of little doubt that the earliest building on the site was erected by Asoka. Near the southern gateway fragments survive of a finely designed Asoka pillar estimated to have stood about forty-two feet in height. The mutilated lions which once crowned the summit are admirable examples of Asokan art, comparable in merit with the Sârnâth capital. Both compositions may be the work of one artist. The damaged inscription at Sânchî is a replica of the more perfect text of Minor Pillar Edict I at Sârnâth. Inasmuch as all the Minor Pillar Edicts date from a late period of the reign and the Sânchî pillar seems to be contemporary with the original *stûpa*, we may assign that building also to the last ten years of Asoka's rule. Other *stûpas* in the neighbourhood are more or less alike in form Some have yielded interesting inscribed relic caskets, as mentioned above in Chapter I[1].

[1] It now suffices to cite only one book, *A Guide to Sânchî* by Sir John Marshall, C.I.E. (Calcutta, 1918), which gives all needful references to other works. Detailed treatises are in preparation.

A very interesting relic, belonging in part to the age of Asoka, was discovered by Sir Alexander Cunningham in 1873 at Bharhut, a village in the Nâgaudh (Nagod) State of Baghelkhand, about ninety-five miles south-west from Allahabad. He found there the remains of a brick *stûpa* of moderate size, nearly 68 feet in diameter, surrounded by an elaborately carved railing bearing numerous dedicatory inscriptions in characters closely resembling those of Asoka's records. The *stûpa* had been covered with a coat of plaster, in which hundreds of triangular-shaped recesses had been made for the reception of lights to illuminate the monument. It was the practice of the Indian Buddhists, as it is that of their co-religionists now in Burma, to decorate their holy buildings on festival days in every possible way, with flowers, garlands, banners, and lights.

The *stûpa* has, I believe, wholly disappeared, and portions of the richly sculptured railing have been saved only by the precaution of removing them to Calcutta, where they now form one of the principal treasures of the Indian Museum. The railing was a little more than 7 feet high, and was divided into quadrants by openings facing the cardinal points, which were framed in elaborate gateways similar to those at Sânchî. The sculptures of the railing and gateways were principally devoted to the illustration of the Buddhist *Jâtakas*, or Birth stories. As at Sânchî, the buildings were of different ages, the *stûpa* itself probably dating from the time of Asoka, while one of the gateways is known to have been erected in the days of the Sunga kings, who succeeded the Mauryas. The railing, which may have been considerably earlier than the gateways, was composed of pillars, three cross-bars or rails, and a heavy coping. Each of the pillars is a monolith bearing a central medallion on each face, with a half medallion at the top and another at the bottom. Every member of the structure is covered with rich and spirited sculpture in low relief, which is of exceptional interest for the history of Buddhism, because it is interpreted to a large extent by contemporary explanatory inscriptions [1].

The more or less similar railing, fragments of which exist at Bodh Gayâ, has been generally designated as the 'Asoka railing,' but really belongs, like the Bharhut gateway, to Sunga times [2]. Bâbû P. C. Mukharjî found at Patna parts of at least three stone railings, some of which must date from Asoka's reign. The inscribed and sculptured railing at Besnagar, near Bhîlsâ or Bhalsâ, and not far from Sânchî, cannot be very far removed from the time of Asoka. The sculptures are similar to those at Bharhut and Sânchî [3].

[1] Cunningham wrote 'Bharhut,' and others spell 'Bharaut,' but the late Dîwân of Rewâ told me that the correct spelling is 'Barhut.' The ruins are not so far from Allahabad as Cunningham estimated. They are described in his special monograph, *The Stûpa of Bharhut* (London, 1879). The inscriptions are dealt with in *Ind. Ant.*, xiv. 138; xxi. 225.

[2] Marshall, *J. R. A. S.*, 1908, p. 1096, Pl. iv.

[3] Cunningham, *Reports*, x. 38, Pl. xiii.

The progress of the excavations at Sârnâth may be expected to disclose many remains of the Maurya age, but they are difficult to get at, being buried under the buildings of later generations.

In ancient India, as is now a common practice in China, both the Buddhists and the Jains were in the habit of defraying the cost of expensive religious edifices by subscription, each subscriber or group of subscribers being given the credit of having contributed a particular pillar, coping-stone, or other portion of the edifice on which the contributor's name was inscribed. The subscriptions, of course, must have been collected in cash, the work being carried out by the architect according to plan. The record of individual donors was intended not only to gratify their vanity and the natural desire for the perpetuation of their names, but also for the practical purpose of securing for themselves and their families an accumulation of spiritual merit to serve as a defence against the dangers of rebirth. This special purpose is frequently expressed in the Indian records. Dedicatory inscriptions were very numerous at Bharhut. It is interesting to observe that the same practice of building by subscription existed in Hellenistic Asia. At the temple of Labranda in Caria, dating from the reign of Nero, or a little later, Sir Charles Fellows found twelve fluted columns, each of which bore a panel recording that it was the gift of such and such a person[1].

[1] Fellows, *Asia Minor* (London, 1838), pp. 261, 331, and plate.

In India statues in the round are rare, relief being preferred, but a few notable examples of figures in the round apparently assignable to the Maurya period are known. The most remarkable is the inscribed colossal statue of a man found at Parkham, a village between Agra and Mathurâ. The figure, executed in grey sandstone highly polished, stands about 7 feet high, and is massive, if not clumsy, in its proportions. The face, unfortunately, is mutilated and the arms have been broken off. The dress, a loose robe confined by two broad bands, one below the breast and the other round the loins, is peculiar. The inscription, which has not been edited properly, seems to be in characters substantially identical with those used in the edicts [1].

A colossal female statue, 6 feet 7 inches in height, uninscribed, but supposed on account of the costume to belong to the same period, was found at Besnagar, and is specially noteworthy as being the only known early female figure in the round. The arms are missing and the face is damaged, but so far as I can judge from a photograph, the work is of considerable merit [2]. The Patna and Didarganj statues (*J. B. O. Res. Soc.*, vol. v (1919), Plates i–iv) seem to be closely related to the Parkham image.

Asoka took special delight in erecting monolithic

[1] Vogel, *Catalogue of the Archaeological Museum at Mathura* (Allahabad, 1910), p. 83, Plate xii. The inscription records the artist's name.

[2] *Hist. of Fine Art in India and Ceylon* (1911), p. 62, Plate xiv.

pillars, inscribed and uninscribed, in great numbers and designed on a magnificent scale, regardless of cost. These pillars, many of which, more or less complete, are known, give us a better notion of the treasure, taste, and skill lavished upon Asoka's architectural works than do any of the other monuments. Hiuen Tsang mentions specifically sixteen of such pillars, four or five of which can be identified with existing monuments more or less convincingly; and, on the other hand, most of the extant pillars are not referred to by the Chinese pilgrim. The inscribed pillars now known number ten, of which only two can be positively identified with those noticed by him. Fortunately, two pillars—one uninscribed, the other bearing a copy of the first six Pillar Edicts—still stand in a condition practically perfect, and a detailed description of these will suffice to give the reader an adequate notion of the whole class. The discovery in 1904–5 of the magnificent capital of the Sârnâth pillar has revealed the finest example of Maurya art known to exist.

The perfect uninscribed pillar at Bakhirâ near Basâr, the ancient Vaisâli, in the Muzaffarpur District, N. Bihâr, is a monolith of fine sandstone, highly polished for its whole length of 32 feet above the water level. A square pedestal with three steps is said to exist under water. The shaft tapers uniformly from a diameter of 49·8 inches at the water level to 38·7 at the top. The principal member of the capital, 2 feet 10 inches in height, is bell-shaped in the Persepolitan style, and is surmounted by an oblong abacus 12 inches high, which serves as a pedestal for a lion seated on its haunches, and 4½ feet in height. Two or three mouldings are inserted between the shaft and the bell capital, and one intervenes between the latter and the abacus. The total height above the level of the water is 44 feet 2 inches. Including the submerged portion the length of the monument cannot be less than 50 feet, and its weight is estimated to be 50 tons [1].

The inscribed Lauriyâ-Nandangarh or Mathiah pillar in the Champâran District, N. Bihâr, resembles that at Bakhirâ in general design, but is lighter and less massive, and consequently very graceful (*Frontispiece*). The polished shaft, 32 feet 9½ inches in height, diminishes from a base diameter of 35½ inches to a diameter of only 22¼ inches at the top. The abacus, which is circular instead of oblong, is decorated on the edge with an artistic bas-relief representing a row of geese pecking their food. The height of the capital including the lion, which faces the rising sun, is 6 feet 10 inches, and consequently the entire monument is nearly 40 feet high. The cable-string courses and 'egg and dart' ovolo which serve as mouldings are admirably executed, and the design and workmanship of the whole are rightly praised as displaying both knowledge and power [2].

[1] Cunningham, *Reports*, i. 56; xvi. 12.

[2] Ibid, i. 73, Pl. xxiv; xvi. 104, Pl. xxvii (copied in frontispiece); Caddy, in *Proc. A. S. B.*, 1895, p. 155. The correct

The circular abacus of the Allahabad pillar is decorated, instead of the geese, with a graceful scroll of alternate lotus and honeysuckle, resting on a beaded astragalus moulding, seemingly of Greek origin. According to tradition the monument was originally surmounted by a lion, and in 1838 a Captain Smith of the Royal Engineers was commissioned to design a new capital in the style of the Bakhirâ and Lauriyâ-Nandangarh pillars. But his attempt was a lamentable failure and resulted in a monstrosity which Cunningham considered to be 'not unlike a stuffed poodle stuck on the top of an inverted flower-pot.' Many years have passed since I saw the thing, but I suppose it is still there.

Two mutilated pillars exist at Râmpurwâ in the Champâran District. The one which bears a copy of the first six Pillar Edicts was surmounted by a finely designed lion, discovered in 1907–8 buried close by. Mr. Marshall notes that the 'muscles and thews of the beast are vigorously modelled, and though conventionalized in certain particulars, it is endowed with a vitality and strength which rank it among the finest sculptures of the Maurya period.' The companion uninscribed pillar had a bull capital, also discovered by research, but unfortunately much injured. The

name of the neighbouring village is Nandangaṛh, not Navandgaṛh, as stated by Cunningham.

[1] Cunningham, *Reports*, i. 298–300; *Inscriptions of Asoka*, p. 37.

bell section of the lion capital was attached to the shaft by a barrel-shaped bolt of pure copper, measuring 2 feet $0\frac{1}{2}$ inch in length, with a diameter of $4\frac{5}{16}$ inches in the centre, and $3\frac{5}{8}$ inches at each end, which was accurately fitted without cement[1].

The line of pillars in the Muzaffarpur and Champâran Districts at Bakhirâ (Vaisâli), Lauriyâ-Ararâj (Radhiah), Lauriyâ-Nandangarh (Mathiah), and Râmpurwâ evidently marks the course of the royal road from the northern bank of the Ganges opposite the capital to the Nepâl valley. The hamlet of Râmpurwâ is not far from the foot of the hills. Three of the five pillars are inscribed with practically identical copies of the first six Pillar Edicts, which were thus published for the edification of travellers along the high road. The other known pillars were all placed in equally conspicuous positions at important cities, places of pilgrimage, or on frequented roads in the home provinces. No pillar has yet been found in the distant provinces, where the Rock Edicts were incised. The pillars are all composed of fine sandstone, quarried in most cases apparently at Chanâr (Chunar) in the Mirzâpur District, and were frequently erected at localities hundreds of miles distant from any quarry capable of supplying the exceptionally choice blocks required for such huge monoliths. Their fabrication, conveyance, and erection bear eloquent testimony to

[1] Cunningham, *Reports*, xvi. 112, Pl. xxviii; xxii. 51, Pl. vi, vii; Marshall, *J. R. A. S.*, 1908, pp. 1085–8, Pl. i. The copper bolt is in the Indian Museum, Calcutta.

the skill and resource of the stonecutters and engineers of the Maurya age.

Sixteen centuries later, in A. D. 1356, the two Asoka pillars which now stand near Delhi on the Kothila and the Ridge respectively were transported by Sultan Fîroz Shah the one from Topra in the Ambâla (Umballa) District, now in the Panjâb, and the other from Mîrath (Meerut) in the United Provinces. The process of removal of the Topra monument has been described by a contemporary author, whose graphic account is worth transcribing as showing the nature of the difficulties so frequently and successfully surmounted by Asoka's engineers.

The historian relates that—

'After Sultan Firoz returned from his expedition against Thatta he often made excursions in the neighbourhood of Delhi. In this part of the country there were two stone columns. One was in the village of Topra in the District of Sâdhaura and Khizrâbâd, at the foot of the hills, the other in the vicinity of the town of Mirath. . . . When Firoz Shah first beheld these columns he was filled with admiration and resolved to remove them with great care as trophies to Delhi.

Khizrâbâd is 90 *kos* from Delhi, in the vicinity of the hills. When the Sultan visited that District and saw the column in the village of Topra, he resolved to remove it to Delhi and there erect it as a memorial to future generations. After thinking over the best means of lowering the column, orders were issued commanding the attendance of all the people dwelling in the neighbourhood, within and without the Doâb, and all soldiers, both horse and foot. They were ordered to bring all implements and materials suitable for the work. Directions were issued for bringing parcels of the *sembal* (silk-cotton) tree[1]. Quantities of this silk-cotton were placed round the column, and when the earth at its base was removed, it fell gently over on the bed prepared for it. The cotton was then removed by degrees, and after some days the pillar lay safe upon the ground. When the foundations of the pillar were examined, a large square stone was found as a base, which also was taken out.

The pillar was then encased from top to bottom in reeds and raw skins, so that no damage might accrue to it. A carriage with forty-two wheels was constructed, and ropes were attached to each wheel. Thousands of men hauled at every rope, and after great labour and difficulty the pillar was raised on to the carriage. A strong rope was fastened to each wheel, and 200 men [$42 \times 200 = 8{,}400$] pulled at each of these ropes. By the simultaneous exertions of so many thousand men, the carriage was moved, and was brought to the banks of the Jumna. Here the Sultan came to meet it. A number of large boats had been collected, some of which could carry 5,000 and 7,000 maunds of grain, and the least of them 2,000 maunds. The column was very ingeniously transferred to these boats, and was then conducted to Fîrozâbâd, where it was landed and conveyed into the Kushk with infinite labour and skill.

At this time the author of this book was twelve years of age and a pupil of the respected Mîr Khân. When the pillar was brought to the palace, a building was commenced for its reception near the Jâmi Masjid [mosque], and the most skilful architects and workmen were employed. It was constructed of stone and chunam [fine mortar], and consisted of several stages or steps. When a step was finished the column was raised on to it, another step was then built and the pillar was again raised, and so on in succession until

[1] *Salmalia Malabarica (pentaphyllum)*. The cotton obtained from this tree was used on account of its elasticity.

it reached the intended height. On arriving at this stage, other contrivances had to be devised to place it in an erect position. Ropes of great thickness were obtained, and windlasses were placed on each of the six stages of the base. The ends of the ropes were fastened to the top of the pillar, and the other ends passed over the windlasses, which were firmly secured with many fastenings. The wheels were then turned, and the column was raised about half a *gaz* [yard]. Logs of wood and bags of cotton were then placed under it to prevent it sinking again. In this way, and by degrees, the column was raised to the perpendicular. Large beams were then placed round it as supports until quite a cage of scaffolding was formed. It was thus secured in an upright position straight as an arrow, without the smallest deviation from the perpendicular. The square stone before spoken of was placed under the pillar[1].'

Asoka erected about thirty or more such monuments. When labour so great was required to move one a distance of a hundred and twenty miles we may imagine how much energy was expended in setting up thirty pillars, some of which were much heavier than that removed by Fîroz Shah, and were transported to distances still greater.

Ten of the pillars known at present are inscribed. Six of these bear copies of the first six Pillar Edicts, the seventh edict, the most important of all, being found on one monument only, the Delhi-Topra pillar, the removal of which has been described. The

[1] Shams-i-Sirâj, quoted in Cunningham, *Reports*, xiv. 78; and Carr Stephens, *Archaeology of Delhi*, p. 131; Elliot, *Hist. India*, iii. 350.

records on two pillars in the Nepalese Tarâi commemorate Asoka's visit to the Buddhist holy places in B.C. 249, and the Sânchî and Sârnâth pillars are inscribed with variant recensions of the Minor Pillar Edict dealing with Church discipline. A detailed list of the inscribed pillars will be found at the end of this chapter.

Many more pillars remain to be discovered. The two great monuments, one surmounted by the figure of a bull and the other by the wheel of the Law, which stood at the entrance of the famous Jetavana monastery near Srâvastî, are said to exist; and notwithstanding certain finds which seem to render my opinion untenable, I have a suspicion that the ruins of Srâvastî may lie buried in Nepalese jungles on the upper course of the Râptî. Pillars which may prove to be those of the Jetavana are located by report near Bairât and Matiâri in Tahsîl Nepâlganj. Other pillars are rumoured to exist in the Nepalese Tarâi to the north of Nichlawal beyond the Gorakhpur frontier, and also at Barewâ and Maurangarh, north of the Champâran District[1].

Only two of the ten inscribed pillars known, namely, those at Rummindeî and Sârnâth, can be identified certainly with monuments noticed by Hiuen Tsang. A third, the Niglîva pillar, which does not occupy its original position, may or may not be the one which he mentions in connexion with the *stûpa* of Konâkamana. There is, however, no doubt that

[1] Mukharjî, *Antiquities in the Tarâi, Nepâl*, p. 59; *Z. D. M. G.*, vol. lxv. (1911), pp. 221–4.

seven out of the ten escaped notice in the pilgrim's memoirs. It is a curious fact that he never makes the slightest allusion to Asoka's edicts, whether incised on rocks or pillars. When he does refer to an alleged inscription of Asoka in the statement that a pillar at Pâtaliputra recorded the donation of all Jambudvîpa to the Church, he is probably only retailing the gossip of local monks, who could not read the inscription and invented an interpretation. Similar fraudulent readings of old inscriptions are constantly offered by local guides; thus, for example, Shams-i-Sirâj relates that 'certain infidel Hindus' interpreted the inscription on the Delhi-Topra pillar to mean that 'no one would be able to remove the obelisk from its place till there should arise in the latter days a Muhammadan king named Sultan Fîroz.' I do not believe for a moment that Asoka ever either perpetrated the folly of professing to give away all Jambudvîpa or recorded on a monument the nonsense attributed to him. His real records are all thoroughly sensible and matter-of-fact. The reason that the Chinese pilgrim ignores them presumably must be that in his time, nine centuries after the execution of the inscriptions, nobody could read them. The alphabets current in India during the seventh century A.D., which are well known, differ widely from those used in the time of Asoka, and the difference is quite sufficient to account for his inscriptions being regarded as illegible. By that time the true personality of the great emperor had been covered up by a mass of mythological legend, and nobody cared to search for the genuine records of his reign.

The wonderful rock inscriptions, although wanting in the artistic interest of the monolithic pillars, are in some respects the most interesting monuments of the reign. They are found at thirteen distinct localities in the more remote provinces of the empire, and the contents may be described generally as sermons on *dharma*, or the Law of Piety. The longer documents are either variant recensions, more or less complete, of the series known as the Fourteen Rock Edicts, or substitutes for certain members of that series. The shorter records include the two documents classed as the Minor Rock Edicts, and the peculiar Bhâbrû Edict. The inscriptions are found over an area extending from 34° 20′ to 14° 49′ N. lat., and from about 72° 15′ to 85° 50′ E. long., that is to say, twenty degrees of latitude, and thirteen of longitude. It is possible, and not improbable, that other examples remain to be discovered in Afghanistan and tribal territory beyond the north-western frontier, or even within the limits of India.

Beginning from the north-west, the first set of inscriptions is found at Shâhbâzgarhi in the Yûsufzai subdivision of the Peshâwar District of the North-West Frontier Province, about forty miles to the north-east of Peshâwar, and more than a thousand miles in a direct line distant from Asoka's capital. The principal inscription, containing all the Fourteen Edicts except the twelfth, is recorded on both the eastern and western faces of a mass of trap rock, 24 feet long and 10 feet high, which lies on the slope of a hill to the south-east of the village.

The Toleration Edict, No. XII discovered a few years ago by the late Sir Harold Deane, is incised on a separate rock about fifty yards distant from the main record. The text of all the documents, being nearly perfect, is of high value to the student[1].

The next recension in order is that at Mânsahra (Mânsera) in the Hazâra District of the North-West Frontier Province, N. lat. 34° 20′, E. long. 73° 13′, about fifteen miles to the north of Abbottabad. The inscription not being near habitations or on any main line of road, the reason for the selection of this site, which is not apparent at first sight, has been made clear by Dr. Stein, who found an ancient road leading to a place of pilgrimage now called Brerî. As at Rûpnâth and Girnâr the inscription was placed so as to catch the eye of pilgrims. The text is less complete than that at Shâhbâzgarhi[2]. Both of the north-western versions agree in giving special prominence to the Toleration Edict, which at Mânsahra has one side of the rock to itself, and at Shâhbâzgarhi is inscribed on a separate

[1] *Ep. Ind.*, i. 16; ii. 447; Cunningham, *Reports*, v. 9–22, Pl. iii–v; Foucher, in 11me *Congrès des Orientalistes*, Paris, p. 93. This recension is sometimes cited by the name of Kapurdagiri, a village two miles distant.

[2] *Ep. Ind.* ii. 447; *Ind. Ant.*, xix (1890), p. 43, giving abstract of M. Senart's article in *J. As.*; Stein, *Prog. Report, A. S. N. W. Frontier Prov.*, 1904–5, p. 17. Brerî is the Kashmîrî equivalent of Bhaṭṭârikâ = Devî or Durgâ. The text is now nearly illegible.

rock. Both the recensions further agree in being inscribed in the form of Aramaic character, now generally called Kharoshthî, which is written from right to left, and appears to have been introduced by Persian officials into the north-western regions of India after the conquest of the Indus valley by Darius, son of Hystaspes, about B.C. 500.

The third version of the Fourteen Edicts, and perhaps the most perfect of all, discovered in 1860, is on a rock about a mile and a half to the south of the village of Kâlsî (N. lat. 30° 32′, E. long. 77° 51′), in the Dehra Dûn District of the United Provinces, on the road from Sahâranpur to the cantonment of Chakrâta, and about fifteen miles westwards from the hill station of Mussoorie (Mansûri). The record is incised on the south-eastern face of a white quartz boulder shaped like the frustum of a pyramid, about 10 feet in diameter at the base and 6 feet at the top, which stands at the foot of the upper of two terraces overlooking the junction of the Jumna and Tons rivers. The confluences of rivers being regarded as sacred the place probably used to be visited by pilgrims, and must have been chosen for that reason as a suitable spot for the inscription. Some pilasters and other wrought stones indicate the former existence of buildings in the vicinity. The text agrees closely with the Mânsahra version, but exhibits certain peculiarities. A well-drawn figure of an elephant labelled 'the superlative elephant' (*gajatama*) is incised on one side of the boulder. The character, as in all the

Asoka inscriptions, excepting those at Mânsahra and Shâhbâzgarhi, is an ancient form of the Brâhmî script, written from left to right, and the parent of the modern Devanâgarî and allied alphabets. The alphabetical forms used in the different inscriptions vary to some extent in details [1].

Two copies of the Fourteen Edicts were published at places on the western coast. The fragment found at Sopârâ, in the Thâna District, to the north of Bombay, consisting of only a few words from the eighth edict, is enough to show that a copy of the set of documents once existed there. Sopâra, still a prosperous country town (N. lat. 19° 25′, E. long. 72° 48′), was an important port and mart under the name of Sopâraka, Sûrpâraka, or Shurpâraka in ancient times for many centuries, and contained some notable Hindu and Buddhist edifices. At one time the sea appears to have come up to the walls of the town, but the channel has been silted up for ages [2].

The famous Girnâr version, first described by Colonel Tod in 1822, lay buried in dense forest and might never have come to light had not a local notable made a causeway through the jungle for the

[1] The correct name is Kâlsî, not Khâlsî, as in the books. Cunningham, *Reports*, i. 244, Pl. xl; *Inscriptions of Asoka*, p. 12, Pl. iv; *Ep. Ind.* ii. 447; *Pioneer Mail*, 23 Sept., 1904. The boulder is not in danger of erosion by the river, as was at one time feared.

[2] *Ind. Ant.*, i. 321; iv. 282; vii. 259; Bhagwân Lâl Indrajî, 'Sopâra' (*J. Bo. Br. R. A. S.*, 1882, reprint); *Prog. Report, A. S. W. I.* for 1897–8, pp. 7–10, with map; *I. G.* (1908), *s.v.*

benefit of pilgrims to the hill, which is one of the most sacred places venerated by the Jains. The ancient town of Jûnâgarh (Ûparkot), capital of a State in the peninsula of Kâthiâwâr or Surâshtra (N. lat. 21° 31′, E. long. 70° 36′), stands between the Girnâr and Dâtâr hills. The Sudarsana Lake constructed under the orders of Chandragupta Maurya and equipped with watercourses and sluices by Asoka's local representatives, filled the whole valley between the Ûparkot rocks on the west and the inscription rock on the east. That rock, a nearly hemispherical mass of granite, therefore stood on the margin of the lake, which disappeared long since. Indeed its very existence had been forgotten, and its limits have been traced with difficulty. The Fourteen Edicts are incised on the north-eastern face of the rock, the top being occupied by the valuable record of the Satrap Rudradâman (*cir.* A.D. 152) and the western face by the important inscriptions of Skandagupta's governor (A. D. 457). The edicts have suffered a good deal of injury, but some care is now taken to protect them. Imperfect copies of them were the materials on which M. Senart was obliged to rely chiefly when writing his classical work on the inscriptions of Asoka; but since then accurate copies have been taken, and in 1899–1900 two fragments, which had been separated from the rock, were recovered by Professor Rhys Davids [1].

[1] *A. S. W. I.*, vol. ii, p. 95, Pl. ix; *Prog. Rep. A. S. W. I.*, 1898–9, p. 15; *J. R. A. S.*, 1900, p. 335.

Two recensions of the Fourteen Edicts, with modifications, exist on the eastern side of India, near the coast of the Bay of Bengal, within the limits of the kingdom of Kalinga conquered by Asoka in B. C. 261. Both recensions agree in omitting Edicts XI, XII, and XIII, which were considered unsuitable locally, and in substituting for them the Borderers' and Provincials' Edicts specially drafted to meet the needs of the newly annexed province, and not published elsewhere.

The northern copy is incised on a rock called Aswastama on the northern face and close to the summit of a hill near the village of Dhauli (N. lat. 20° 15′, E. long. 85° 50′), about seven miles to the south of Bhuvanesvar, in the Purî District, Orissa. The inscription occupies the prepared surface of a sloping sheet of stone, which is watched over from above by the well-executed fore-part of an elephant, about 4 feet high, cut out of the solid rock. The viceregal town of Tosali appears to have been in the neighbourhood [1].

The southern version is engraved on the face of a rock situated at an elevation of about 120 feet in a mass of granitic gneiss rising near the centre of an ancient walled town called Jaugada or Jogadh (N. lat. 19° 33′, E. long. 84° 50′) in the Ganjâm District,

[1] *Imp. Gazetteer* (1908), *s. v.* Dhauli; Cunningham, *Inscriptions of Asoka*, p. 15; *Reports*, xiii. 95. A photograph of the elephant forms the frontispiece of *E. Hist. of India*.

Madras, which probably is the town Samâpâ mentioned in the local edicts[1].

The Minor Rock Edicts, which are believed for the reasons stated in Chapter I (*ante*, p. 26) to be the earliest of the Asoka inscriptions, are found, like the Fourteen Rock Edicts, only in the remoter provinces. The second Minor Edict, consisting of a short summary of the Law of Piety, expressed in a style different from that of the other edicts, occurs in Mysore only, where three copies of it exist as a supplement to the first edict. Probably this supplementary document was composed in the office of the Prince of Suvarnagiri and published on his viceregal authority. The Mysore recensions of both the edicts were incised in three localities, all close to one another, in the Chitaldûrg District of northern Mysore, namely, Siddâpura (N. lat. 14° 49′, E. long. 76° 47′), Jatinga-Râmesvara, and Brahmagiri, near the site of a large ancient town. Variant recensions of Edict I occur at Sahasrâm (N. lat. 24° 57′, E. long. 84° 1′) in the Shâhâbâd District, S. Bihâr; Rûpnâth in the Jabalpur District, Central Provinces; Maski in the Nizam's Dominions; and at Bairât (N. lat. 27° 27′, E. long. 76° 12′) in Râjputâna. That document gives a valuable account of the emperor's religious history and

[1] Cunningham, *Inscr. of Asoka*, p. 17; *Reports*, xiii. 112; Sewell, *Lists of Antiq., Madras*, i. 4; *Ind. Ant.* i. 219; Sir W. Elliot in *Mad. J. Lit. and Science*, April–Sept. 1858, p. 75; *Prog. Rep. A. S. Madras*, 1903–4, 1904–5, 1906–7. The inscription is now protected by a roof and iron railing.

is devoted to the inculcation of his favourite precept. 'Let small and great exert themselves.' Thus it appears that Edict I was published in five widely separated regions, a clear proof that much importance was attached to its teaching.

The Rûpnâth inscription was placed in a singularly wild and out-of-the-way glen, 'a perfect chaos of rocks and pools overshadowed by rugged precipices fifty to sixty feet high, in whose clefts and caverns wild beasts find a quiet refuge.' Indeed, while Mr. Cousens was taking a photograph, he was being watched by a panther crouching less than twenty yards away. The spot, which is still visited by pilgrims who worship the local deity as a form of Siva, became sacred by reason of the three pools one above another, which are connected in the rainy season by a lovely waterfall. The detached boulder upon which the edict is inscribed lies under a great tree just above the western margin of the lowest pool, and may have fallen from its original position higher up [1].

The Sahasrâm recension is engraved on the face of the rock in an artificial cave near the summit of a hill to the east of the town, now surmounted by a shrine

[1] Rûpnâth is 14 miles west of Sleemanâbâd Railway Station. Cousens, *Prog. Rep. A. S. W. I.*, 1903-4, para. 113; Bloch, *Annual Rep. A. S. E. Circle*, 1907-8, p. 19. Dr. Bloch obtained a good impression, which has not yet been published. See also Cunningham, *Reports*, vii. 58; ix. 38; and *Inscr. of Asoka*, p. 21, Pl. xxix; *Ind. Ant.*, xxii. 298.

of a Muhammadan saint. In Asoka's time the place must have been visited by Hindu pilgrims [1].

The Bairât version, discovered by Mr. Carlleyle in 1872–3, is engraved on the lower part of the southern face of a huge block of volcanic rock 'as big as a house' at the foot of the 'Pândus' hill' close to the very ancient town of Bairât [2].

The peculiar Bhâbrû Edict, giving the list of Asoka's favourite passages of scripture, was incised on a boulder within the precincts of a Buddhist monastery on the top of another hill near the same town. The boulder is now preserved in Calcutta [3].

The cave dwellings excavated in the refractory gneiss of the Barâbar and Nâgârjuni hills near Gayâ by Asoka and his grandson for the use of the Âjîvikas, although not beautiful as works of art, are wonderful monuments of patient skill and infinite labour, misapplied as it seems to the modern observer. The largest is the Gopikâ cave dedicated by Dasaratha, which is 46 feet 5 inches long by 19 feet 2 inches broad, with semicircular ends and a vaulted roof 10½ feet in height. The whole of the interior is highly polished. The cost of such a work must have been enormous, and the expenditure of so much treasure on the Âjîvikas is good evidence of the influential position held in

[1] *Imp. Gazetteer* (1908), *s. v.* Sasarâm; Cunningham, *Inscr. of Asoka*, p. 20.

[2] Cunningham, *Reports*, vi. 97; *Inscr. of Asoka*, p. 22. The hill has other names.

[3] The 'second Bairât rock' of Cunningham, *Inscr. of Asoka*, p. 24; *Reports*, ii. 247.

Asoka's days by that now forgotten order of ascetics, who, although detested by orthodox Buddhists, were able to win favour from the sovereign who did 'reverence to all denominations[1].'

The arts in the age of Asoka undoubtedly had attained to a high standard of excellence.

The royal engineers and architects were capable of designing and executing spacious and lofty edifices in brick, wood, and stone, of constructing massive embankments equipped with convenient sluices and other appliances, of extracting, chiselling, and handling enormous monoliths, and of excavating commodious chambers with burnished interiors in the most refractory rock. Sculpture was the handmaid of architecture, and all buildings of importance were lavishly decorated with a profusion of ornamental patterns, an infinite variety of spirited bas-reliefs, and meritorious statues of men and animals. The rare detached statues of the human figure have been noticed. But the

[1] The caves are described by Cunningham, *Inscr. of Asoka*, pp. 30–2; *Reports*, i, pp. 40–52, Pl. xviii–xx; and by Caddy, *Proc. A. S. B.*, 1895, pp. 156–8. 'The Ajîvikas or naked ascetics. Tradition tells us that behind Jetavana [at Srâvastî] they used to practise false austerities. A number of the Brethren seeing them painfully squatting on their heels, swinging in the air like bats, reclining on thorns, scorching themselves with five fires, and so forth, in their various false austerities, were moved to ask the Blessed One whether any good resulted therefrom. "None whatever," answered the Master.' (Cowell and Francis, *transl. Jâtakas*, Introd. to No. 144, vol. i, p. 307.) See D. R Bhandarkar, *Ind. Ant.*, xli (1912), p. 286; Hoernle, *Encycl. Religion and Ethics*, *s.v.*

lions on the monolithic pillars are better. The newly discovered capital at Sârnâth is described by Mr. Marshall in the following somewhat bold language, which is, however, justified by the photographs: 'Lying near the column were the broken portions of the upper part of the shaft and a magnificent capital of the well-known Persepolitan bell-shaped type with four lions above, supporting in their midst a stone wheel or *dharmachakra*, the symbol of the law first promulgated at Sârnâth. Both bell and lions are in an excellent state of preservation and masterpieces in point of both style and technique—the finest carvings, indeed, that India has yet produced, and unsurpassed, I venture to think, by anything of their kind in the ancient world [1].'

The skill of the stone-cutter may be said to have attained perfection, and to have accomplished tasks which would, perhaps, be found beyond the powers of the twentieth century. Gigantic shafts of hard sandstone, thirty or forty feet in length, were dressed and proportioned with the utmost nicety, receiving a polish which no modern mason knows how to impart to the material. Enormous surfaces of the hardest gneiss were burnished like mirrors, bricks of huge dimensions were successfully fired, and the joints of masonry were fitted with extreme accuracy. White ants and other destructive agencies have prevented the preservation of any specimens of woodwork, save a few posts and beams buried in the silt of the rivers at Patna, but

[1] *Annual Rep. A. S.*, 1904-5, p. 36.

the character of the carpenter's art of the period is well known from the bas-relief pictures and from the railings and other forms in stone, which, as Fergusson so persistently urged, undoubtedly are copied from wooden prototypes. Burma teaches us that wooden architecture need not be lacking in dignity or magnificence, and we may feel assured that the timber structures which preceded the Bharhut rail and the Sânchî gateways were worthy of a powerful sovereign, a stately court, and a wealthy hierarchy. The beads, jewellery, and seals of the Maurya period and earlier ages which have been found from time to time prove that the ancient Indian lapidaries and goldsmiths were not inferior in delicacy of touch to those of any other country. The recorded descriptions and sculptured representations of chariots, harness, arms, accoutrements, dress, textile fabrics, and other articles of necessity or luxury indicate, that in the third century B.C. the Indian empire had attained a stage of material civilization fully equal to that reached under the famous Mughal emperors eighteen and nineteen hundred years later.

The sculptures in bas-relief, even if they cannot be often described as beautiful, although some may be, are full of life and vigour, and frankly realistic. No attempt is made to idealize the objects depicted, although the artists have allowed their fancy considerable play in the representations of tritons and other fabulous creatures. The pictorial scenes, even without the help of perspective, tell their stories vividly, and many of the figures are drawn with much spirit. The purely decorative elements exhibit great variety of design, and some of the fruit and flower patterns are extremely elegant. Images of the Buddha were not known in the time of Asoka, and are consequently absent from his sculptures. The Teacher is represented by symbols only, the empty seat, the pair of foot-prints, the wheel.

The Greek accounts, read along with the Edicts, leave on my mind the impression that the civil and military government of the Mauryas was better organized than that of Akbar or Shahjahân. It is certain that the Greek authors speak with the utmost respect of the power and resources of the kingdoms of the Prasii and Gangaridae, that is to say, Magadha and Bengal, that Alexander considered Pôros to be a formidable opponent, and that Chandragupta was able to defeat first the Macedonian garrisons and then Seleukos. The military strength of the government was reflected in the orderly civil polity and the developed state of the arts.

The care taken to publish the imperial edicts and commemorative records by incising them in imperishable characters, most skilfully executed, on rocks and pillars situated in great cities, on main lines of communication, or at sacred spots frequented by pilgrims, implies that a knowledge of reading and writing was widely diffused, and that many people must have been able to read the documents. The same inference may be drawn from the fact that the inscriptions are composed, not in any learned scholastic tongue, but in vernacular dialects intelligible to the common people, and modified when necessary to suit local needs. It is probable that learning was fostered by the numerous monasteries, and that the boys and girls in hundreds of villages learned their lessons from the monks and nuns, as they do now in Burma from the monks. Asoka, it should be noted, encouraged nunneries, and makes particular reference more than once to female lay disciples as well as to nuns. I think it likely that the percentage of literacy among the Buddhist population in Asoka's time was higher than it is now in many provinces of British India. The returns of 1901 show that in the United Provinces of Agra and Oudh, which include many great cities and ancient capitals, the number of persons per 1000 able to read and write amounts to only 57 males and 2 females. In Burma, where the Buddhist monasteries flourish, the corresponding figures are 378 and 45 [1]. I believe that the Buddhist monasteries and nunneries in the days of their glory must have been, on the whole, powerful agencies for good in India, and that the disappearance of Buddhism was a great loss to the country.

Two scripts, as before observed, were in use. The Aramaic Kharoshthî, written from right to left, was ordinarily confined to the north-western corner of India, but the scribe of the Brahmagiri version of the Minor Rock Edicts showed off his knowledge by writing part of his signature in that character. The Brâhmî script,

[1] *The Indian Empire, Imp. Gazetteer*, vol. iv (1907), p. 416.

the parent of the Devanâgarî and most of the existing Indian alphabets, appears in the Asoka inscriptions and the nearly contemporary records at Bhattiprolu and in Ceylon in so many varieties that it must have been already in use for several centuries, although no extant example can be cited which is certainly earlier than Asoka. Bühler seems to have been right in deriving this script from Mesopotamia, and the date of its introduction into India may have been about B.C. 700 or 800, or earlier.

The story of the origins of the early civilization of India has been very imperfectly investigated and still remains to be written. We can perceive dimly the main lines of communication by sea and land along which the elements of the arts and sciences travelled to India from Egypt and the continent of Asia, but our actual knowledge of the subject is extremely fragmentary. The imposing fabric of the Achaemenian empire evidently impressed the Indian mind, and several facts indicate the existence of a strong Persian influence on the Indian civilization of the Maurya age.

The free use of pillars was the dominant feature of Achaemenian architecture and Asoka's fondness for columns is in itself an indication of Persian influence. But no indirect inference is needed to prove the Persian suggestion of his monoliths which recall the motive of the Persepolitan bell-capital surmounted by animals, frequently placed back to back. The Sârnâth capital described above (*ante*, p. 136), while in a certain sense Persepolitan, is far less conventional than its prototypes, and much superior in both design and execution to anything in Persia, so far as I can ascertain.[1] The Persepolitan capital long continued to be used as a decorative element in Indian sculpture, and is common in the reliefs from Gandhâra, the so-called Graeco-Buddhist school.

The idea of issuing long proclamations engraved on the rocks most likely was suggested by the practice of Darius, and the special variation of using the proclamations as sermons may have been originated by the inscription of that monarch at Naksh-i-Rustam, which is supposed to be 'preceptive not historical,' and to contain 'the last solemn admonition of Darius to his countrymen with respect to their future conduct in policy, morals, and religion.' But the text of that document, apparently, has not been published, so it cannot be compared in detail with the Edicts of Asoka.[2] The opening phrases of the Edicts, 'Thus saith his Sacred and Gracious Majesty,' and the like, recall, as has often been observed, the style of the Achaemenian records.

Several minor details confirm the impression that the Maurya court was very sensible to the influence of the great empire to the west, so recently conquered

[1] Examples of Persian lion capitals may be seen in the Louvre, or reproduced in Perrot and Chipiez, *History of Art in Persia* (London, 1902).

[2] Sir H. Rawlinson, *Memoir on the Cuneiform Inscriptions*, vol. i, p. 312; Canon Rawlinson, *Transl. of Herodotus*, vol. iv, p. 177.

by Alexander. The Persian word *nipi* for 'writing' occurs in the Shâhbâzgarhi version of the Edicts; the penalty of cropping the hair (*ante*, p. 100) was a Persian punishment [1]; and the ceremonial washing of the king's hair, which Strabo, no doubt transcribing Megasthenes, mentions as an Indian custom, seems to be copied from the similar ceremony performed by Xerxes, as related by Herodotus [2]. The Persian title of Satrap, which continued to be used in Western India as late as the closing years of the fourth century A. D., is not recorded for Maurya times. But the monolithic pillars alone are enough to prove the reality of the Persian influence, and M. Le Bon seems to be right in maintaining that early Indian art was very largely indebted to Persia for its inspiration [3]. The Hellenistic decorative motives, acanthus leaves, and so forth, which are common in ancient Indian sculpture, may have come through either Persia or Alexandria, or by both ways. The problems concerning the relation between Indian, Asiatic, and Hellenistic art have never been threshed out, and are too complex for discussion in these pages, but I may say that I am inclined to regard the early Indian bas-reliefs as translations, so to speak, of Alexandrian motives; by which I mean that the scheme of composition is Hellenistic of the Alexandrian school, while the

[1] *Athenaeum*, July 19, 1902.

[2] Strabo, Bk. xv, ch. 69; transl. McCrindle, *Ancient India*, p. 75; Herodotus, Bk. ix. 110; *Ind. Ant.* xxxiv (1905), p. 202.

[3] Le Bon, *Les Monuments de l'Inde* (Paris, 1893), p. 15.

spirit, subject, and details are pure Indian. M. Le Bon truly observes that 'la puissance de déformation du génie hindou est en effet si grande, que les formes empruntées subissent des transformations qui les rendent bientôt méconnaissables.' Many illustrations of this proposition in both plastic art and literature might be cited. When the Indians adopt and adapt a foreign suggestion they do it so cleverly and transmute the spirit of the work so completely that the imitation seems to be indigenous and original.

It is, perhaps, advisable to remind the reader that the Persian art referred to was itself based upon Assyrian models, so that in a sense the Indian capitals may be described as Assyrian. But the bas-reliefs, while closely related to those of Alexandria, differ completely in style from the stiff formal bas-reliefs of Assyria and Persia. I believe it to be probable that India was never, up to quite recent times, more exposed to the impact of foreign ideas than it was during the Maurya age. All these matters, however, require much more attentive consideration than they have yet received, and here can be merely alluded to. But it seems clear that Indian art in the Maurya and Sunga periods, whatever may have been the nationality of the artists employed, attained a high standard of merit when compared with anything except the masterpieces of Greek genius, and that it deserves an honourable place in the history of the artistic achievements of the world.

The inscriptions dispersed throughout the empire

as described were written either at the capital or at the head quarters of one or other of the viceroys, and then made over to skilled stone-cutters for incision on the rocks and pillars. In the extreme north-west the Kharoshthî alphabet was used as being the best known locally; throughout the rest of the empire the Brâhmî script was employed. The language was invariably a form of Prâkrit, the vernacular language of the day, closely allied to Sanskrit, especially that of the Vedic variety, on the one hand, and to the modern vernaculars of the country on the other. The proclamations published in the home provinces are in the dialect of Magadha; those issued in more remote regions exhibit local peculiarities in spelling, vocabulary, and grammar. The various texts of the same edict sometimes differ to a small extent in substance, certain versions being fuller than others.

Repetitions, after the manner of the Buddhist scriptures, are frequent, and were inserted designedly, as is explained in the Epilogue to the Fourteen Rock Edicts. The style was supposed by the earlier interpreters to be exceedingly uncouth and to display lack of facility in prose composition. But now that accurate texts are available and the language is better understood, the style is found to possess a considerable amount of force and simple dignity. The desire to give the sovereign's own words often, especially in the Kalinga Edicts, involves transitions from the third person to the first, which are embarrassing to the translator, but do not imply want of skill in composition. The following versions are as literal as differences of idiom will permit, and, if considered at all successful renderings, will, I hope, support my view of the style of the originals. The accuracy of the texts is wonderful. A clerical error or engraver's blunder very rarely occurs, and the beauty of the lettering may be judged from the facsimile of the Rummindeî inscription in Plate II. I have seen the original twice, and can certify that it is quite as clear as the reduced copy of the impression.

The reasons for treating all the inscriptions as the work of one author and for adopting the renderings chosen for the royal titles have been stated in Chapter I (*ante*, pp. 20, 22). The subject headings, of course, are not in the originals. All modern studies of the inscriptions known to me have been utilized in the preparation of the revised versions, which differ materially from those published in the earlier editions. References will be found in the Bibliographical Note appended to Chapter V.

Assuming the correctness of the chronology accepted by M. Senart, Mr. F. W. Thomas, and myself, which is not admitted by all scholars, the extant inscriptions may be classified in order of date as follows:—

EDICTS.

	'Regnal Year.'	B.C.
Minor Rock Edicts	13th	257.
Bhâbrû Edict	? ditto	? ditto.
Fourteen Rock Edicts	13th & 14th	257 & 256.

	'Regnal Year.'	B.C.
Kalinga Edicts	?14th or 15th	?256 or 255.
Seven Pillar Edicts	27th & 28th	243 & 242.
Minor Pillar Edicts	29th to 38th	241 to 232.
MISCELLANEOUS INSCRIPTIONS.		
Cave Dedications of Asoka	13th & 20th	257 & 250.
Tarâi Commemorative Inscriptions	21st	249.
Cave Dedications of Dasaratha	1st	?232.

EXISTING INSCRIBED PILLARS OF ASOKA

Serial No.	Name.	Position.	Remarks.
1	Delhi-Topra	On summit of Kothila in the ruined city of Fîrozâbâd near Delhi; transported from Topra in Ambâla District in A.D. 1356 by Sultan Fîroz Tughlak.	'Delhi-Sivâlik' (Cunningham); 'lâṭ of Fîroz' or 'D^{1}.' (Senart). Pillar Edicts I–VII nearly complete. Capital modern.
2	Delhi-Mîrath (Meerut)	On ridge at Delhi, broken; removed from Mîrath in A.D. 1356 by Sultan Fîroz, and set up in the grounds of his hunting-lodge near its present position, where it was re-erected by the Indian Government in 1867.	'D^{2}.' (Senart). Pillar Edicts I–VI much mutilated. Capital missing.
3	Allahabad	Near Ellenborough Barracks in the Fort; evidently removed from Kauśâmbî, possibly by Sultan Fîroz.	Pillar Edicts I–VI; Queen's Edict; Kauśâmbî Edict, all imperfect. Capital modern, except the abacus.
	Lauṛiyâ-Ararâj	At hamlet of Lauṛiyâ, 1 mile SW. of temple called Ararâj-Mahadeo, 20 miles NW. of Kesariyâ	'Radhiah' or 'R.' (Senart). Pillar Edicts I–VI practically perfect. Capital lost. According to

Serial No.	Name.	Position.	Remarks.
		stûpa, on the way to Bettia, in the Champâran District, N. Bihâr. It is 2½ miles ESE. of Radhia or Rahariya.	the miniature reproduced by Foucher (*Icon. Bouddhique*, p. 55) the pillar was surmounted by a *Garuḍa*, or winged monster.
5	Lauriyâ-Nandangaṛh	Near the large village of Lauṛiyâ, on the direct road from Bettia to Nepâl, 3 miles N. of Mathiah, and 15 miles NNW. of Bettia, in the Champâran District.	'Mathiah' or 'M.' (Senart). Pillar Edicts I–VI practically perfect. Lion capital slightly damaged by a cannon-shot in Aurangzeb's time (*Frontispiece*).
6	Râmpurwâ	At Râmpurwâ hamlet and more than a mile NE. of Piparîyâ village, about 20 miles NNE. of No. 5, in same District, 84° 34′ E. long., 27° 15′ 45″ N. lat. Prostrate.	Pillar Edicts I–VI well preserved. Bell-capital now detached from the pillar; the crowning lion recently found buried at a short distance. The 'bull' pillar near is not inscribed.
7	Sânchî	At southern entrance to great *stûpa* of Sânchî, in Bhopâl State, Central India, 23° 29′ N. lat., 77° 45′ E. long. Fallen and broken.	Minor Pillar Edict, imperfect, a variant of the edict on the Sârnâth pillar, and also of the Kauśâmbî Edict on the Allahabad pillar. The fine capital with four lions lies near.
8	Sârnâth	NNW. of 'Jagat Singh's *stûpa*' at Sârnâth, about 3½ miles N. of Benares. Broken.	Minor Pillar Edict, nearly complete, being a fuller form of the Sânchî and Kauśâmbî Edicts. The magnificent capital with four lions formerly supported the 'wheel of the Law.' Discovered by Mr. Oertel in 1905.

Serial No.	Name.	Position.	Remarks.
9	Rummindeî	At shrine of Rummindeî, about 1 mile N. of Paḍaṛia, 2 miles N. of Bhagwânpur in the Nepalese Tahsîl of that name, and about 6 miles NE. of Dulhâ in the British District of Bastî.	'Paderia' (Bühler). Split by lightning, but standing, the bell member of the capital lies apart, but the crowning member is missing. The commemorative inscription (Plate II) is absolutely perfect.
10	Niglîva	On west bank of Niglîva (Nigâlî) Sâgar, near Niglîva village in Nepalese Tarâi, north of the Bastî District, and about 13 miles NW. of No. 9, but not in original position. Broken.	Imperfect commemorative inscription in form similar to that of No. 9, and apparently of same year.

CHAPTER IV

The Rock Edicts

SECTION 1

The Minor Rock Edicts

EDICT I

THE FRUIT OF EXERTION

(Brahmagiri text. The best facsimile is in Rice, *Ep. Carn.*, vol. xi, plate facing No. 21, p. 164; reproduced on a smaller scale in *Mysore and Coorg from the Inscriptions*, Constable, 1909.)

ACCORDING to the words of the Prince and High officers of Suvarnagiri the High officers in Isila are to be addressed with salutations and addressed in the manner following:—

'His Sacred Majesty (*Devānaṁpiya*) gives these instructions:—

"For more than two-and-a-half years I was a lay disciple, without, however, exerting myself strenuously. But a year—in fact, more than a year ago—I entered the Order, and since then have exerted myself strenuously.

During that time the men in India who had been unassociated with the gods became associated with them. For this is the fruit of exertion. Nor is this to be attained by greatness only, because even by the small man who chooses to exert himself, immense heavenly bliss may be won.

For that purpose has this proclamation been proclaimed:

'Let [small] and great exert themselves to this end.'

My neighbours, too, should learn this lesson, and may this lesson long endure!

And this purpose will increase—yea, it will increase vastly, at least half as much again will it increase."

And this proclamation was proclaimed by the body of missioners (*vyûthena*), [to wit], 256 [persons].'

EDICT II

SUMMARY OF THE LAW OF PIETY OR DUTY

(Brahmagiri text; incised continuously with Edict I, as a supplement to it, in the original, beginning in the middle of line 8.)

Thus saith His Sacred Majesty (*Devânampiya*):—

'Father and mother must be hearkened to; similarly, respect for living creatures must be firmly established; truth must be spoken.

These are the virtues of the Law which must be practised. Similarly, the teacher must be reverenced by the pupil, and fitting courtesy must be shown to relations.'

This is the ancient nature of things—this leads to length of days, and according to this men must act.

Written by Paḍa the scribe.

EDICT I

(Rûpnâth text. The best facsimile is in *Ind. Ant.*, vol. xxii (1892), facing p. 298.)

Thus saith His Sacred Majesty:—

'For more than two-and-a-half years I was a lay disciple, without, however, exerting myself strenuously. But it is more than a year since I joined the Order, and have exerted myself strenuously.

The gods who up to this time had been unassociated [with men] in India (*Jambudvîpa*) have now become associated.

For this is the fruit of exertion. Nor is this to be obtained by greatness only; because even by the small man who exerts himself immense heavenly bliss may be won.

For this purpose has the proclamation been made:—

"Let small and great exert themselves."

My neighbours, too, should learn this lesson, and may such exertion long endure!

And this purpose will increase—yea, it will increase immensely—at least half as much again will it increase.

And this purpose must be written on the rocks as opportunity offers (*vâlata*). And measures must be taken to have it engraved upon stone pillars, wherever there are stone pillars in my dominions [lit. "here"].

And according to this text, so far as your jurisdiction extends, you must send it out everywhere.'

By the body of missioners (*vyûthena*) was the proclamation made—to wit, 256 persons [were] missioners.

Comment

The first Minor Rock Edict is perhaps the most difficult of the Asoka inscriptions. Discussion has gone on for many years. Even if perfect unanimity among scholars has not been attained, most of the puzzles may now be regarded as solved. The readings translated as 'more than two-and-a-half years' and 'more than a year since' may be accepted as established. The phrase *saṁghe upayîte* (with slight variants) interpreted by me as 'joined the Order,' in the sense that Asoka became a monk for a time, is understood by some scholars in a less definite manner. The passage about the gods and men was formerly rendered wrongly owing to an erroneous etymology of the words *amisâ* and *misâ*. I think that everybody now accepts M. Sylvain Lévi's opinion that those words mean 'unmixed' or 'unassociated' and 'mixed' or 'associated' respectively. The meaning seems to be that true teaching raises men to the level of the gods. 'Ye shall be as gods.' The word *deva* in the passage certainly means 'gods,' and not either 'kings' or 'Brahmans.' The words *iyaṁ sâvaṇe*, 'this proclamation' or 'precept,' refer, I believe, only to the phrase 'Let small and great exert themselves' and not to the whole document. The words 'half as much again' represent the literal version 'one-and-a-half fold.'

Controversy has raged for years around the concluding sentence, which is found more or less complete with considerable variation in the Rûpnâth, Sahasrâm, Brahmagiri, and Jaṭṭinga-Râmeśvara texts. The words and numerals are wanting in the Bairât, Siddâpura, and Maski texts.

In the second edition of this work I followed Dr. Thomas, but now I recognize the force of the criticisms by Mr. D. R. Bhandarkar (*Ind. Ant.*, vol. xli (1912), p. 171), and my translation substantially agrees with his and Senart's explanation.

It seems desirable to exhibit the three legible texts in a form which brings out the necessity of applying one interpretation to all:—

Sahasrâm (*Ind. Ant.*, xxii, 298)—

Iyaṁ cha sâvane vivuṭhena	*luve Sapaṁnâ lâti* [? to be read as *s-âti*, another *satâ* being accidentally omitted] *vivuthâ ti* 256.

Rûpnâth—

Vyûṭhenâ sâvane kaṭe	256 *satavivâsâ t*[*i*].

Brahmagiri—

Iyaṁ cha sâvaṇe sâv[*â*]*p*[*i*]*te vyûthena*	256.

The first clause clearly means that the 'proclamation' or 'precept' was 'proclaimed' or 'made' by the *vyûtha* or *vivutha*. In the second clause the bare figures 256 of Brahmagiri must be interpreted to mean the same as both the full wording of Sahasrâm and the intermediate phraseology of Rûpnâth. The numeral 256 is expressed also in words at Sahasrâm. I agree with Bhandarkar in holding that *lâti* is a clerical error and that one word *satâ* meaning 'hundreds' has been accidentally omitted. The second *satâ* connected with *virâsâ* must be the Sanskrit *sattva*, meaning 'person.' Thus we get the renderings:—

Sahasrâm—'And this proclamation [was made] by the body of missioners; to wit, two hundred and fifty-six, 256 missioners.'

Rûpnâth—'By the body of missioners the proclamation was made; to wit, 256 persons [were] missioners.'

Brahmagiri—'And this proclamation was proclaimed by the body of missioners; [to wit], 256 [persons].'

Vyûtha (*vivutha*) in the first clause is a collective noun. The meaning of the second clause at Rûpnâth is clear and determines the interpretation of the other texts. It is impossible to discuss the problem further in this place. The interpretation now offered recurs to that of Senart, who long ago translated *vyûtha* by 'missionaries' (i. 188).

The interpretation of Edict II is easy, and my earlier version stands. The style differs from that of all the other inscriptions, and it seems plain that the document was composed in the secretariat of the Viceroy of the South at Suvarṇagiri. Probably that town ('Golden Hill') was somewhere near the gold mines in the Nizam's territory.

The new version of Edict I discovered in 1915 at Maski in the Râichûr District of the Nizam's Dominion is close to ancient gold workings. The much mutilated text of that document is interesting chiefly because it begins with the words,

Devanaṁpiyasa Asokasa.

No other inscription gives the emperor's personal name Asoka. The text nearly agrees with Rûpnâth and Sahasrâm, but is too much damaged to admit of continuous translation. Edited with plates in *Hyderabad Archaeological Series*, No. 1, Calcutta, 1915.

The addition of the scribe's signature at the end of the Mysore texts is curious, and it is specially remarkable that he wrote the last word 'scribe' (*lipikarena*) in the Kharoshṭhî character of the North-Western frontier. He seems to have been a northerner. The town of Isila must have been at or near Siddâpura. The Prince, no doubt, was a son of Asoka, and Viceroy of the Deccan.

The number 256 is significant as being the square of 16, a number much favoured by Hindu usage. It may also be analysed as 64 × 4 or as 32 × 8, all favourite numbers. The notion that the numerals should be interpreted as a date is certainly erroneous. The scholars who believed in the date theory were led into many baseless speculations, now wholly obsolete, which need no further notice.

SECTION 2

The Bhâbrû or Second Bairât Rock Edict

ASOKA'S FAVOURITE PASSAGES OF SCRIPTURE

(Facs. in *J. As.*, 1887; text (requiring some amendment) by Senart in *Ind. Ant.*, vol. xx (1891), p. 165.)

His Grace the King of Magadha addresses the Church with greetings and bids its members prosperity and good health.

'You know, Reverend Sirs, how far extend my respect for and faith in the Buddha, the Sacred Law, and the Church.

Whatsoever, Reverend Sirs, has been said by the Venerable Buddha, all of that has been well said.

However, Reverend Sirs, if on my own account I may point out (a particular text), I venture to adduce this one:—

"Thus the Good Law will long endure."

Reverend Sirs, these passages of the Law, to wit:—

[1] The Exaltation of Discipline (*Vinaya-samukkase*);
[2] The Course of Conduct of the Great Saints (*Aliya-vasâni*);
[3] Fears of what may happen (*Anâgata-bhayâni*);
[4] The Song of the Hermit (*Muni-gâthâ*);
[5] The Dialogue on the Hermit's Life (*Moneya-sûte*);
[6] The Questioning of Upatishya (*Upatisa-pasine*);
[7] The Address to Râhula, beginning with the Subject

of Falsehood (*Lâghulovâde musâvâdaṁ adhigidhya*)—

spoken by the Venerable Buddha—these, Reverend Sirs, I desire that many monks and nuns should frequently hear and meditate; and that likewise the laity, male and female, should do the same.

For this reason, Reverend Sirs, I cause this to be written, so that people may know my intentions (*abhipretaṁ*).'

Comment

The Bhâbrû Edict, or Second Bairât Rock Edict, as Cunningham called it, is incised on a small boulder now preserved in the Indian Museum, Calcutta, which had lain on the lower platform of the 'Inscription Hill' at Bairât, twelve miles from Bhâbrû, the nearest camping ground. Major Burt, the discoverer, seems to have encamped at Bhâbrû, to which place the boulder was brought. Thus it became known by the name of his camp. The correct spelling is Bhâbrû, not Bhâbrâ (*Pros. Rep. A. S. W. Circle* for 1909-10, p. 45). The Bairât copy of Minor Rock Edict I seems to have been made within the precincts of the monastery where the so-called Bhâbrû Edict also was incised. Probably Asoka was resident during a rainy season early in his reign at that monastery. I think that the two Bairât inscriptions must both date from the one year, most likely the 13th regnal year, when Asoka began the publication of inscriptions.

The Bhâbrû Edict is unique. It differs in both phraseology and subject-matter from all the other inscriptions, and is avowedly Buddhist. The text is well preserved, so that the controversies which long raged concerning its interpretation were not due in any serious degree to textual defects. Most of the difficulties formerly discussed may now be regarded as settled. The translation of the body of the inscription given in the second edition of this work consequently holds good, although differences of opinion may still exist concerning the identification of some of the seven canonical passages recommended for special study.

Asoka calls himself *Priyadasi lâjâ Mâgadhe*, 'Priyadasi, Râjâ of Magadha.' The form is *Mâgadhe*, not *Mâgadhaṁ* (Bloch), and the *r* is preserved in *Priyadasi* as well as three other words, (Hultzsch, *J. R. A. S.*, 1911, p. 1113). I translate the royal style or *protocole* as 'His Grace the King of Magadha.'

The declaration of faith in Buddha, the Sacred Law (*dhaṁma*), and the Church (*saṁgha*) may be illustrated by the formula of the Three Refuges or the Three Jewels as still used in Ceylon at the ordination of a monk, which is:—

'I put my trust in Buddha;
I put my trust in the Law;
I put my trust in the Priesthood;
Again I put my trust in Buddha;
Again I put my trust in the Law;
Again I put my trust in the Priesthood;
Once more I put my trust in Buddha;
Once more I put my trust in the Law;
Once more I put my trust in the Priesthood.'
(Warren, *Buddhism in Translations*, 1900, p. 396.)

The remark that 'whatsoever has been said by the Venerable Buddha has been well said' is in substance a quotation from *Aṅguttara*, iv, p. 163, as cited by Poussin in *The Way to Nirvâṇa*, Cambridge, 1917, p. 106.

The text 'Thus the Good Law will long endure' occurs in both the *Mahâvyutpatti* and the *Aṅguttara Nikâya* of the Pâli Canon.

The main purpose of the document is to enumerate the seven passages in the Canon which Asoka considered to be the most important as guides of conduct, and to recommend those passages to the earnest study of all classes in the church, monastic or lay, male or female. Some difficulty has been experienced in identifying the passages referred to. I think that Mr. A. J. Edmunds rightly identifies the first passage with the famous First Sermon at Benares, on the grounds that that discourse is one of the most ancient Buddhist documents, that it could not well be ignored by Asoka, and that the Four Truths expounded in it are described in *Udâna*, v, 3, as *Sâmukaṁsikâ dhammadesanâ*, a phrase which recalls the title given to the text No. 1 by Asoka (*J. R. A. S.*, 1913, p. 387).

The list of passages 2–7, originally drafted by Rhys Davids, *J. R. A. S.*, 1898, p. 639, and amended by Professors Dharmananda Kosambi and Lanman, *Ind. Ant.*, vol. xli (1912), pp. 37–40, now stands thus:—

(2) *Aliya-vasâni* = *Ariya-vaṁsâ* (*Aṅguttara*, vol. ii, p. 27);
(3) *Anâgata-bhayâni* = *Anâgata-bhayâni* (*Aṅguttara*, vol. iii, p. 103, *Sutta* 78);
(4) *Muni-gâthâ* = *Muni-sutta* (*Sutta-nipâta*, i, 12, p. 36);
(5) *Moneya-sûte* = *Nâlaka-sutta* (ibid., iii, 11, pp. 131–4);
(6) *Upatisa-pasine* = *Sâriputta-sutta* (ibid., iv, 16, pp. 176–9);
(7) *Lâghulovâde*, &c. = *Râhulo-vâda sutta* (*Majjhima-nikâya*, ii, 2. 1, vol. i, p. 414). The word translated 'beginning' is *adhigidhya*, not *adhigichya* (Michelson, *Indo-germ. Forsch*, Strassburg, 1910, p. 194).

The references are to the Pâli Text Society's editions.

It is needless to explain the importance of such a list, approximately dated, for the history of the Buddhist Canon.

The reader will not fail to note Asoka's anxiety that the moral law as expounded in the Buddhist scriptures should obtain the utmost possible publicity. Women as well as men concerned him.

A collection of the seven passages cited, including both text and translation, would be of much interest as constituting an authoritative compendium of the Law of Duty or Piety as conceived by Asoka. The inscriptions are all devoted to the exposition, exaltation, and dissemination of that Law. Such a collection would serve as a commentary on the whole series. One form of No. 3 has been rendered into English in *J. Pâli Text Soc.*, 1896. M. Senart has printed the text of No. 7. A Chinese version of the same has been translated by M. Sylvain Lévi (*J. As.*, 1896, mai-juin) and an English rendering by Beal will be found in Sec. xxxi of *Texts from the Buddhist Canon, commonly known as Dhammapada* (London, 1902). The substance of the First Sermon is given in *Buddhism* (American Lectures, first series, 1896), pp. 135–9, by Rhys Davids, who believes that the very words of the preacher have been transmitted.

SECTION 3

The Fourteen Rock Edicts

(*Abbreviations* D., Dhauli; G., Girnâr; J., Jaugada; K., Kâlsî; M., Mânsahra; Sh., Shâhbâzgarhi.)

EDICT I

THE SACREDNESS OF LIFE

(Sh. text, as in Bühler's transcript in *Ep. Ind.* ii. 448, slightly amended.)

This scripture of the Law of Duty has been written by command of His Sacred and Gracious Majesty the King:

'Here no animal may be slaughtered for sacrifice, nor shall any merry-making be held. Because in merry-makings His Sacred and Gracious Majesty sees much offence, although certain merry-makings are excellent in the sight of His Sacred and Gracious Majesty the King. Formerly, in the kitchen of His Sacred and Gracious Majesty the King each day many hundred thousands of living creatures were slaughtered to make curries. But now, when this scripture of the Law is being written, only three living creatures are slaughtered for curry [daily], to wit, two peacocks and one antelope—the antelope, however, not invariably. Even those three living creatures shall not be slaughtered in future.'

Comment

Mr. Harit Krishna Deb is, I think, right in regarding the term 'scripture of the Law of Duty' 'or Piety' (*dhaṁmalipi* or *-nipi*) as applying to the whole series of the Fourteen Rock Edicts, which must be read together as a single document. The term, which recurs in R. E. VI, and in the Epilogue, is also applied to the Six Pillar Edicts collectively, as well as to the distinct Seventh Pillar Edict. Those are the only documents so designated (*Asoka's Dhammalipis*, Calcutta, Temple Press, 1919). The word *-nipi* in the M. and Sh. texts was formerly read erroneously as *-dipi*. Similarly in R. E. IV, *nipista* is to be read, not *dipista* (Hultzsch in *J. R. A. S.*, 1913, p. 653). The words are Iranian; cf. modern Persian, *narishta*, 'written'. 'Scripture' seems to be the best rendering. 'Rescript,' which has been suggested, is incorrect. Asoka's instructions are not 'rescripts' or imperial decisions on points referred for orders. The royal *protocole* (*Devânaṁ priyo Priyadasi*), with slight variations in different texts, is rendered by the formula which I have adopted.

The word 'here' (*hida*, or *idha*, G.) is ambiguous. It may be understood as meaning 'in my dominions,' as in R. E. XIII, or 'ici-bas,' 'here below' (Senart), or possibly, 'at the capital,' as in R. E. V.

'Merry-making' seems to be the best rendering of *samâja* in its various spellings. The meaning of the term has been thoroughly elucidated by D. R. Bhandarkar in *Ind. Ant.*, vol. xlii (1913), pp. 253-8, and N. G. Majumdar (ibid., vol. xlvii (1918), pp. 221-3). The word was used in both Brahmanical and Buddhist literature to mean 'merry-making' or 'festival' generally, and in certain cases to mean a 'semi-religious theatrical performance.' It was also applied to the place, building, or stage where the performance was given. The use of the English word 'theatre' may be compared. The *samâja* was of two kinds. The popular festival kind, accompanied by animal fights, heavy drinking and feasting, including much consumption of meat, was necessarily condemned by Asoka, as being inconsistent with his principles. The other kind, the semi-religious theatrical performance, sometimes given in the temples of Sarasvatî, the goddess of learning, was commended. Full details will be found in the convincing articles cited. See also F. W. Thomas in *J. R. A. S.*, 1914, p. 393.

'Offence,' *doshaṁ* or *dosaṁ*, Bühler translates by 'evil.'

'Hundreds of thousands' (*śatasahasrani*). K. has simply 'thousands' (*sahasâni*). The meaning is satisfactorily explained by Bhandarkar (loc. cit.), who cites chap. 208, *Vana-*

parwan of *Mbh.* to show that King Rantideva used to have 2,000 cattle and 2,000 kine slain daily in his kitchen (*mahânasa*, the word used by Asoka) in order to provide doles of meat for his people, by which liberality he gained incomparable fame. Asoka evidently had done the same in his unregenerate days. Asoka at first restricted the killing to the small quantity required for the royal table, and then abolished it altogether.

The precise dates of his action cannot be fixed, as this particular edict is not expressly dated.

Antelope (*mrugo* or *murgo*, Sh.; *mrige*, M.; *mago*, G.; and *mige*, K.) is the Sanskrit *mṛiga*, which may be rendered either 'deer' or 'antelope.' If the 'black buck' (*Antilope bezoartica* or *cervicapra*) is meant, as seems probable, 'antelope' is the more accurate. The popular term 'deer' includes many animals, none of which is so widely diffused and commonly eaten as the 'black buck.'

The meaning of this edict has now been satisfactorily cleared up in all its expressions.

EDICT II

PROVISION OF COMFORTS FOR MEN AND ANIMALS

(G. Text.)

'Everywhere in the dominions of His Sacred and Gracious Majesty the King, as well as among his frontagers, the Choḷas, Pâṇḍyas, the Satiyaputra, the Ketalaputra [Keraḷa-, Sh.], as far as the Tâmbaparṇi, Antiochos the Greek king, or even the kings the neighbours of that Antiochos—everywhere have been made the healing arrangements of His Sacred and Gracious Majesty the King in two kinds, [namely], healing arrangements for men and healing arrangements for beasts. Medicinal herbs also, both medicinal herbs for men and medicinal herbs for beasts, wheresoever lacking, have been everywhere both imported and planted. Roots also and fruits, wheresoever lacking, have been everywhere imported and planted.

On the roads, too, wells have been dug and trees planted for the enjoyment of man and beast.'

Comment

The fullest form of the text (G), which is well preserved, has been translated. The edict, like No. XIII, is of special interest for its bearing upon political history. 'Frontagers,' *prachaṁteshu* of G.=Sanskrit *prâty-anteshu*. Choḷa is written *Choḍâ* in text, the *ḍ* being certain. The letters *ḍ* and *ḷ* are interchangeable, and in many cases *ḷ* has been misread as *ḍ* (Lüders, *J.R.A.S.*, 1911, p. 1037). Pâṇḍya is written *Pâḍâ*, and in Sh. *Paṁḍiya*. The kingdom of the Choḷas was on the SE. or Madras side of the peninsula, the Coromandel (*Choḷamaṇḍala*) coast. The ancient capital was at Uṛaiyûr (variously spelt), near Trichinopoly. The kingdom of the Pâṇḍyas corresponded roughly with the modern Madura and Tinnevelly Districts, but sometimes extended further to the west. The early capital, Korkai, at the mouth of the Tâmraparṇi river, was replaced by Madura. It is not certain which place was the capital in Asoka's time. The Satiyaputra people, kingdom, or country is not mentioned elsewhere. In all probability it is represented by the Satyamangalam Tâlûk or sub-division of the Coimbatore District, lying along the Western Ghâts, and bordering on Mysore, Malabar, Coimbatore, and Coorg. The town of the same name commands the Gazalhatti Pass from Mysore, which used to be of strategical importance. Beryls and gold formerly were mined in the region, which still yields some corundum. The Coimbatore District is full of megalithic structures and prehistoric remains. The ancient kingdom may have extended beyond the limits of the present Tâlûk, which has an area of 1,177 square miles. The Satyamangalam country was included in the territory colonized by the Great Migration (*Bṛihad-charaṇaṁ*), possibly that led by Bhadrabâhu in the days of Chandragupta Maurya. See *I.G.* (1908) *s.v.*; *Ind. Ant.*, vol. xli (1912), p. 231; ibid., vol. xlv (1916), p. 200; ibid., vol. xlvi, 1917, pp. 22-67. The Keralaputra kingdom, country, or people, equivalent to Chera, is Malabar, now partly in the Bombay, and partly in the Madras, Presidency.

The G. reading *Ketala-* is quite clear and certain. The phonetic change is curious. The most ancient capital was Vanji, Vanchi, or Tiru-Karûr, about 28 miles ENE. of Cochin. See *The Tamils Eighteen Hundred Years Ago*, Madras, 1904, p. 15. The list of 'frontagers' indicates the extent of Asoka's empire. Tâmraparṇi (*Tambapaṁṇi*) here seems to mean the river in Tinnevelly. The ports (Korkai, and later Kâyal) at its mouth had an ancient and lucrative trade in pearls, gems, and conch shells. G. alone reads *â Tambapaṁṇi* 'as far as [the] Tâmbaparṇi,' a phrase which indicates that the river is meant, not Ceylon. I now apply the same interpretation to Edict XIII. The reference in the *Arthaśâstra* to pearls from Tâmraparṇi certainly is to the river. The pearls from it are distinguished from the Kauleya pearls of Ceylon. See my article in *Ind. Ant.*, vol. xlvii (1918), p. 48, and *I. G.* (1908), *s.v.* Tâmbraparṇi. *Yona* in *Yonarâja* (Yavana) is to be interpreted here as 'Greek'. Antiochos is A. Theos, king of Syria or Western Asia (261–246 B.C.), grandson of Seleukos Nikator, the contemporary of Asoka's grandfather, Chandragupta Maurya. The identity of the 'neighbours' is uncertain. They are not necessarily the same as the foreign kings named in R. E. XIII. *Sawîpaṁ*, 'neighbourhood,' of G. is a collective neuter noun (Michelson), equivalent to *sâmaṁtâ* of K.

Chikîchha is a general term, not meaning in itself 'hospitals,' as Bühler renders, but inclusive of them. The wording of the passage about healing arrangements, medicinal herbs, roots, fruits, trees, and wells varies in the different texts. It is most detailed in G. and K. See P. E. VIII, sec. 5. Asoka's system of state medicine was based on the institutions of his predecessors. Hospitals are mentioned in the *Arthaśâstra*, Bk. ii, chap. 4, as part of the equipment of a fortified town. A physician was called *chikitsika*. The interpretation of the edict as a whole may be regarded as finally settled.

EDICT III

THE SYSTEM OF QUINQUENNIAL OFFICIAL TRANSFERS

(G. text; the variations in other texts are unimportant.)

Thus saith His Sacred and Gracious Majesty the King:—

'When I had been consecrated twelve years this command was issued by me:—

"Everywhere in my dominions the subordinate officials, the Governor, and the District Officer must every five years proceed in succession (*anu*) on transfer, as well for their other business, as for this special purpose, the inculcation of the Law of Duty (or Piety)," to wit:—

"An excellent thing is the hearkening to father and mother; an excellent thing is liberality to friends, acquaintances, relatives, Brahmans, and ascetics; excellent is abstention from the slaughter of living creatures; excellent is small expense with small accumulation."

The Council also will inculcate [the same] on the officials in the Accounts Department, with regard both to the principle and the text [of the order].'

Comment

'Thus saith.' The formula may have been suggested by the inscriptions of Darius. For the various forms of royal correspondence and orders see *Arthaśâstra*, Bk. ii, chap. 9.

'Twelve years.' The date of the original order here quoted *may* be earlier than that of the publication of the Fourteen R. E. as a collection.

The meaning of *yukta* (*yuto*), first recognized by F. W. Thomas, is now admitted as certain. It is the most general term for officials of minor or intermediate rank. The Râjûka had extensive powers over hundreds of thousands of persons (P. E. IV), and so may be translated by 'Governor.' The Prâdesika, an 'officer charged with executive duties of revenue collection and police' (Thomas, *J. R. A. S.*, 1914, p. 385), must have been more or less equivalent to the District officer or magistrate and collector of modern India, the Âmil of Mogul times.

The chief difficulty in the document is the interpretation of the technical term *anusaṁyâna*, which has not been met with elsewhere than in the edicts. It cannot possibly mean 'assembly,' as supposed at one time, nor does the rendering 'circuit' seem to be tenable. Jayaswal rightly points out that the whole administrative staff from the Governor down to the clerks could not possibly all go on circuit at once every five years. He is probably correct in referring to the *Sukranîti* and interpreting the term as signifying a regular system of transfer from one station or district to another, designed to prevent the abuses apt to arise when officials remain too long in a particular locality (*J. B. O. Res. Soc.*, iv. 37). That interpretation fits in with the etymology of the term and with the language of the concluding paragraphs of the Provincials' Edict. The summary of the Law is repeated elsewhere, more than once, in slightly variant language, as in R. E. IV. The other difficulty concerns the word *parishad* (*palisâ*, &c.), of which the general meaning is 'session' or 'assembly.' In the law books it is usually applied to an advisory council composed of from three to ten Brahmans learned in the sacred law. Here again I agree with Jayaswal in believing that the reference must be to the *Mantri-parishad*, or Council of Ministers mentioned in the *Arthaśâstra* (Bk. i, ch. 15).

Gaṇanâ certainly is the Accounts Department, as interpreted by D. R. Bhandarkar. The intention may be that the Accountant-General or Controller should see that the transfers were carried out, and salaries only paid in case of obedience. But it must be confessed that the connexion of the final sentence with the rest of the document remains obscure, and some improvement in the rendering may be hoped for. The old interpretations were clearly wrong, and need not be discussed. The phrase *hetuto cha vyaṁjanato cha* undoubtedly refers to the principle and the wording of the imperial commands. A suggested, nearly equivalent, rendering is 'the spirit and the letter.' Another is 'idée par idée et mot par mot.' *Vyanjana* in the sense of 'text' has been already met with in the Rûpnâth Minor R. E.

I am not yet satisfied that the exact meaning of this Edict has been thoroughly ascertained.

EDICT IV

THE PRACTICE OF THE LAW OF PIETY OR DUTY

(G. text; the variations in the other versions are not important.)

'For a long period past, even for many hundred years, have increased the sacrificial slaughter of living creatures, the killing of animate beings, unseemly behaviour (or "discourtesy") to relatives, unseemly behaviour to Brahmans and ascetics.

But now, by reason of the practice of piety by His Sacred and Gracious Majesty the King, the reverberation of the war-drums has become the reverberation of the law, while he exhibits spectacles of the dwellings of the gods, spectacles of elephants (or "the elephant"), bonfires ("illuminations," Sh.), and other representations of a divine nature.

As for many hundred years before has not happened, now at this present, by reason of the inculcation of the Law of Piety by His Sacred and Gracious Majesty the King, have increased abstention from the sacrificial slaughter of living creatures, abstention from the killing of animate beings, seemly behaviour (or "courtesy") to relatives, seemly behaviour to Brahmans and ascetics, hearkening to father and mother, hearkening to elders.

Thus, and in many other ways the practice of the Law has increased, and His Sacred and Gracious Majesty the King will make such practice of the Law increase further.

The sons, grandsons, and great-grandsons of his Sacred and Gracious Majesty the King will cause this practice of the Law to increase until the aeon of universal destruction (other texts omit "of universal destruction"). Standing firm in the Law of Piety and in morality they will inculcate the Law. For this is the best of deeds—even the inculcation of the Law. Practice of the Law is not for the immoral man. Both increase and non-diminution in this matter are excellent.

For this purpose has this [document] been caused to be written that they may strive for increase and not give countenance to diminution.

When he had been consecrated twelve years His Sacred and Gracious Majesty the King had this written.'

Comment

Ârambho means specially sacrificial slaughter (Thomas). *Dhammacharaṇa* is 'practice' of the Law. The phrase 'drum of the Law' is familiar in Buddhist literature. Buddha said: 'I am going to Varâṇasî to sound the drum of the Law . . . to turn the wheel of the Law' (Rockhill, *Udânavarga*, xxi, 6, p. 91; Trübner, 1892). 'Has become', as the rendering of *aho* (= *abhavat*), is preferable to taking that word either as an interjection, 'oh', or 'lo', or as a conjunction, 'or'. *Vimâna*, a representation by a processional car or otherwise of the gods' abodes. 'Elephant' may refer either to the representation of Buddha as the white elephant, or to images of the four celestial elephants, the vehicles of the Lokapâlas. Dh. has the plural form *hathîni*. *Agikhandâni* (G.) apparently means 'bonfires' or 'fireworks', and possibly a special kind of bonfire, such as the burning palmyra trunk set up at a popular festival to Indra in S. India (*Ind. Ant.*, 1915, p. 203). Burnouf rendered 'feux de joie' (*Introd.*, 2nd ed., 1876, p. 568). The corresponding word *jotikaṁdhana* in Sh. means 'illuminations'. Asoka sought to engage the interest of his people in edifying spectacles concerning things divine rather than in martial display. The spectacles referred to should be regarded as terrestrial exhibitions, not as celestial phenomena. The general meaning is plain. Fa-hien's description of a grand Buddhist procession at Pâṭaliputra, although centuries later in date, serves as a commentary.

'Every year,' he says, 'on the eighth day of the second month they celebrate a procession of images. They make a four-wheeled car, and on it erect a structure of five storeys by means of bamboos tied together. . . . They make figures of *dêvas*, with gold, silver, and lapis lazuli grandly blended, and having silken streamers and canopies hung out over them. On the four sides are niches, with a Buddha seated in each, and a Bodhisattva standing in attendance on him. There may be twenty cars, all grand and imposing, but each one different from the others. On the day mentioned, the monks and laity within the borders all come together; they have singers and skilful musicians; they pay their devotions with flowers and incense. The Brahmans come and invite the Buddhas to enter the city. These do so in order and remain two nights in it. All through the night they keep lamps burning, have skilful music, and present offerings. This is the practice in all the other kingdoms as well' (*Travels*, ch. xxvii, tr. Legge).

Other descriptions of Buddhist edifying spectacles might be quoted. The details, of course, varied from time to time and from place to place.

'The aeon of universal destruction,' *saṁvarta-kalpa* in Sanskrit, as described in *Mbh.* 3, Yanap., sec. 188, 12869–90, quoted by Fleet in *J.R.A.S.*, 1911, p. 485 note. 'At the end of the 1,000 Yugas (which make the daytime of a day of the Creator) there will appear seven blazing suns, which will dry up all the waters in the rivers and the oceans. They will be followed by the *saṁvartaka* fire, the "fire of destruction," accompanied by a great wind,' &c. See R.E. V, where the term recurs. Ordinary morality (*sîla*) is distinguished from Asoka's Buddhist form of the Law of Piety or Duty (*dhamma*). 'Give countenance to,' or more literally 'behold.' Bühler renders 'permit,' and Senart 'qu'ils n'en voient (or 'qu'on n'en voie') point.'

Little doubt now remains concerning the interpretation of the whole edict

EDICT V

THE CENSORS OR HIGH OFFICERS OF THE LAW OF PIETY OR DUTY

(M. text, which is the most complete; material variations exist in other texts.)

Thus saith His Sacred and Gracious Majesty the King:—

'A good deed is a difficult thing. He who is the author of a good deed does a difficult thing. Now by me many good deeds have been done.

Should my sons, grandsons, and my descendants after them until the end of the aeon ["of universal destruction," G.] follow in this path, they will do well; but in this matter he who shall neglect a part of his duty [or "the commandment"] will do ill, because sin easily develops ["is an easy thing," G.].

Now in all the long time past, officers known as Censors [or "High Officers"] of the Law of Piety never had existed, whereas such Censors were created by me when I had been consecrated thirteen years.

Among people of all [non-Buddhist] sects they are employed for the establishment of the Law of Piety, for the increase of that Law, and for the welfare and happiness of the subordinates of the Law of Piety Department [or ? "the faithful of the true religion," Senart], as well as of the Yavanas, Kambojas, Gândhâras, Râshṭrikas, Pitinikas, with other nations on my western frontier.

Among servants and masters, Brahmans and the wealthy, among the helpless and the aged, they are employed in freeing from worldly cares ["greed," G.] their subordinates [in the department] of the Law of Piety.

They are also employed on the revision of [sentences of] imprisonment or execution, in the reduction of penalties, or [the grant of] release, on the grounds of motive, having children, instigation, or advanced years.

Here [in the capital; "at Pāṭaliputra," G.], and in all provincial towns, in the female establishments of my brothers and sisters, as well as of other relatives, they are everywhere employed. These Censors of the Law of Piety are engaged everywhere in my dominions, among the subordinate officials of that Law, with regard to the concerns of the Law, the establishment of the Law, and the business of almsgiving.

For that purpose has this scripture of the Law been written, that it may long endure, and that my subjects may act accordingly.'

Comment

The subject of the Censors is further treated in R.E. XII and P. E. VII. They are styled the High Officers or Ministers of the Law of Piety to distinguish them from their colleagues of equal rank who were the High Officers (*mahâ-mâtrâḥ*) for the ordinary business of administration. Probably they had the power of life and death, so that a strict administration of their office might easily result in intolerable tyranny, and it is likely that in practice it did so result. Asoka dwells only upon the humane, merciful side of their jurisdiction, which extended even to the ladies of his own family. The appointment of more or less similar officials by various Hindu governments in times and localities widely apart is recorded, and it is known that in such cases the prescribed rules of conduct were enforced by tremendous penalties, including death.

Professor D. R. Bhandarkar points out that in the Deccan of the Ândhra or Sâtavâhana period, before and after the Christian era, persons of the highest social rank are distinguished in sundry inscriptions as Mahâ-raṭhis, Mahâ-bhojas, and Mahâ-senapatis. All the three terms seem to be applied to 'feudatory chieftains.' The Mahâ-bhojas appear to have held the present Ṭhâṇâ and Kolâbâ Districts of the Bombay

Presidency, while the Mahâ-raṭhis controlled Poona and the neighbouring Districts.

By detaching the honorific prefix *mahâ-* or 'great', Raṭhi and Bhoja can be easily recognized as the Râstika and Bhoja of Asoka's R. E. V and R. E. XII respectively. The professor suggests that, in accordance with a passage in the *Aṁguttara-Nikâya* as interpreted by the commentator (iii, 70 and 300), the word *pitenika* (variously spelt) should not be read as a separate name, but as an adjective meaning 'hereditary,' qualifying Râstika in R. E. V and Bhoja in R. E. XIII. The respective renderings, therefore, would be 'hereditary Râstikas' and 'hereditary Bhojas' (*Ind. Ant.*, vol. xlviii (1919), p. 80). The suggestion deserves consideration, although it may not be absolutely convincing.

'Sect' or 'denomination' (*pâshaṇḍa*) connotes especially a non-Buddhist, heretical sect. See P. E. VII, where Brahmans, Jains, and Âjîvikas are specified, and also the Toleration Edict, R. E. XII.

'Subordinates of the Law of Piety' (*dhaṁmayuta*) seems to be the right rendering, not 'the faithful of the true religion,' as translated by Senart, before the meaning of *yukta* as 'subordinate official' had become known and accepted. The High Officers or Censors were charged with the duty of keeping their subordinates in order. The five tribes or nations named as requiring the services of the Censors probably were not either generally Buddhists or much inclined to observe the rules of conduct laid down by the imperial moralist. Yavana (Yona) must mean the Greek or Hellenized people on the north-western frontier. The Kambojas are supposed to have occupied the western Himalayas and to have spoken an Iranian tongue. The Gândhâras certainly were the inhabitants of Gandhâra, equivalent to the N.W. Panjâb and adjoining regions. Râshṭrikas probably mean the people of Mahâ-râshṭra. The position of the Pitinikas (variously spelt) is uncertain. The supposed connexion with Paithan on the Godâvarî is not proved. These last two names are omitted by K.

'On my western frontier,' *aparânta*.

'Servants and masters,' *bhaṭamayeshu*. *Bhaṭa*, Sanskrit

bhṛita, should be taken here to mean 'hired servant,' as in the *Arthaśâstra*. *Ayeshu* = *âryeshu*, 'masters,' the inserted *m* being euphonic (Franke). Other less convincing interpretations have been offered. *Bhaṭa* (*bhṛita*) sometimes means 'soldier.'

'Rich,' *ibhyeshu*. *Anatheshu* = *anâthesu*, 'helpless' (Michelson). Cf. the name *Anâthapiṇḍika*, 'feeder of the poor,' nearly equivalent to the Hindostânî *gharîb-parwar*.

The next clause is the most difficult in the edict. Jayaswâl (*J. B. O. Res. Soc.*, iv. 144-6) rightly explains the technical terms as referring to the Censors' power of modifying the sentences of convicts on the specific grounds authorized by the law-books. *Badha* (*vadha*) seems to mean 'execution with torture'. The *Arthaśâstra* distinguishes instantaneous death as *suddha vadhah*. *Ambandha* certainly means the criminal's 'motive' or 'intention,' as in Manu, viii. 126, compared with ibid., vii. 16, and other legal texts. *Paja* (and variants) apparently means 'having children.' *Apalibodhaye* here may be interpreted as 'reduction of penalty.' The word occurs above in the sense of 'freeing from worldly cares,' but in that case the G. text has the preferable reading *aparigodhâya*, 'freeing from greed,' which probably represents the original draft. The two forms are fully discussed by F. W. Thomas in *J.R.A.S.*, 1915, pp. 99-106. *Karṭabhikara* is, I think, correctly interpreted by Jayaswal (loc. cit.) as meaning 'acting under instigation.' The word *abhikâra* occurs early in this edict in the sense of 'author.' 'Female establishments,' *orodhaneshu*, is better than Bühler's 'harem.' Although the seclusion of females was not unknown in ancient India (*Arthaśâstra*, Bk. ii, chap. 23), it was not the rule apparently. See R. E. XII for the special *mahâmâtras* or Censors of Women, whose exact functions are not known. The word 'Here' in this passage evidently means 'the capital,' as the G. reading shows. In other edicts it has to be interpreted differently. The mention of Asoka's 'brothers and sisters' proves the baselessness of the legends accusing him of the slaughter of his brothers. 'In my dominions.' Dh. has the variant 'in the whole earth.'

Although this difficult document is now fairly intelligible as a whole, some details of the interpretation may be regarded as still doubtful.

EDICT VI

THE PROMPT DISPATCH OF BUSINESS

(G. text; Sh. repeats one clause by mistake.)

* Thus saith His Sacred and Gracious Majesty the King:—

'A long period has elapsed during which in the past business was not carried on or information brought in at all times. So by me the arrangement has been made that at all times, when I am eating, or in the ladies' apartments, or in my private room, or in the mews, or in my [?] conveyance, or in the pleasure-grounds, everywhere the persons appointed to give information should keep me informed about the affairs of the people.

And in all places I attend to the affairs of the people. And, if, perchance, by word of mouth I personally command a donation or injunction; or, again, when a matter of urgency has been committed to the High Officers, and in that matter a division or adjournment takes place in the Council, then without delay information must be given to me in all places, at all times. Such is my command.

Because I never feel satisfaction in my exertions and dispatch of business. For work I must for the welfare of all the folk; and of that, again, the root is energy and the dispatch of business; for nothing is more essential than the welfare of all the folk. And whatsoever efforts I make they are made that I may attain release from my debt to animate beings, so that while in this world I make some persons happy, they may win heaven in the world beyond. For that purpose have I caused this scripture of the Law to be written in order that it may endure, while my sons, grandsons, and great-grandsons may take action for the welfare of all folk. That, however, is difficult save by the utmost exertion.'

Comment

The older interpretations of this edict, as in my previous editions, were largely erroneous. The true purport of it has been made clear by the *Arthaśâstra*, which Mr. Jayaswal has applied with satisfactory results. Asoka, in accordance with the precepts of the text-books on state-craft, declares his readiness to attend to business concerned with the public welfare, at all times and in all places, even at the cost of much personal inconvenience. He requires the proper officers (*paṭivedakâ*) to keep him fully informed without delay on all public affairs, and gives special directions that when a matter of urgency discussed in the Council of Ministers (*parisâyain*) occasions a division of opinion or adjournment, he must be informed without delay. He then explains the principles on which his action is based.

The best commentary is presented by *Arthaśâstra*, Bk. i. chap. 19, entitled 'The Duties of a King.' The following passages are specially relevant:

'When in court he shall never cause his petitioners to wait at the door, for when a king makes himself inaccessible to his people and entrusts his work to his immediate officers, he is sure to engender confusion in business, and to cause thereby public disaffection, and make himself a prey to his enemies.

He shall, therefore, personally attend to the business of gods, of heretics, of Brahmans learned in the Vedas, of cattle, of sacred places, of minors, the aged, the afflicted, and the helpless, and of women . . .

All urgent calls he shall hear at once, but never put off; for when postponed, they will prove too hard or impossible to accomplish. . . . Of a king the religious vow is his readiness for action; satisfactory discharge of his duties is his performance of sacrifice; equal attention to all is the presentation of fees and the ablution of consecration.

In the happiness of his subjects lies his happiness; in their welfare his welfare; whatever pleases himself he shall not consider as good, but whatever pleases his subjects he shall consider as good.

Hence the king shall ever be active and discharge his duties; the root of wealth is activity, and of evil its reverse.

In the absence of activity acquisitions present and to come will perish; by activity he can achieve both his desired ends and abundance of wealth.'

Thus it is apparent that Asoka's sententious maxims were not original, but were copied from the approved text-books on state-craft. The *Arthaśâstra* had had many predecessors. Some special points require brief exposition. Jayaswal translates *paṭivedakâ* by 'ushers,' such as the Gentlemen Ushers of the English court, but the rendering is not quite satisfactory.

The different texts express 'eating' by three distinct verbs. 'Private room' accurately represents *garbhâgâra*, a term sometimes applied to the sanctuary of a temple. We learn from *Arthaśâstra*, Bk. i, chap. 6, that such a room might be underground, and might be made secure by secret stairs and passages.

The word 'mews' is the best representation I can find for *vachamhi* (*vrachaspi*, Sh.). Jayaswal certainly is right in taking *vracha* as dialectic for Sanskrit *vraja*. The same phonetic change occurs again in this edict in *vrachayaṁ*, Sh. (*vrajeyaṁ*), equivalent to *gachheyaṁ*, G. *Vraja* (*Arth.*, Bk. ii, chap. 6) means 'a herd of cattle,' including 'cows, buffaloes, goats, sheep, asses, camels, horses, and mules.' The king was bound to inspect his live-stock, and I use the word 'mews' to include stables, cowsheds, and the like.

The meaning of *vinîta* is uncertain. The rendering 'conveyance,' signifying especially 'litter' or 'palanquin,' is highly probable (Senart, ii. 280 note). Jayaswal's 'drill' is not tenable.

'Some persons happy.' The word 'some' (*nâni*) is clear in G. only.

'Scripture of the Law.' Sh. omits 'scripture of.'

'Sons,' &c. Sh. and M. omit 'great-grandsons.' K. has 'sons and wives.'

Except for the one doubtful word *vinîta* the whole edict is now clearly intelligible, and the new version may be accepted as correct.

EDICT VII

IMPERFECT FULFILMENT OF THE LAW

(Sh. text ; no important variations.)

'His Sacred and Gracious Majesty the King desires that in all places men of every denomination (or "sect") may abide, for they all desire mastery over their senses and purity of mind. Man, however, is various in his wishes and various in his passions. They (*scil.* the denominations) will perform either the whole or only a part of the commandments. Even for a person to whom lavish liberality is impossible, mastery over the senses, purity of mind, gratitude, and steady devotion are altogether indispensable.'

Comment

The first clause apparently means that no restriction should be placed upon the residence of the adherents of any particular sect or denomination, Asoka's reason being that all the sects alike mean well. Restrictions of the kind hinted at are indicated in *Arthaśâstra*, Bk. i, chap. 36, by the rule that

'Managers of charitable institutions shall send information (to Gopa or Sthânika) as to any heretics (*pâshaṇḍa*) and travellers arriving to reside therein. They shall allow ascetics and men learned in the Vedas to reside in such places only when those persons are known to be of reliable character.'

'Passions' is a better rendering of *râga* than 'likings,' as in my last edition, or 'attachements,' as Senart.

The chief difficulty lies in the words *niche* (*nichâ*, G.) *bâḍhaṁ*, rendered by Burnouf as 'toujours bien,' by Senart as 'toujours excellent,' and by Jayaswal as 'always desirable.' Those renderings rest on the hypothesis that *niche* (*nichâ*) represents the Sanskrit adverb *nityam*, 'always.' Thomas agrees that the word meant is *nityam*, but takes it to be an adjective with the sense of 'permanent' or 'indispensable.' He translates therefore 'altogether indispensable.' Michelson raises phonetic difficulties, but fails to suggest an alternative. Other suggestions have been made, which are not convincing. On the whole, the rendering by Mr. Thomas still seems to me to be the best.

Part of the 'commandment' is the duty of liberality, but obedience to that part may be dispensed with.

EDICT VIII

PIOUS TOURS

(Sh. text.)

'In times past Their Sacred Majesties used to go out on so-called "tours of pleasure." In those tours hunting and other similar amusements used to be practised.

His Sacred and Gracious Majesty the present King, after he had been consecrated ten years went out to Bôdh Gaya or "towards supreme knowledge"). Thence arose "tours of piety." In them this is the practice—visiting ascetics and Brahmans, with liberality to them; visiting elders, with largess of gold; visiting the people of the country, with instruction in the Law of Piety, and discussion of that Law.

Consequently, since that time a different portion constitutes the pleasuring of His Sacred and Gracious Majesty the King.'

Comment

'Their Sacred Majesties' (*deranam priya*), replaced by 'Kings' (*râjâns*) in G. and Dh. The passage is interesting as proving conclusively that the style *devânâm priya* was an established royal title borne by several of Asoka's predecessors. G. omits 'so-called' (*nama*). 'In those tours' seems to me to be the meaning of 'here' (*atra; eta*, G.; *iha*, M.; *hidâ*, K.). In the later sentence beginning 'In them' the word is *atra*, Sh. and M.; *etayam*, G.; and *hetâ*, K. 'The present King,' *so*, Sh.

and M.; *se*, G.; omitted in G. Fleet rendered 'this same king.'

The puzzle lies in the words *nikrami* (*ayâya*, G.) *sambodhim.* Most scholars take them to mean that Asoka entered on the 'eight-fold path' of 'right views, right feelings,' &c., which leads to *saṁbodhi*, or supreme knowledge in the Buddhist sense. The person starting on that path is described as *saṁbodhi-parâyaṃo*, 'intent on *saṁbodhi*' (Rhys Davids, *Dialogues*, 1st ser., p. 190; *Buddhism* (1899), p. 108). That interpretation may be correct. But D. R. Bhandarkar contends that the verbs must be interpreted in a physical sense, so that *saṁbodhi* should be taken as equivalent either to *bodhi*, meaning the *bodhi* tree, or to *Mahâbodhi*, meaning the temple at Bōdh Gayā (*Ind. Ant.*, vol. xlii (1913), p. 159). That interpretation seems to be possible, but I am inclined to accept the general opinion.

Asoka in his programme for 'pious tours,' as usual, followed prescribed rules. The *Arthaśâstra* (Bk. i, chap. 21) directs that the king 'attended by trusty bodyguards armed with weapons shall give interviews to saints and ascetics.' Compare also the passage from ibid., chap. 19, quoted in the comment on R. E. VI. The moralists treated hunting as one of the four heinous vices due to desire, namely, hunting, gambling, women, and drinking, some writers considering hunting to be worse than gambling, but the author of the *Arthaśâstra* (Bk. viii, chap. 3) points out that the practice of the chase has its good side. 'Elders' presumably mean the honoured senior members of the Buddhist *saṁgha*. The concluding words *bhâge* (*bhagi*) *aṁñe* (*aṁñi*) are nominatives in apposition to *rati*, 'pleasuring.' Senart and Bühler's rendering 'in exchange' is not strictly accurate, although it gives the general sense. Asoka seems to mean that his virtuous conduct has given him a different and better share of what is really worth having than that enjoyed by his frivolous predecessors.

Except for the doubt about *saṁbodhi* the translation of this edict may be accepted as settled.

EDICT IX

TRUE CEREMONIAL

(K. text, which is practically perfect, and in substantial agreement with Sh. and M. The G., Dh., and J. texts form a distinct group.)

Thus saith His Sacred and Gracious Majesty the King:—

'People perform various ceremonies. In sickness, at the weddings of sons, the weddings of daughters, the birth of children, departure on journeys—on those and other similar occasions people perform many ceremonies. Nay, the womankind perform many, manifold, trivial, and worthless ceremonies.

Ceremonies, however, have to be performed, although that kind bears little fruit. This sort, on the other hand, to wit, the ceremonial of piety, bears great fruit. In it are included proper treatment of slaves and servants, honour to teachers, gentleness towards living creatures, and liberality towards ascetics and Brahmans. These things and others of the same kind are called the Ceremonial of Piety.

Therefore ought a father, son, brother, master, friend, or comrade, or even a neighbour to say: "This is excellent, this is the ceremonial to be performed until the attainment of the desired end."

This I will perform, for the ceremonial of this world is of doubtful efficacy; perchance it may accomplish the desired end, perchance it may not, and it remains a thing of this world. This Ceremonial of Piety, on the contrary, is not temporal; because, even if it fails to attain the desired end in this world, it certainly produces endless merit in the world beyond. If it happens to attain the desired end here, then both gains are assured, namely, in this world the desired end, and in the world beyond endless merit is produced by that Ceremonial of Piety.'

Instead of the passage from 'This I will perform' to the end, G., Dh., and J. have :—

'And it has been said—"Excellent is liberality." But there is no such liberality or favour as the liberality of piety, the favour of piety. Therefore should a friend, lover, relative, or comrade exhort, saying, "This is to be done, this is excellent, by this it is possible for you to win heaven." And what is better worth doing than the winning of heaven?'

Comment

The variations between the texts in both substance and language are larger than usual. Bühler translated the Sh. text, but his readings and version require some correction.

Maṁgalaṁ includes all rites and ceremonies performed for luck or to avert possible calamity. Sometimes such rites include animal sacrifices, which Asoka abhorred. Buddha's condemnation of all omen-taking or other superstitious practices is expressed in the *Maṅgala-Jâtaka* (No. 87, Cambridge transl., vol. i, p. 215). *Abakajani*, which I have rendered 'womankind,' is expressed by the more or less equivalent terms, *balika janika* in M., *mahiḍâya* in G., and by *striyaka* in Sh. The last two terms certainly mean 'womankind.' The phrase in K. might be rendered 'mothers and wives.' 'Nurses,' too, has been suggested for the first element. *Âbâdha*, which I have translated 'sickness,' following Senart, is rendered 'misfortunes' by Bühler, and 'troubles' by Thomas, perhaps more accurately. For the Maurya law concerning slaves and hired servants see *Arthaśâstra*, Bk. iii, chap. 13. 'Teachers' (*guru*); but the word may be rendered 'elders,' so as to agree with other similar passages. Either translation is verbally correct. The correct reading of the passage 'This I will do' is due to Hultzsch (*J. R. A. S.*, 1913, p. 654). Sh. inserts the words 'even after it is actually attained' (*nivutaspi va puna*); M. has the like. Bühler's and other early readings and renderings are wrong. 'The desired end' (*taṁ athaṁ*); the idiom occurs in the *Arthaśâstra* and elsewhere.

The text and translation may now be accepted as settled, subject to doubts as to the exact meaning of *abakajaṁyo*. The purport of the document is sufficiently plain.

EDICT X

TRUE GLORY

(G. text; the other texts do not vary materially.)

'His Sacred and Gracious Majesty the King does not believe that glory or renown brings much profit unless in both the present and the future my people obediently hearken to the Law of Piety and conform to its precepts. For that purpose only does His Sacred and Gracious Majesty the King desire glory or renown.

Whatsoever exertions His Sacred and Gracious Majesty the King makes, all are for the sake of the life hereafter, so that every one may be freed from peril, and that peril is vice.

Difficult, verily, it is to attain such freedom, whether by people of low or of high degree, save by the utmost exertion, giving up all other aims. That, however, for him of high degree is difficult.'

Comment

This and the next document are the easiest of the R. E. The translation of Edict X in the second edition stands unaltered.

'My people,' *me jans*. In the other texts *me* refers to the royal teaching. 'Freed from peril,' *apa-parisrave*, more literally 'with as little (*alpa*) peril as possible.' Some of the ideas are repeated in R. E. XIII.

Milton offers a strikingly close parallel:—

> 'They err who count it glorious to subdue
> By conquest far and wide, to overrun
> Large countries, and in field great battles win,
> Great cities by assault. . . .

But, if there be in glory aught of good,
It may by means far different be attained,
Without ambition, war, or violence—
By deeds of peace, by wisdom eminent,
By patience, temperance.' . . .
(*Paradise Regained*, III, 71-92).

EDICT XI

TRUE ALMSGIVING

(Sh. text; there are no material variations in the other texts.)

Thus saith His Sacred and Gracious Majesty the King:—

'There is no such almsgiving as is the almsgiving of the Law of Piety, friendship in piety, liberality in piety, kinship in piety.

Herein does it consist—in proper treatment of slaves and servants, in hearkening to father and mother, in giving to friends, comrades, relations, ascetics, and Brahmans, in abstaining from the sacrificial slaughter of living creatures.

This ought to be said by father, son, brother, master (omitted by G.), friend, or comrade, nay, even by a neighbour—"This is excellent, this ought to be done."

Acting thus a man both gains this world and in the other world produces endless merit, by means of this almsgiving of piety.'

Comment

This edict also is easy to understand, and my former version holds good without substantial change. The matter is almost a verbal repetition of the conclusion of Edict IX as given in G.

'Almsgiving of the Law of Piety' means the free communication of good advice and teaching in the spirit of that Law. I think *sambandho* is better rendered by 'kinship' than by 'association,' which Mr. Thomas prefers. The concluding clause is phrased differently in G. without change of meaning.

The document is aptly illustrated by an inscription of Niśśanka Malla, King of Ceylon (A.D. 1187–96), which records that 'this pious monarch enjoyed the bliss of almsgiving, as he sat granting largess with great happiness, hearing many joyous shouts of "*sâdhu*" and the like, and imparting the gift of piety (*dâna-dharmma*), which is the noblest of all gifts' (*Arch. S. Rep. Ceylon*, for 1902 (lxvii of 1907), p. 11). Niśśanka Malla, like Asoka, bestowed his bounty alike on all sects and classes, on Brahmans and Buddhists, on natives and foreigners.

Another illustration comes from an unexpected place, the first extant letter of Cromwell, dated at St. Ives, Jan. 11, 1635 (Carlyle), which lays down the propositions that 'building of hospitals provides for men's bodies; to build material temples is judged a work of piety; but they that procure spiritual food, they that build up spiritual temples, they are the men truly charitable, truly pious.'

EDICT XII

TOLERATION

(G. text; no material variations in other texts.)

'His Sacred and Gracious Majesty the King does reverence to men of all sects, whether ascetics or householders, by gifts and various forms of reverence.

His Sacred Majesty, however, cares not so much for gifts or external reverence as that there should be a growth of the essence of the matter in all sects. The growth of the essence of the matter assumes various forms, but the root of it is restraint of speech, to wit, a man must not do reverence to his own sect or disparage that of another without reason. Depreciation should be for specific reasons only, because the sects of other people all deserve reverence for one reason or another.

By thus acting a man exalts his own sect, and at the same time does service to the sects of other people. By acting contrariwise a man hurts his own sect, and does disservice to the sects of other people. For he who does reverence to his own sect while disparaging the sects of others wholly from attachment to his own, with intent to enhance the splendour of his own sect, in reality by such conduct inflicts the severest injury on his own sect.

Concord, therefore, is meritorious, to wit, hearkening and hearkening willingly to the Law of Piety as accepted by other people. For this is the desire of His Sacred Majesty that all sects should hear much teaching and hold sound doctrine.

Wherefore the adherents of all sects, whatever they may be, must be informed that His Sacred Majesty does not care so much for gifts or external reverence as that there should be growth in the essence of the matter and respect for all sects.

For this very purpose are employed the Censors of the Law of Piety, the Censors of the Women, the (?) Superintendents of pastures, and other [official] bodies. And this is the fruit thereof—the growth of one's own sect and the enhancement of the splendour of the Law of Piety.'

Comment

'Sects' (*pâsamda*) is a more convenient word when often repeated than the longer term 'denomination,' which is preferred in R. E. VII and XIII. 'Reverence,' *pûjâ*. Compare R. E. IX and P. E. VI, VII, sec. 7. 'Reason' is used in the sense of 'particular occasion' or 'justification,' the 'légitime occasion' of Senart.

'Concord' (*samavâyo*) suits the context better than the *samayo*, 'self-restraint,' of Sh.

'Growth in the essence of the matter and respect for all sects.' I follow Senart in taking *bahukâ* as a substantive, meaning 'respect,' contrasted with *lahukâ*, 'depreciation,' in an earlier passage. *Bahukâ* was treated as an adjective meaning 'large' by Bühler.

The Censors or High Officers of the Law of Piety have been fully discussed in the comment on R. E. V. The similar officers appointed specially to look after the morals of the women evidently were a later institution, because when R. E. V was issued the duty of superintending the female establishments of the royal family was left in the hands of the officials responsible for the general enforcement of the *Dhamma*.

Nobody knows the exact meaning of *vachabhûmikâ*, equivalent to *vraja-°*, as in R. E. VI. The officials alluded to may be the Superintendents of Pastures, whose duties are defined in *Arthaśâstra*, Bk. ii, chap. 34. That work contains many provisions about the regulation of pasture lands. *Vraja*, as we have seen, means a herd of domestic animals. It would be possible to treat *Vraja-bhûmi* as a proper name, the land of Braj near Mathurâ (Muttra). But it is not apparent why the *vajrabhûmikas* should be selected for mention here. *Nikâya* is a general term for a class, body, or community. Here it evidently refers to official bodies or boards. With the exception of the one obscure term above noticed, this edict, although expressed in unusually abstract language, is fully intelligible.

All the Indian sects, creeds, or forms of religion had much in common; and most of the ancient Indian kings were tolerant of religious or sectarian differences. The persecutions which occurred occasionally were exceptional, as observed *ante*, pp. 62, 63.

The subject of the edict is illustrated by one of the 'Happy Sayings' of Akbar, that 'every sect favourably regards him who is faithful to its precepts, and in truth he is to be commended' (*Âîn*, transl. Jarrett, vol. iii, p. 391). The *Arthaśâstra* (Bk. xiii, chap. 5) goes so far as to advise that the king who annexes foreign territory should follow his new subjects 'in their faith with which they celebrate their national, religious, and congregational festivals or amusements. . . . He should always hold religious life in high esteem.' Readers of Machiavelli will remember the similar counsels in *The Prince*.

The edict was engraved on a separate boulder at Shâhbâzgarhi, a peculiarity which suggests that its principles must have been regarded as being of exceptional importance for the people in that region.

EDICT XIII

TRUE CONQUEST

(Sh. text, which is almost perfect; some variation in K.; the other texts very imperfect.)

'Kalinga was (or "the Kalingas were") conquered by His Sacred and Gracious Majesty the King when he had been consecrated eight years. One hundred and fifty thousand persons were thence carried away captive, one hundred thousand were there slain, and many times that number died.

Directly after the Kalingas had been annexed began His Sacred Majesty's zealous protection of the Law of Piety, his love of that Law, and his inculcation of that Law. Thence arises the remorse of His Sacred Majesty for having conquered the Kalingas, because the conquest of a country previously unconquered involves the slaughter, death, and carrying away captive of the people. That is a matter of profound sorrow and regret to His Sacred Majesty.

There is, however, another reason for His Sacred Majesty feeling still more regret, inasmuch as the Brahmans and ascetics, or men of other denominations, or householders who dwell there, and among whom these duties are practised, [to wit], hearkening to superiors, hearkening to father and mother, hearkening to teachers (or "elders"), and proper treatment (or "courtesy to") of friends, acquaintances, comrades, relatives, slaves, and servants, with steadfastness of devotion—to these befalls violence (or "injury"), or slaughter, or separation from their loved ones. Or violence happens to the friends, acquaintances, comrades, and relatives of those who are themselves well protected, while their affection [for those injured] continues undiminished. Thus for them also that is a mode of violence, and the share of this distributed among all men is a matter of regret to His Sacred Majesty, because it never is the case that faith in some one denomination or another does not exist.

So that of all the people who were then slain, done to death, or carried away captive in Kalinga, if the hundredth part or the thousandth part were now to suffer the same fate, it would be matter of regret to His Sacred Majesty. Moreover, should any one do him wrong, that too must be borne with by His Sacred Majesty, so far as it can possibly be borne with. Even upon the forest folk in his dominions, His Sacred Majesty looks kindly, and he seeks to make them think [aright], for [otherwise] repentance would come upon His Sacred Majesty. They are bidden to turn from their [evil] ways that they be not chastised. Because His Sacred Majesty desires for all animate beings security, self-control, peace of mind, and joyousness.

And this the chiefest conquest in the opinion of His Sacred Majesty, that conquest of the Law of Piety, which, again, has been won by His Sacred Majesty both here [in his own dominions] and among all his neighbours as far as six hundred leagues, where the king of the Greeks named Antiochos dwells, and to the north of that Antiochos [where dwell] the four (4) kings named severally Ptolemy, Antigonos, Magas, and Alexander—[likewise] in the south, the Cholas and Pâṇḍyas as far as the Tamraparni [river]—and here, too, in the King's dominions—among the Greeks, Kâmbojas, the Nâbhapantis of Nâbhaka; among the Bhojas, Pitinikas, ndhras, and Pulindas—everywhere they follow the instruction of His Sacred Majesty in the Law of Piety.

Even where the envoys of His Sacred Majesty do not penetrate, these people, too, hearing His Sacred

Majesty's ordinance based upon the Law of Piety and his instruction in that Law, practise and will practise the Law.

And, again, the conquest thereby won everywhere is everywhere a conquest full of delight. Delight is won in the conquests of the Law. A small matter, however, is that delight. His Sacred Majesty regards as bearing much fruit only that which concerns the other world.

And for this purpose has this scripture of the Law been recorded, in order that my sons and grandsons, who may be, may not think it their duty to conquer a new conquest.

If, perchance, a conquest should please them (?) they should take heed only of patience and gentleness, and regard as a conquest only that which is effected by the Law of Piety. That avails for both this world and the next. Let all their joy be that which lies in effort; that avails for both this world and the next.'

Supplement in G. only (Senart, vol. i, p. 323).

. . . 'the white elephant bringing indeed happiness to the whole world.'

Comment

This long, important, and interesting edict, which was imperfectly known when Senart wrote in 1881, is now fully intelligible, except in certain small details. The decipherment of the well-preserved Sh. text has cleared up most of the difficulties.

'Kalinga,' 'the Kalingas,' or 'the Three Kalingas,' the province on the coast of the Bay of Bengal between the Mahânadî and Godâvarî, nearly equivalent to Orissa. The early history of the kingdom at various periods is treated in the Khâravela inscription (*J. B. O. Res. Soc.*, vols. iii, iv). The date of the conquest by Asoka in his ninth regnal year would fall approximately in 261 B.C.

'Inasmuch as the Brahmans and ascetics . . . to these befalls.' The reading and interpretation have been corrected by Hultzsch (*J. R. A. S.*, 1913, p. 655).

'Because it never is the case,' &c. M. supplies an interesting variant, 'There is no country where these (two) classes, (viz.) the Brâhmaṇas and the Sramaṇas, do not exist, except among the Greeks (*Yoneshu*)' (Hultzsch, ibid.).

'Should any one do him wrong.' This remarkable sentiment recurs in the Kalinga Borderers' Edict. R. E. XIII was not published in Kalinga. For the 'true conquest' idea see comment on R. E. X.

Antiochos, *scil.* Theos (261–246 B.C.), has been already mentioned in R. E. II.

'The four (4) kings.' The numeral figure is in the text. Ptolemy (*Turumaye*), *scil.* Philadelphos of Egypt (285–247 B.C.). Antigonos (*Aṁtikini*), *scil.* Gonatas of Macedonia (278 or 277–239 B.C.); Magas (*Maka*) of Cyrênê to the west of Egypt, half-brother of Ptolemy Philadelphos. He declared his independence of Egypt about 285 B.C., and died in 258 B.C. Alexander is usually identified with a king of Epirus (272–? 258 B.C.), who opposed Antigonos Gonatas, but Beloch prefers to see a reference to a certain Alexander of Corinth.

'In the south,' *nicha* (Senart). For the Cholas and Pâṇḍyas see comment on R. E. II. The Keralaputra and Satiyaputra are not mentioned in this edict. Tâmraparṇi (*Taṁbapaṁni*) here, as in R. E. II, means the river in Tinnevelly, and not Ceylon. *Yonas* (Yavanas) mean, as in R. E. II, the Greek or Hellenized people on the NW. frontier. We have already met the Kâmbojas and Pitinikas in R. E. V. The Bhojas occupied the Ilichpur (Ellichpur) region in Berar or Vidarbha (Collins, *Geogr. Data of the Raghuvaṁśa*, Leipzig, 1907, p. 37).

The 'Nabhapantis of Nâbhaka' (*Nabhake Nabhitina*, the *Nâbhake Nabhapaṁtishu* of K.) have not been identified. The *Arthaśâstra* (Bk. i, chap. 6) mentions an ancient king named Nâbhâga. The Ândhras are well known. They were a powerful nation mentioned by Pliny, and after Asoka's death established a great kingdom stretching across India, which lasted for over four centuries, with fluctuations of dominion. See

E. H. I., latest ed. The term Pulinda was used vaguely to denote wild hill-tribes. Here it probably refers to people like the Bhîls in the Vindhya and Sâtpura hills.

The next sentence shows that Asoka's envoys or missioners, *dûta*, carried on his propaganda among all the peoples named.

'Scripture of the Law,' *dhramanipi*, or *dhaṁmalipi*, K., as in other passages. *Nipi*, not *dipi*, is the correct reading (Hultzsch).

'If, perchance, a conquest should please them.' The translation has been suggested by Hultzsch, but the meaning is uncertain. Senart and Bühler took *sara* as 'by arrows,' or 'by arms,' a forced interpretation not likely to be right. 'Patience' seems to be the best rendering of *kshânti* (*chhâtiṁ*), but 'mercy' and 'forbearance' are alternatives. Asoka, as elsewhere, proclaims that his teaching results in 'delight,' 'joy,' or 'joyousness,' and insists on the superior claims of the next world.

The supplementary imperfect inscription appended only at G. seems to refer to the lost figure of an elephant, such as is incised on the rock at K. with the legend Gaj[o]tame (*gajottama*), 'the most excellent elephant.' At Dh. an elephant carved in relief looks down upon the inscriptions (*E. H. I.*, frontispiece). The elephant was a familiar symbol of Buddha.

EDICT XIV

EPILOGUE

(G. text, which is slightly fuller than Sh.; all three, K. being the third, are well preserved.)

'This scripture of the Law of Piety has been written by command of His Sacred Majesty the King, [in a form] sometimes condensed, sometimes of medium length, and sometimes expanded; and everything is not brought together everywhere. For great is my dominion, and much has been written, and much shall I cause to be written.

And certain phrases have been uttered again and again by reason of the honeyed sweetness of this topic or that, in the hope that the people may act accordingly. It may be that something may have been written incompletely by reason of mutilation of a passage, or of misunderstanding, or by a blunder of the writer.'

Comment

This epilogue serves as an official commentary on the Fourteen Edicts described collectively as a Scripture of the Law of Piety. No attentive reader can fail to see the application of Asoka's remarks. The verbal repetitions are numerous to a wearisome degree, and many examples of the condensed, medium, and expanded expositions might be cited. 'Brought together' is offered as a rendering of the Sanskrit *ghaṭitam* (G.), *ghaṭiti* (Sh.), *ghaṭite* (K.). Senart translates *réuni*, that is to say 'gravé complet et sans omission.'

I do not understand how Bühler got the sense 'suitable,' which I adopted formerly.

'Much has been written' applies apparently to the Minor R. E., the Fourteen R. E., and the Kalinga E. The inscriptions to be written seem to mean the Pillar and Minor Pillar E. 'Mutilation of a passage.' The words, equivalent to Sanskrit *deśaṁ saṁkhyāya*, are susceptible of several interpretations. *Deśaṁ* may be taken to mean a 'part,' or 'commandment,' or 'space.' I follow Senart's rendering, 'soit qu'un passage ait été tronqué.'

As a matter of fact, blunders in the extant copies of the edicts are rare. Most of the apparent errors assumed by the early interpreters to exist were due to defective facsimiles. But mistakes do occur, as, for example, at Shâhbâzgarhi, passages are accidentally repeated in at least two instances.

The 'copy' from which the stone-cutter worked must have been scrupulously accurate as a rule, and the cutting of the letters on the rock is beautifully executed in most cases.

SECTION 4

The Kalinga Edicts

(Separate or Detached Edicts of earlier authors.)

EDICT I

THE BORDERERS' EDICT

(Separate or Detached Edict No. 2 of Prinsep, Bühler, &c.; J. text, facs. and transcript in *A. S. S. I.* (Amarâvati vol., 1887), p. 127, Pl. lxix.)

THE DUTIES OF OFFICIALS TO THE BORDER TRIBES

Thus saith His Sacred Majesty:—

At Samâpâ the High Officers are to be addressed in the King's words, as follows:—

'Whatsoever my views are I desire them to be acted on in practice and carried into effect by certain means. And in my opinion the chief means for attaining this purpose are my instructions to you.

"All men are my children;" and, just as I desire for my children that they may enjoy every kind of prosperity and happiness both in this world and in the next, so also I desire the same for all men.

[If you ask] "With regard to the unsubdued borderers what is the king's command to us?"

[The answer is that—] "The King desires that 'they should not be afraid of me, that they should trust me, and should receive from me happiness, not sorrow.' Moreover, they should grasp the truth that 'the King will bear patiently with us,' and that 'for my sake they should follow the Law of Piety and so gain both this world and the next.'"

And for this purpose I give you instructions. Thereby being freed from my debt, giving instructions to you and making known my will, my inflexible resolve and promise.

Now you, acting accordingly, must do your work, and must make these people trust me and grasp the truth that "the King is to us even as a father; he loves us even as he loves himself; we are to the King even as his children."

By instructing you and intimating my will, my inflexible resolve and promise, I shall be provided with [trained] local officials for this business, because you are in a position to make these people trust me and to ensure their prosperity both in this world and in the next, and by so doing you may win heaven and also effect my release from debt [or "discharge your debt to me"].

And for this purpose has this scripture of the law of piety been written here, in order that the High Officers may strive without ceasing both to secure the confidence of these borderers and to set them moving on the path of piety.

And this scripture must be recited at the beginning of each season of four months on the Tishya day. In the intervals also it may be recited. On occasion it may be recited even to one person.

By acting this you should endeavour to fulfil my instructions.'

Comment

This edict is now fully understood, and my former version stands almost unchanged. It and the companion document possess special interest as recording avowedly the very words of Asoka, who thus speaks to us from the rocks in his own person across the centuries. The translation of the two Kalinga Edicts is difficult by reason of the frequent changes from the third to the first person involved in the quotations from the sovereign's words. The two documents concern only the conquered province of Kalinga and the wild tribes dwelling on its borders, as they still dwell. These two edicts take the place of R. E. XI, XII, XIII, not published in Kalinga. The composition which I call the Borderers' Edict comes first upon the rock, following R. E. XIV. The text at Jaugaḍa in the Ganjâm District, Madras, is substantially in perfect condition. That at Dhauli, in the Puri District, Orissa, is much mutilated. The texts agree in almost every detail, except that the Dhauli proclamation is addressed to the Prince and High Officers at Tosali, the capital of the newly-annexed province, whereas that at Jaugaḍa is addressed to the High Officers of Samâpâ. Dhauli, according to M. M. Haraparshad Śâstrî, is a phonetic equivalent of Tosalî. The ancient ruins surrounding the inscription rock at Jaugaḍa evidently are to be identified with Samâpâ. The Prince (*Kumâra*) at Tosalî, presumably was one of Asoka's sons, the offspring of one of the lawful Queens; see P. E. VII, sec. 7.

Both of the Kalinga Edicts were intended solely for the guidance of the officials of high rank entrusted with the administration of a country lately hostile and continually troubled by the presence on its borders of wild, half-savage tribes, who needed firm, though kindly, paternal government. The principles inculcated are admirable, and it is curious to find the leading propositions repeated in a proclamation issued in 1848 by an English officer who is not likely to have been acquainted with the Kalinga Edicts. Mr. Cust's proclamation at Hoshyârpur in the Panjâb includes the following passages: 'What is your injury, I consider mine; what is gain to you, I consider my gain . . . Tell those who have joined in the rebellion to return to me, as children who have committed a fault return to their fathers, and their faults will be forgiven them' (Aitchison, *John Lawrence*, p. 46, Rulers of India series).

A few points of detail require brief notice.

'Views'—literally, 'whatever I see' (*dakhâmi*).

'All men are my children;' an echo of the saying 'All beings are my children,' ascribed to Buddha, and found both in the *Lotus de la bonne Loi*, Burnouf, p. 89, and in the *Dharma-saṅgraha*, II, as quoted by Kern, *Manual of Indian Buddhism* (Strassburg, 1896), p. 61.

'Bear patiently;' compare R. E. XIII. The phrase 'discharge of debt' occurs also in R. E. VI

'I shall have (trained) local officials,' *desâ âyutike hosâmi*, literally, 'I shall be local-officialed,' an odd phrase. The *âyuktas* were the subordinate civil service.

The Tishya day is the day on which the moon is supposed to be in conjunction with the constellation so named. The three seasons are still recognized in parts of India. In the *Arthaśâstra* the division into six seasons is adopted. Bühler points out that Asoka's practice accords with that prescribed in the ancient Brahmanical *sûtras.* The few innovations introduced by Asoka into the established system of government were all directed to the propagation of *dharma*, as viewed by him from a Buddhist stand-point.

EDICT II

THE PROVINCIALS' EDICT

(References as for Edict I; Dh. text.)

THE DUTIES OF OFFICIALS TO THE PROVINCIALS

In the words of His Sacred Majesty the High Officers administering the town are to be addressed as follows:—

'Whatsoever my views are I desire them to be acted on in practice and carried into effect by certain means. And in my opinion the chief means for this purpose are my instructions to you, because you have been set over many thousands of living beings that you may gain the affection of good men.

"All men are my children;" and, just as I desire for my children that they may enjoy every kind of prosperity and happiness both in this world and in the next, so also I desire the same for all men.

You, however, do not grasp this truth to its full extent. Some individual, perchance, pays heed, but to a part only, not the whole. See then to this, for the principle of government is well established.

Again, it happens that some individual incurs imprisonment or torture, and when the result is his imprisonment without due cause, many other people are deeply grieved. In such a case you must desire to do justice.

However, with certain natural dispositions success is impossible, to wit, envy, lack of perseverance, harshness, impatience, want of application, laziness, indolence. You must desire that such dispositions be not yours. The root of the whole matter lies in perseverance and patience in applying this principle of government. The indolent man cannot rouse himself to move, yet one must needs move, advance, go on.

In the same way you must see to your duty, and be told to remember:—"See to my commands; such and such are the instructions of His Sacred Majesty." Fulfilment of these bears great fruit, non-fulfilment brings great calamity. By those who fail neither heaven nor the royal favour can be won. Ill performance of this duty can never gain my regard, whereas in fulfilling my instructions you will gain heaven and also pay your debt to me.

This scripture must be recited every constellation of Tishya day, and in the intervals between the Tishya days, on fit occasions it may be recited even to a single hearer. By such action you must endeavour to fulfil my intentions.

For this purpose has this scripture been here inscribed in order that the administrators of the town may strive without ceasing [lit. "all the time"] that the restraint or torture of the townsmen may not take place without due cause.

And for this purpose, in accordance with the Law of Piety, I shall send forth in rotation every five years such persons [lit. "a person"] as are of mild and temperate disposition, and regardful of the sanctity of life, who knowing this my purpose will comply with my instructions.

From Ujjain, however, the Prince for this purpose will send out a similar body [of officials], and will not over-pass three years.

In the same way—from Taxila.

When the High Officers aforesaid . . . proceed on transfer in rotation, then without neglecting their own [ordinary] business, they will attend to this matter also, and thus will carry out the king's instructions.'

Comment

The Jaugaḍa text is addressed to the corresponding officers at Samâpâ. The Prince is not mentioned in either text, apparently because he was too exalted to be concerned. In so far as this document is identical with Kalinga Edict I, the Borderers' Edict, see the comment on that edict.

'Administering,' *viyohâlikâ*.

'Principle of government,' *nîti*. Bühler renders 'maxims of government,' Senart, 'obligations morales.' I understand that Asoka alludes to the *Nîti-śâstras*, or treatises on the principles of government, which are either closely related to or identical with the class of works called *Arthaśâstra*. The existing treatises professedly devoted to *Nîti*, although much later than Asoka, must be based, like the *Arthaśâstra* of Kauṭilya, on lost ancient books.

'Torture;' the word corresponding with the Sanskrit *parikleśa* should be rendered 'torture,' not 'ill-usage,' as in my earlier version. Senart long ago rightly translated 'torturé.' The discovery of Kauṭilya's *Arthaśâstra* has exposed the horrible Maurya law on the subject of judicial torture, which had come down from much earlier times, 'in the Śâstras of great sages,' as Kauṭilya affirms. The subject is fully treated in Bk. iv, chapters 8, 9, 11. Chapter 10 deals with mutilation and alternative fines, supposed to be equivalent. Chapter 8, which is devoted to 'trial and torture to elicit confession,' provides that 'those whose guilt is believed to be true shall be subjected to torture,' of which eighteen appalling kinds are enumerated. The victim might be compelled to endure any or all of those kinds. When Asoka refers to 'torture without due cause' he seems to mean arbitrary torture applied without regard to the law. The irregularities of officials such as those denounced in general terms by Asoka are dealt with specifically in chapter 9, which enacts among other things that the superintendent of a jail who subjects a prisoner to unjust torture shall be fined 48 (silver) *paṇas*, probably nearly equivalent to either shillings or francs. If such an officer shall have beaten a prisoner to death, the fine was 1,000 *paṇas*. Execution was often accompanied by deliberate legal torment, as explained in chapter 11. It is clear that Asoka maintained the ferocious criminal code of the *Arthaśâstra* and of his grandfather. He merely tried to remedy abuses in administration by admonition and supervision, but no man can now tell how far he succeeded or failed.

For the meaning of *anusaṁyâna* see comment on R. E. III.

'Regardful of the sanctity of life.' The word used, as Bühler points out, represents the curious Sanskrit compound *ślakshṇârambhaḥ*, which means 'sparing in sacrificial slaughter.'

Both Taxila and Ujjain were the capitals of princely Viceroys, ordinarily sons of the sovereigns by principal queens. Literary tradition represents Asoka as having served his father at both cities before his accession. We cannot explain with certainty why it was thought necessary to transfer the officials in the outlying provinces every three years. 'Similar body [of officials];' the word used represents the Sanskrit *varga*.

I think it may be said both that this document is now completely intelligible, and that the translation offered is entitled to acceptation as being correct.

CHAPTER V

THE PILLAR EDICTS AND MISCELLANEOUS INSCRIPTIONS

SECTION I

The Seven Pillar Edicts

EDICT I

THE PRINCIPLES OF GOVERNMENT

(Bühler's ed. of the series with facs. in *Ep. Ind.* ii. (1894), pp. 245-74. The various texts are mostly well preserved, and in substantial agreement for Edicts I-VI. Edict VII is extant in one text only.)

Thus saith His Sacred and Gracious Majesty the King:—

'When I had been consecrated twenty-six years I caused this scripture of the Law of Piety to be written.

Both this world and the next are difficult to secure save by intense love of the Law of Piety, intense self-examination, intense obedience, intense dread, intense effort. However, owing to my instructions, this yearning for the Law of Piety, this love of the Law from day to day, have grown and will grow.

My Agents, too, whether of high, low, or middle rank, themselves conform to my teaching and lead others in the right way—fickle people must be led in the right way—likewise also the Wardens of the

Marches. For this is the rule: "protection by the Law of Piety, regulation by that Law, felicity by that Law, guarding by that Law."'

Comment

In the Pillar Scripture recorded at a late date in his reign Asoka continues, develops, and reviews the instructions which he had first recorded in his thirteenth regnal year. His principles had not changed, and many things said before are repeated. This first Pillar Edict may be regarded as a preamble or introduction to the series. Senart treats it as being specially addressed to the imperial officials, but to me it seems intended for more general application by all concerned, official or non-official. The text and translation present no difficulties, except that there is room for some difference of opinion concerning the shade of meaning of some of the terms. *Parîkshâ* (*palikkâ*) is rendered 'self-examination,' the *paṭivekhe* of P. E. III. Bühler translates 'circumspection,' and Senart, in conformity with his notion that officials only are addressed, translates 'surveillance rigoureuse.'

The word *pulisâ*, literally 'men,' translated 'agents,' here occurs for the first time. It may be intended to include all the superior officials, or, more probably, it may refer to special supervising officers, like the *missi dominici* of Charlemagne. The term recurs in P. E. IV and VII. The latter passage, if Bhandarkar's probable emendation be accepted, would seem to distinguish the *pulisâ* from the 256 *vyûthas* of Minor R. E. I.

The 'Wardens of the Marches,' *aṁta-mahamâtâ*, or 'High Officers of the Frontiers,' also have not been heard of before by name, although Asoka had laid down in the Kalinga Borderers' Edict the principles which should guide frontier officers.

Compare Charlemagne's *Markgrafen* (Bryce, *The Holy Roman Empire*, p. 68). 'Fickle people,' *chapalaṁ*, with the secondary sense of 'ill-behaved' or 'sinners.' 'Protection,' *pâlanâ*; 'guarding,' *goti*. All those terms admit of slight variations in translation.

EDICT II

THE ROYAL EXAMPLE

Thus saith His Sacred and Gracious Majesty the King:—

'"The Law of Piety is excellent." But wherein consists the Law of Piety? In these things, to wit, little impiety, many good deeds, compassion, liberality, truthfulness, purity.

The gift of spiritual insight I have given in manifold ways; whilst on two-footed and four-footed beings, on birds and the denizens of the waters, I have conferred various favours, even unto the boon of life; and many other good deeds have I done.

For this my purpose I have caused this scripture of the Law of Piety to be written, that men may walk after its teaching and that it may long endure. And he who will thus follow its teaching will do well.'

Comment

The edict presents no serious difficulty. *Âsinave* is a technical term, like the Jain *aṇhaya*, best rendered by 'impiety.' See the next edict. It is the exact contrary of *dhaṁma*. 'Good deeds,' *kayânâni*, Sanskrit *kalyâṇâni*. Compare *kalaṇa-kramasa* as a translation of εὐεργέτου on a coin of Telephos. A pious Buddhist does not regard himself as an 'unprofitable servant,' but frankly boasts of his good deeds. 'Nothing was so calming to a man's soul as to think of even one deed he had done well in his life' (Fielding Hall, *The Soul of a People*, p. 296). See R.E. V and P.E. VII. Bühler explained the true meaning of *chakhu-dâne* as 'the gift of spiritual insight,' and pointed out that the metaphorical use of *chakhu* (*chakshus*) is common to both Hindus and Buddhists. Compare *dhaṁma-dâne* in R. E. XI.

EDICT III

SELF-EXAMINATION

Thus saith His Sacred and Gracious Majesty the King:—

'A man sees only his good deed and says, "This good deed has been done by me." In no wise does he see his ill deed (or "sin") and say, "This ill deed have I done, this act called impiety."

Difficult, however, is self-examination of this kind.

Nevertheless, a man should see to this that brutality, cruelty, anger, pride, jealousy, are the things leading to impiety, [and should say], "By reason of these may I not fall."

This is chiefly to be seen to—"The one course avails me for the present world, the other course avails me also for the world to come".'

Comment

This document is easily understood. The word 'impiety,' *âsinave*, connects it closely with the preceding edict.

'Brutality' is Rhys Davids's rendering of *chamdiye*.

'Self-examination,' *paṭivekhe*, seems to mean nearly the same thing as *parîkshâ* in P. E. II. 'Also,' *mana*, is Michelson's translation.

EDICT IV

THE POWERS AND DUTIES OF GOVERNORS

Thus saith His Sacred and Gracious Majesty the King:—

'When I had been consecrated twenty-six years I caused this scripture of the Law of Piety to be written.

To my Governors set over many hundred thousands of people I have granted independence in the award of honours and penalties in order that the Governors confidently and fearlessly may perform their duties. bestow welfare and happiness upon the people of the country, and confer favours upon them.

They will ascertain the causes of happiness or unhappiness, and through the subordinate officials of the Law of Piety will exhort the people of the country so that they may gain both this world and the next.

My Governors, too, eager to serve me; my Agents, also, acknowledging my will, shall serve me, and they, too, on occasion, will give exhortations so that the Governors will be eager to win me.

For, just as a man, having made over his child to a skilful nurse, feels confident and says to himself, "The skilful nurse is eager to care for the happiness of my child," even so my Governors have been created for the welfare and happiness of the country, with intent that fearlessly, confidently, and quietly they may perform their duties. For that reason I have granted to my Governors independence in the award of honours and penalties.

Forasmuch as it is desirable that there should be uniformity in judicial procedure and uniformity in penalties, from this time forward my rule is this:—

"To condemned men lying in prison under sentence of death a respite of three days is granted by me."

[During that interval] the relatives in some cases will arrange for a revision in order to save their lives, or in order to obtain a revision will give alms with a view to the next world, or will observe fasting.

For my desire is that even when their time is irrevocably fixed they [the condemned] may gain the next world, while among the people various pious practices may increase, including self-control and liberality.'

Comment

The meaning of this rather difficult edict, which had been discussed and misunderstood for many years, has now been cleared up to my satisfaction in all essential points. It deals with two subjects, the independent discretion vested in the Governors (*Râjûkas*), and the reprieve of three days granted to convicts lying under sentence of death.

As to the Râjûkas, I believe that the word is etymologically connected with Râja, and that Bühler's notion of its relation to *rajju*, a measuring rope, was mistaken. Considering the extent of those officers' powers over hundreds of thousands of subjects, and the unfettered discretion allowed to them, the rendering 'Governors' is preferable to 'Commissioners.' I understand that the rank of Râjûka had long existed, and that Asoka's innovation consisted in granting them extensive powers without the necessity of obtaining sanction for particular acts by reference to the Crown. The designation *Râjûka* does not occur in the *Arthaśâstra*.

The imperfectly understood term 'Agents' (*pulisâ*) recurs here. We cannot at present define the exact position of those officers.

'Confidently, and quietly,' Michelson's rendering, is, I think, right.

'Uniformity,' *samatâ*, as Senart, not 'equity,' as Bühler. 'Judicial procedure,' *viyohâla*, is indicated by the context as the correct translation here. Bühler preferred the more general words 'official business,' and is supported by Kalinga Provincials' Edict, where *viyohâlika* seems to mean 'administrators' rather than 'judges,' although the latter rendering is not excluded.

In interpreting the last two paragraphs I have been helped by the remarks of Thomas in *J. R. A. S.*, 1916, pp. 120-3. I venture to think that my version gives the real meaning. If a revision should be granted, the convicts would save their lives. If it should be refused, both they and their relations would at any rate gain spiritual advantages. I take it that the Râjûkas were empowered and required to grant invariably the three days' delay before execution. That interpretation connects the two subjects discussed in the document.

EDICT V

REGULATIONS RESTRICTING SLAUGHTER AND MUTILATION OF ANIMALS: JAIL DELIVERIES

Thus saith His Sacred and Gracious Majesty the King:—

'When I had been consecrated twenty-six years the following species [or "creatures"] were declared exempt from slaughter, namely these:—parrots, starlings, (?) adjutants, "Brahmany ducks," geese, *nandîmukhas*, *gelâtas*, bats, queen-ants, female tortoises, "boneless fish," *vedaveyakas*, *gangâpuputakas*, (?) skate, river tortoises, porcupines, tree squirrels, (?) *bârahsingha* stags, "Brahmany bulls," (?) monkeys, rhinoceros, grey doves, village pigeons, and all four-footed animals which are neither utilized nor eaten.

She-goats, ewes, and sows, that is to say, those which are with young or in milk, are exempt from slaughter, as well as their offspring up to six months of age.

The caponing of cocks must not be done.

Chaff must not be set on fire along with the living things in it.

Forests must not be set on fire either wantonly or for the destruction of life.

The living must not be fed with the living.

At each of the three seasonal full moons and at the full moon of Tishya (December–January) for three days in each case, namely, the fourteenth and fifteenth days of the first fortnight and the first day of the second fortnight, as well as on fast-days throughout the year, fish is exempt from slaughter, and must not be sold.

On the same days in elephant-forests and fish-ponds other classes of animals whatsoever are not to be destroyed.

On the eighth, fourteenth, and fifteenth days of each

fortnight, as well as on the Tishya and Punarvasu days, on the full-moon days of the three seasons, and on festivals, the castration of bulls must not be performed, nor may he-goats, rams, boars, or other animals liable to castration be castrated.

On the Tishya, Punarvasu, and seasonal full-moon days, and during the fortnights of the seasonal full-moons the branding of horses and oxen must not be done.

During the period that elapsed until I had been consecrated twenty-six years twenty-five jail deliveries have been effected.'

Comment

My former translation stands, except for slight verbal emendations. The animals, of which the names remain untranslated, have not been identified.

The code of regulations, although based on ancient Brahmanical practices, bears the impress of Asoka's personal decisions. It applied to the whole empire. R. E. I was concerned only with the animals previously slaughtered for the royal kitchen and for the distribution of meat doles at merry-makings. The legislator does not attempt to forbid either the killing of animals generally, or the use of meat and fish for food. He contents himself with hampering and restricting those practices by stringent regulations which must have been extremely oppressive (*ante*, p. 57). It is probable that the existence of such an irritating code may have had much to do with the break-up of the Maurya empire after Asoka's death.

The identity of the animals mentioned has been discussed at length by Bühler (*Ep. Ind.*, ii. pp. 259–61); and by Manmohan Chakravarti in his monograph, 'Animals in the Inscriptions of Piyadasi' (*Mem. A. S. B.*, vol. i (1906), pp. 861–74). My translation gives the results, certain or probable. 'Female tortoises,' *ḍuḷi* (not *duḍi* as previously read, Lüders). 'Monkeys' seems to be the most plausible rendering of *okapiṃde*. The creature is said to have been a thief of monks' rations, a character which suits the monkey best. 'Grey doves,' *setakapote*, the whitish-grey dove, common in some parts of India (*Columba* (?) spec.). 'Village-pigeons,' the common 'blue-rock' (*Columba intermedia*), which frequents wells, mosques, &c.

'Utilized,' for their skins or in other ways.

'Caponing,' forbidden as a practice not essential, and intended merely to improve the flavour of the flesh.

'Chaff,' as that lying on a threshing-floor, sometimes burnt to get rid of vermin. 'Forests.' Burma supplies an illustration. 'During the progress [of the first rise of the river] some hunters went to one of these islands where many deer were to be found, and set fire to the grass to drive them out of cover, shooting them as they came out' (Fielding Hall, *The Soul of a People*, p. 299).

'The living must not be fed with the living;' as hawks with the blood of living pigeons, a cruel practice said to be still in vogue. Other cases readily occur to the mind.

For elephant-preserves, see the rules in *Arthaśâstra*, Bk. ii, chap. 2, 31. Asoka no doubt had a 'superintendent of elephants,' as his predecessors had. 'Fish-pond,' *keraṭabhoge*, a piece of water reserved for the use of the Kewats or fishermen. The close days for fish amounted to fifty-six in the year.

'Castration,' an unholy, although necessary operation. I-tsing asserts that 'the Buddha did not allow even castration' (transl. Takakusu, p. 197). 'The Hindus of Bengal, before the Muhammedan conquest, are said never to have castrated the bull. In fact, I found that any questions on this subject were exceedingly disagreeable, and that although the landlords and their agents tolerated the practice in the Muhammedans and impure tribes, yet they considered it as very illegal and disgraceful, and not fit to be mentioned' (Buchanan in Martin, *Eastern India*, 1838, vol. ii. p. 891). 'Branding,' of cattle, see *Arthaśâstra*, Bk. ii, chap. 29; and for the ancient practice in Ceylon, see *Ceylon Nat. Review*, 1907, p. 334.

As to Tishya days and the seasons see comment on Kalinga Borderers' Edict. 'Punarvasu' is the seventh lunar asterism or *nakshatra*. Bühler (loc. cit.) discusses the subject fully.

The *Arthaśâstra*, Bk. i, chap. 26, headed 'The Superintendent of Slaughter-house' (transl., p. 152), gives a list of protected animals, which agrees with that of Asoka in exempting from slaughter the 'Brahmany duck,' parrot, starling, and goose, among the creatures specified.

The same chapter enacts that 'cattle such as a calf, a bull, or a milch cow shall not be slaughtered.' But other cows might be killed and eaten. Book ii, chap. 29 (transl., p. 160) expressly mentions 'cattle that are fit only for the supply of flesh.' The reader will hardly fail to observe that horned cattle, cows included, are *not* included in Asoka's list of protected animals. There is, as is well known, abundant evidence that the meat of such beasts was largely used in ancient India. In 326 B. C. the king of Taxila gave Alexander '3,000 oxen fatted for the shambles.' See the valuable paper by W. Crooke, 'The Veneration of the Cow in India' (*Folk-Lore*, Sept. 1912, pp. 275–306). The Maurya documents are of special interest as marking at a definite period a transitional stage in the cult of the cow.

The final paragraph of the edict shows that Asoka was in the habit of releasing prisoners once a year, presumably on his birthday; i. e. 'the day to which his birth-star is assigned,' as phrased in *Arthaśāstra*, Bk. ii, chap. 36 (transl., p. 185). That text enumerates nine occasions or reasons which would justify the release of prisoners, the first being the king's birthday.

The whole document, except for the failure to identify some of the animals named, is now completely understood, and the translation may be accepted as correct.

EDICT VI

THE NECESSITY FOR A DEFINITE CREED

Thus saith His Sacred and Gracious Majesty the King:—

'When I had been consecrated twelve years I caused a scripture of the Law of Piety to be written for the welfare and happiness of mankind, with the intent that they, giving up their old courses, might attain growth in piety, one way or another.

Thus, aiming at the welfare and happiness of mankind, I devote my attention alike to my relatives, to persons near, and to persons afar off, if haply I may guide some of them to happiness, and to that end I make my arrangements.

In like manner I devote my attention to all communities, because all denominations are reverenced by me with various forms of reverence. Nevertheless, personal adherence to one's own creed is the chief thing in my opinion.

When I had been consecrated twenty-six years I had this scripture of the Law of Piety written.'

Comment

This short edict, reasserting the doctrine of R. E. IV and XII, offers few difficulties. My former translation stands without substantial change. The elliptic phrase, *taṁ apahata*, is construed in accordance with Bühler's view. Senart renders 'taking away some part of the teaching.' 'Arrangements;' this clause was accidentally omitted from Bühler's version. The indefinite term *nikâya* is best rendered by 'communities,' equivalent to 'denominations,' and not by 'corporations,' as Bühler, or 'the whole body of my officers,' as Senart. Compare R. E. XIII. The Pâli *Kośa* defines *nikâya* as a 'body of co-religionists,' while *kula* means a community of persons related by birth or caste. *Sajâtinaṁ tu kulaṁ, nikâyo tu sadharminaṁ* (Bhagwân Lâl, *J. Bo. Br. Rut. S.*, xii. 408).

'Personal adherence;' my version follows Senart, in preference to Bühler, who renders 'the approach through one's own free will' of one sect to another.

Subject to the differences of opinion noted, the whole edict is completely understood, and my version may be accepted as satisfactory.

EDICT VII

REVIEW OF ASOKA'S MEASURES FOR THE PROPAGATION OF THE LAW OF PIETY IN HIS EMPIRE

I. Thus saith His Sacred and Gracious Majesty the King:—

'The kings who lived in times past desired that men might grow with the growth of the Law of Piety. Men, however, did not grow with the growth of the Law of Piety in due proportion.'

II. Concerning this thus saith His Sacred and Gracious Majesty the King:—

'This [thought] occurred to me:—In times past kings desired that men might grow with the growth of the Law of Piety in due proportion; men, however, did not in due proportion grow with the growth of the Law.

By what means, then, can men be induced to conform? by what means can men grow with the growth of the Law of Piety in due proportion? by what means can I lift up at least some of them through the growth of that Law?'

III. Concerning this thus saith His Sacred and Gracious Majesty the King:—

'This [thought] occurred to me:—

"Proclamation of the Law of Piety will I proclaim; with instruction in that Law will I instruct; so that men hearkening thereto may conform, lift themselves up, and mightily grow with the growth of the Law of Piety."

For this my purpose proclamations of the Law of Piety have been proclaimed; instructions in that Law of many kinds have been disseminated; my [?] missioners, likewise my Agents set over the multitude, will expound and expand my teaching.

The Governors, also, set over many hundred thousands of souls have received instructions—"In such and such a manner expound my teaching to the body of subordinate officials of the Law."'

IV. Thus saith His Sacred and Gracious Majesty:—

'Considering further the same purpose, I have set up pillars of the Law, appointed Censors (High Officers) of the Law, and made a proclamation of the Law.'

V. Thus saith His Sacred and Gracious Majesty the King:—

'On the roads, too, I have had banyan-trees planted to give shade to man and beast; groves (or "gardens") of mango-trees I have had planted; at every half-*kôs* I have had wells dug; rest-houses, too, have been erected; and numerous watering-places have been provided by me here and there for the enjoyment of man and beast.

A small matter, however, is that so-called enjoyment. With various blessings has mankind been blessed by former kings, as by me also; by me, however, with the intent that men may conform to the Law of Piety, has it been done even as I thought.'

VI. Thus saith His Sacred and Gracious Majesty:—

'My Censors (or "High Officers") of the Law of Piety, too, are employed on manifold objects of the royal favour affecting both ascetics and householders, and are likewise employed among all denominations. On the business of the Church, too, they are employed, as well as among the Brahmans and Jains are they employed. Similarly, they are employed among the Jains; among miscellaneous sects, too, are they employed.

The High Officers of various kinds shall severally superintend their respective charges, whereas the High Officers of the Law of Piety (Censors) are employed both on such things and also among other denominations.'

VII. Thus saith His Sacred and Gracious Majesty the King:—

'Both these and many other officers, heads of

departments, are employed in the distribution of alms, both my own and those of the Queens; and in all my female establishments both here [*scil.* "at the capital"] and in the provinces they indicate in divers ways sundry places where satisfaction may be given.

Those same officers are also employed in the distribution of the alms of my sons, and likewise of the other Princes, sons of the Queens, in order to promote the practice of the Law of Piety and conformity to that Law.

The practice of the Law of Piety and the conformity referred to are those whereby compassion, liberality, truth, purity, gentleness, and saintliness will thus grow among mankind.

VIII. Thus saith His Sacred and Gracious Majesty the King:—

'Whatsoever meritorious deeds have been done by me, those deeds mankind will conform to and imitate, whence follows that they have grown and will grow in the virtues of hearkening to father and mother, hearkening to teachers (or "elders"), reverence to the aged, and seemly treatment of Brahmans and ascetics, of the poor and wretched; yea, even of slaves and servants.'

IX. Thus saith His Sacred and Gracious Majesty the King:—

'Among men, however, when the aforesaid growth of piety has grown, it has been effected by twofold means, to wit, by regulations of the Law of Piety and by reflection. Of these two, however, regulations of the Law are of small account, whereas reflection is superior.

Nevertheless, regulations of the Law of Piety have been made by me to the effect that such and such species are exempt from slaughter, not to speak of numerous other regulations of the Law of Piety which have been made by me.

Yet the superiority of reflection is shown by the

growth of piety among men and the more complete abstention from killing animate beings and from the sacrificial slaughter of living creatures.

So for this purpose has this been recorded, in order that my sons and descendants (lit. "great grandsons") may conform thereto, and by thus conforming may win both this world and the next.

When I had been consecrated twenty-seven years I had this scripture of the Law written.'

X. Concerning this His Sacred Majesty saith:—

'This scripture of the Law of Piety, wheresoever pillars of stone or tables of stone exist, must there be recorded so that it may long endure.'

Comment

General.—This edict, the longest and most important of the whole collection, is extant only on a single monument, the Delhi-Topra pillar. Part, which is inscribed all round the shaft, used to be erroneously described as a separate edict, No. VIII. The text, happily, is almost perfect, and the difficulties of interpretation are few. Many of the ideas and phrases, being repeated from the earlier inscriptions, have been sufficiently explained already. The subject is a comprehensive review of Asoka's religious efforts within his empire up to the twenty-eighth year of his reign. Although he lived some nine or ten years longer, and certain minor inscriptions to be noticed presently belong to those years, no later precise date is recorded.

Asoka, who speaks in his own person, divided his review into ten sections, each prefaced by the formula 'Thus saith His Sacred and Gracious Majesty the King,' slightly abbreviated in some cases. All persons concerned are addressed, whether officials or the general public. In my last edition I expressed surprise that no mention is made of the foreign missions, but I now perceive the reason for the omission to be that the emperor, who was addressing only his own subjects, confined himself to recounting the principal measures which he had taken for propagating *Dhamma*, or the Law of Piety, throughout his dominions. Evidently he wished to record what he had done for his own people, and did not feel called upon to treat of his dealings with foreign states. The general observations upon propaganda in Section III may be understood as including the foreign missions.

Section I recites the failure of former kings to teach or enforce the Law of Piety. In Section II Asoka formulates his desire to do better, and in Section III enumerates the arrangements made by him for instruction in the Law. Section IV recalls his appointment of special High Officers for the teaching and enforcement of the Law of Piety (Censors), the erection of pillars, and the formal proclamation of his doctrine.

In Section V the sovereign summarizes his efforts to promote the comfort of travellers, adding that, after all, mere enjoyment is a small matter. Section VI explains the nature of the duties entrusted to the Censors. Section VII deals with the Royal Almoner's Department. In Section VIII, as in P. E. II, Asoka expounds the efficacy of the royal example. Section IX, while admitting that detailed regulations, such as those of P. E. V, have their uses, asserts the doctrine that reflection on the moral law is far superior to formal rules issued in order to enforce that Law. The tenth and concluding section directs that effective measures should be taken to secure the publication and perpetuation of the imperial scripture of the Law by having it incised upon pillars and tables of stone, wherever such might be available. When P.E. VII was published P.E. I-VI must have been already incised on the various columns now surviving, and others also; but, for some unknown reason, the seventh edict was not multiplied by copies, so far as appears. Of course, it is possible that copies no longer extant may have existed, and it is further not altogether improbable that another copy of this edict may yet be discovered. I believe that many more Asoka inscriptions are in existence.

The style of the review, although marred by tiresome repetitions, is not devoid of dignity. Certain details remain to be elucidated.

Section I. Asoka's predecessors are described simply as Râjâs.

The use of the plural inflexion shows that he alludes to more than two.

Section III. It is better to translate *sâvanâni* by 'proclamations' than by 'sermons' or 'precepts.'

The words(?) 'my missioners' are in accordance with a brilliant conjecture of D. R. Bhandarkar, who fills up a small lacuna by the word *vyûthâ* (*vyuthâ*) instead of the unsuitable *yathâ* supplied by Bühler. The emendation is not in conflict with the facsimile (*Ind. Ant.* xiii (1884), p. 310, where there seems to me to be an indication of *v*, not *y*); gives good sense, which *yathâ* does not; and is supported by the use of the word *vyûthâ* in Mino R.E. I. I think the emendation almost certain, and adopt it (ibid., vol. xli (1912), p. 172). There is no doubt that, as Senart pointed out, P.E. VII is intimately connected by this passage with Minor R.E. I.

The Agents (*pulisâ*) would seem to have been special superintending emissaries sent out by Asoka, as the *missi dominici* were by Charlemagne.

Section IV. The reference to 'a proclamation' in the singular may be to the maxim 'Let small and great exert themselves,' which is quoted in Minor R. E. I.

Section V. 'Half-*kôs*,' *aḍhakosikyâni*. Fleet, in opposition to all other commentators, argued that *aḍha* here must be taken to represent *ashṭa*, 'eight,' and not *âdha*, 'half.' I consulted Dr. Michelson, who replied: 'It is not absolutely impossible that *aḍha* means "8," as we find *libi* for *lipi*; but in view of Kâlsî *atha*, it is highly improbable. I, for one, still consider *aḍha* means "half."' We may now also compare the form *diyaḍhiya*, '1½,' in the new Maski edict, corresponding with the Hindî *deṛh*. Further, in the Rummindêî Pillar inscription (*post*) *aṭha* undoubtedly represents *ashṭa*, 'eight.' Whatever may have been the exact length of Asoka's *kôs*, he certainly dug his wells at intervals of half a *kôs*. In many cases they may have been merely earthen wells, without masonry, or they may have been cheaply lined with terra-cotta tiles.

Section VI. The special functions of the Censors, as differentiated from other High Officers, are emphasized.

Section VII. 'Heads of departments' seems to be the correct rendering of *mukhâ* (*J. R. A. S.*, 1915, p. 97). 'Sundry places where satisfaction may be found.' The phrase, which is obscure, is supposed to mean 'opportunities for charity,' but I am not quite satisfied.

The Queens (*devî*) may have been four, as later in Burma. Asoka sharply distinguishes between the Princes, sons of the lawful Queens, and his offspring by women of lower degree. One of the Princes is known to have been named Tîvara (Queen's Edict).

Section IX. 'Reflection,' as Mr. Thomas has shown, is the best rendering of *nijhati* (*J. R. A. S.*, 1916, p. 122), meaning 'reflection on the *dhamma*' and heartfelt acceptance of its principles.

'Sun and moon endure.' The phrase, which became a commonplace in later land grants, recurs in the Cave Inscriptions (*post*).

The whole edict, save for the small exceptions noted above, is fully intelligible, and the translation may be accepted as sound. The variations from my earlier version are mostly designed to give greater precision.

SECTION 2

The Four Minor Pillar Edicts

1. THE SÂRNÂTH EDICT

THE PENALTY OF SCHISM

(Ed. with good facsimile by Vogel, *Ep. Ind.* viii, p. 168.)

[Thus saith] His Sacred [and Gracious] Majesty [the King]:—

(I) '[Both] at Pâṭa[liputra and in the provinces, His Sacred Majesty instructs the High Officers that] the Church may not be rent in twain by any person.... Whosoever, be it monk or be it nun, shall mislead [lit. "deflect"] the Church shall be vested in white garments and compelled to dwell in an external residence. Thus should this order be made known, both in the congregation of the monks and in the congregation of the nuns.'

(II) Thus saith His Sacred Majesty:—

'One copy of this order (*sâsane*) accessible to you has been posted in the *saṁsaraṇa*. See that you have another copy posted so as to be accessible to the lay-disciples. Those lay-disciples, too, on every fast-day must make themselves acquainted with this ordinance (*sâsane*). On every fast-day throughout the year the High Officers must attend the fast-day service in order to make themselves acquainted and familiar with the order. And so far as your jurisdiction extends you must, in accordance with this text, everywhere carry out the expulsion. Similarly, in all fortified towns and Districts you must see that the expulsion is effected according to the text.'

Comment

This edict, discovered in the cold season of 1904–5, unfortunately is mutilated in the first three lines. It is to be read with the help of the still more damaged Sânchî and Kauśâmbî Edicts dealing with the same subject, and its meaning is partially elucidated by the discussion of Minor R. E. i.

The Kauśâmbî Edict shows that the persons primarily addressed must have been the High Officers, presumably the *Dhaṁma-Mahâmâtâ*, or Censors, who were to make it their business to suppress schism in the Buddhist Church or *Saṁgha*. Schism was one of the deadly sins of Buddhism, a *kappaṭhikam kibbisam*, 'a sin enduring for a *kalpa* or aeon,' coupled with matricide, parricide, murder of a saint, and the wounding of a Buddha. It may be compared with the *αἰώνιον ἁμάρτημα*, the 'eternal sin' of Mark iii. 29, in Revised Version (Edmunds, *Buddhist and Christian Gospels*, 4th ed., vol. ii, pp. 228, 229). In the civil guilds and corporations which flourished extensively in ancient India, the mischief-maker who stirred up discord (*bheda-kârî*) was similarly punished by expulsion. Brihaspati lays down the rule that 'an acrimonious or malicious man, and one who causes dissension or does violent acts, or who is inimically disposed towards the guild (*śrenî*), association (*pûga*), or the king shall be instantly expelled from the town or the assembly of the corporation.'

Asoka takes upon himself as Head of the Church to eliminate schismatics and maintain ecclesiastical unity among both monks and nuns. No definite indication of the date of this edict can be discerned, but it is certainly later than the Pillar Edicts, as is proved by the Kauśâmbî replica. I am inclined to associate its issue with the traditional Council of Pâṭaliputra, which is not mentioned in the review of pious acts recorded in P. E. VII. I assume, therefore, that the Council, which was assembled to correct the evils caused by schism, took place at some time in the last nine or ten years of Asoka's life. The syllables *Pâṭa-*, surviving at the beginning of line 3, can mean nothing but Pâṭaliputra and suggest that the orders must have been in the first instance directed to the High Officers of the imperial capital.

The edict, it will be observed, comprises two sections or distinct documents, each introduced by the customary formula, 'Thus saith,' &c.

The first section prescribes the penalty for schism. The schismatic was to be 'unfrocked' by being deprived of the monastic yellow robe and compelled to assume white garments like the laity. His expulsion from the holy society was further to be marked by his exclusion from the monastic precincts and his enforced dwelling in a 'non-residence' (*anâvâsa*), which I translate as 'an external residence.' 'Mislead' (or 'deflect') renders *bhokhati*, now recognized rightly as the true reading. The root is *bhuj*, in the sense of 'bending.'

The meaning of the first section, so far as it is extant, may be regarded as clear and finally settled.

The second section, dealing with the publication and enforcement of the imperial decree, has excited much difference of opinion, and the interpretation is not yet unanimously accepted.

The *saṁsaraṇa* certainly meant a place, a building of some sort, but whether it should be translated 'office' or 'cloister,' or otherwise, nobody knows exactly. *Aṁtikaṁ* is fairly rendered as 'in an accessible position,' or simply 'accessible.'

The fast-days were four in each month.

'Acquainted with;' the word *visvaṁsayitave* is from the root *śvas*.

The meaning of *âhâle* (*âhâra*) as 'jurisdiction' is now settled. Early attempts at interpreting it as 'food' made nonsense of the whole document.

The causal *vivâsayâtha* and the double causal *vivâsâpayâthâ* are interpreted by some scholars as referring to the 'sending out,' 'circulation,' or 'publication' of the text, and in my last edition that view was adopted. Now I prefer to agree with Mr. F. W. Thomas (*J. R. A. S.*, 1915. p. 112) and to regard the words as meaning 'expel.' The double causal is needed with reference to the 'fortified towns' and 'Districts,' because each such jurisdiction was in charge of a locally autonomous chief, whether a Râjâ or an official, but probably the former. For 'forts' see *Arthaśâstra*, Bk. ii, chap. 3, 4.

The general purport of the second section of the edict is clearly ascertained, although the details above noted are still unsettled.

2. THE KAUSÂMBÎ EDICT

THE SAME SUBJECT; THE PENALTY OF SCHISM

(Facsimile and transcript in *Ind. Ant.*, xix (1890), pp. 125, 126.)

The first line clearly reads that

'His Sacred Majesty, [*Devânaṁpi*]*ye*, commands the High Officers of Kosaṁbi.'

The second line contains the word *saṁgha*.

The third and fourth lines enact that

'Whosoever, be it monk or be it nun, shall mislead the Church, shall be vested in white garments and compelled to dwell in an external residence.'

Comment

This short, imperfect, and much mutilated record exists on the Allahabad Asoka pillar, where it is mixed up with and defaced by later inscriptions. Cunningham was the first person to note its existence. It was engraved below the text of P. E. I–IV, and is followed by the Queen's Edict. Both of the short inscriptions evidently were added after the incision of the six P. E., but the precise date cannot be fixed. As the document is a replica of the first part of the Sârnâth Edict, it shows that that ordinance also must be later in date than the 28th regnal year, when the main series of P. E. was published.

The pillar originally stood at Kauśâmbî (Kosaṁbi), but was removed to Allahabad, probably in the fourteenth century by Fîrôz Tughlak. The Jain town of Kauśâmbî is represented by Kosam in the Allahabad District. The Buddhist Kauśâmbî may be identified with the *Vana-* or 'forest' Kauśâmbî of Pâṇini (see Fleet in *J. R. A. S.*, 1907, p. 511, note). It was distant seven days' journey through 'a great desert waste' from Prayâg or Allahabad, and must have stood at or near Barhut (Bharhut), as proved by me in *J. R. A. S.*, 1898, pp. 507–19. The Allahabad pillar presumably came from that site and not from Kosam.

3. THE SÂNCHÎ EDICT

THE SAME SUBJECT; THE PENALTY OF SCHISM

(Facsimile in *Ep. Ind.*, ii, plate facing p. 369; and transcript, not quite correct, ibid., p. 367.)

I avail myself of Professor Hultzsch's corrected reading and translation in *J. R. A. S.*, 1911, pp. 167–9. His version is:—

. . . 'path is prescribed both for the monks and the nuns.

As long as (my) sons and great-grandsons (shall reign and) as long as the sun and moon (shall shine), the monk or nun who shall cause divisions in the Saṁgha should be caused to put on white robes and to reside in a non-residence. For what is my desire? That the Saṁgha may be united and of long duration.'

Comment

This mutilated record on a broken column at Sânchî has been known since Prinsep's time. It is now seen to be a replica, although not an exact verbal copy, of part of the Sârnâth edict. But I would not render *bhokhati* by 'cause divisions,' as Hultzsch does. The order probably was addressed to the High Officers of a town at or near Sânchî.

4. THE QUEEN'S EDICT

THE DONATIONS OF THE SECOND QUEEN

(Good facsimile and transcript in *Ind. Ant.*, xix (1890), p. 125.)

According to the words of His Sacred Majesty, the High Officers everywhere are to be addressed:—

'" Whatever gift has been given here by the Second Queen—be it a mango-garden, or pleasure-grove, or almshouse, or aught else—is reckoned as proceeding from that queen."

[Thus is the request] of the Second queen, the Kâruvâkî, mother of Tîvara.'

Comment

This brief and nearly complete record on the Allahabad pillar follows the replica of the Sârnâth edict. The script, as Bühler pointed out, exhibits sundry cursive and peculiar forms. I would date the inscription in the closing years of Asoka's reign. It seems to me to be the latest record extant. Its purpose is to secure to the Second Queen, mother of a prince named Tîvara (Tîvala), the merit of any donations she might be pleased to make. The blank is filled up by Hultzsch with the words [*he*]*vaṁ* [*vi*]*nati*, translated as above (*J. R. A. S.*, 1911, p. 1113). Prince Tîvara seems to have predeceased his father. The queen, in accordance with custom, is designated, not by a personal name, but as belonging to a particular *gotra* or family. The second clause gives the royal order in Asoka's words (*vachanena*). He passed the order at the request of his consort, and addressed it to his officers throughout the empire. 'Here' probably means 'in the empire.'

SECTION 3

The Commemorative Inscriptions on the Pillars in the Tarai

1. THE RUMMINDÊÎ INSCRIPTION

ASOKA'S VISIT TO THE BIRTHPLACE OF BUDDHA

FACSIMILE

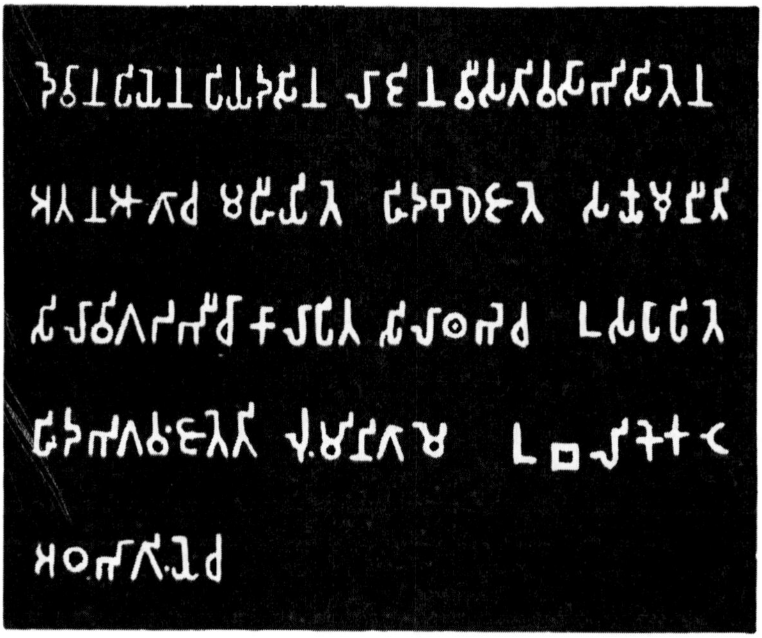

TRANSLITERATION

1. Devānapiyena piyadasina lājina vīsativasābhisitena
2. atana āgācha mahīyite hida budhe jāte sakyamunīti
3. silā vigaḍabhīchā kālāpita silāthabhecha usapāpite
4. hida bhagavaṁ jāteti luṁminigāme ubalikekaṭe
5. athabhagiyecha

ASOKA'S INSCRIPTION AT RUMMINDÊÎ

[*From impression taken by Dr. Führer*]

'By His Sacred and Gracious Majesty the King when he had been consecrated twenty years, having come in person and reverence having been done—inasmuch as "Here was born Buddha, the sage of the Sâkyas"—a stone bearing a horse was caused to be made and a stone pillar was erected.

Inasmuch as "Here the Holy One was born," the village of Lummini was released from religious cesses and required to pay [only] one-eighth as land revenue.'

Comment

This curious record, discovered in 1896 and perfectly preserved, has been the subject of much discussion. Several of the important words are not known to occur elsewhere. The purpose of the inscription is to record Asoka's visit to the birthplace of Gautama Buddha, and also the favours which he was pleased to bestow on the village of Lummini. In the revised translation I have retained the construction of the text at some sacrifice of elegance. I follow Charpentier in taking *mahîyite* as a locative absolute, 'reverence having been done' and in holding that the puzzling word *rigaḍabhîchâ* must signify 'bearing a horse,' or something to that effect. The pillar is known to have been once surmounted by the effigy of a horse. That animal was regarded in northern India as the guardian of the west, and in Ceylon as the guardian of the south. Similarly, the lion watched over the north in both countries; the elephant over the south in northern India, and over the east in Ceylon; while the bull or ox was guardian of the east in northern India, and of the west in Ceylon. All the four creatures appear on Asoka columns. (V. A. Smith, *Z. D. M. G.*, 1911, p. 238. For Dr. Charpentier's views see *Ind. Ant.*, xliii (1914), pp. 17-20.)

Bali, as shown by the *Arthaśâstra*, meant specially, but not exclusively, religious cesses. *Bhâga* meant 'land-revenue' of modern official language, *mâl* in Persian, the crown's share of the produce. Thus, in *Arthaśâstra*, Bk. ii, chap. 12 (transl., p. 9), *shaḍbhâga* means 'one-sixth of the produce paid as land-revenue.' Consequently, *ashṭa* (*aṭha*) *bhâga* means 'one-eighth of the produce paid as land-revenue.' The boon conferred on Lumminî clearly was that the village had to pay only one-eighth of its produce as land-revenue. If Asoka was in the habit of taking one-fourth, the concession amounted to the remission of half the assessment. The proportion taken by the government varied at different times and places. One-sixth was the normal approved rate, but one-fourth was common. Akbar claimed a third, and the Kashmîr kings extracted a half. Probably Asoka ordinarily took one-fourth and in Lumminî remitted half of that. The *Arthaśâstra* makes the interpretation of the word *aṭhabhagiye* certain.

It will be observed that the record does not claim to have been incised by royal command. Presumably it was both drafted and engraved by a local authority to commemorate Asoka's visit and the favours conferred by him on that occasion.

Lummini is now Rummindêî, also called Rûpadêî, a small hamlet named after the shrine of Rummindêî, 'the goddess of Rummin.' The little modern shrine (*Early History of India*, 3rd ed., plate facing p. 168) seems to mark the exact traditional birthplace. The Asoka pillar is only a few yards distant. I have visited the spot twice. It is four miles inside the Nepalese frontier, a little to the west of the Tilâr river (Hiuen Tsang's 'river of oil'), and approximately in 85° 11′ E. long., 25° 58′ N. lat. Paḍaria is a neighbouring village. The identification of the site is beyond doubt. The pillar has been broken by lightning and the horse capital has not been found. *Lummini* in the Mâgadhî dialect represents Rumminî.

The phrases 'Here was born Buddha, the sage of the Sâkyas,' and 'Here the Holy One was born' are quotations. The latter is put by tradition in the mouth of Upagupta, Asoka's guide on his pilgrimage or 'pious tour'. See chap. vii *post* and R. E. VIII.

Bhagavaṁ (***Bhagavân***) is perhaps best rendered by 'the Holy One' (Schrader, *J. R. A. S.*, 1911, p. 194). The date of the inscription is approximately 249 B.C.

2. THE NIGLÎVA PILLAR INSCRIPTION

ASOKA'S VISIT TO THE STÛPA OF KONÂKAMANA

(Facsimile and transcript, *Ep. Ind.*, v, pp. 4–6.)

'His Sacred and Gracious Majesty the King, when he had been consecrated fourteen years, enlarged for the second time the *stûpa* of Buddha Konâkamana; and, when he had been consecrated [twenty years], having come in person, did reverence, and erected [a stone pillar].'

Comment

This imperfect inscription evidently must be assigned to the same year as the Rummindêî inscription, and must mark another stage in the imperial 'pious tour.' It seems to have been drafted by the author of its companion record. It is incised on a broken pillar now lying on the bank of an artificial lake about thirteen miles in a north-westerly direction from Rummindêî. I have visited the spot. The pillar, which once stood beside the *stûpa* of Konâkamana, has been moved a few miles from its original position, which is not known exactly. Führer's pretended identification is a forgery. He published many falsehoods about the locality. On the probable sites of the towns and *stûpas* of the 'previous Buddhas,' Konâkamana and Krakuchanda, see my discussion in the Prefatory Note to Mukhurji's *Report on the Antiquities in the Tarai, Nepâl*, Calcutta, 1901, p. 16.

The inscription, brief and mutilated though it is, has much importance for the history of Buddhism. It proves the early existence of the cult of the 'previous Buddhas' and the fact of Asoka's persistent devotion to them as well as to Gautama Buddha. It may be that the cult of the 'previous Buddhas' and, consequently, Buddhism itself originated in the sub-Himalayan tract now called the Nepalese Tarâi centuries before the time of Gautama Buddha. The subject deserves investigation.

SECTION 4

The Cave Dedications of Asoka in the Barâbar Hills, and of his grandson Dasaratha in the Nâgârjuni Hills, Bihâr.

(Facs. and ed. of all by Bühler in *Ind. Ant.*, xx (1891), p. 361.)

A. THE ASOKA DEDICATIONS

1. THE BANYAN-TREE OR SUDÂMA CAVE

'This Banyan-tree cave was granted to the Âjîvikas by the King's Grace (*lâjinâ Piyadasinâ*) when he had been consecrated twelve years.'

2. THE KHALATIKA OR VIŚVA-JHOPRÎ CAVE

'This cave in the Khalatika Hill was granted to the Âjîvikas by the King's Grace, when he had been consecrated twelve years.'

3. THE SUPIYÂ OR KARṆA-CHAUPÂR CAVE

'The King's Grace (*lâjâ Piyadasi*), when he had been consecrated nineteen years, granted the (?) Supiyâ Cave in the (?) Khalatika Hill for as long as sun and moon endure.'

Comment

For brief notice of the caves and the Âjîvika sect of ascetics, see *ante*, pp. 134, 135.

The second inscription is almost perfect; the first is damaged; and the third is almost illegible.

The script is somewhat cursive.

Two approximately contemporary inscriptions, discovered by Mr. V. H. Jackson in 1913 and 1914, give the name of the hill as Goratha-giri, which occurs in *Mbh.*, *Sabhâ Parva*, xx, 30 (Madras text). The name Khalatika is found in the Vârttika to Pâṇini, i. 2, 52. The new inscriptions consist simply of the name *Gorathagiri* incised twice on the rocks near the Asoka caves. The final vowel is uncertain (*J. B. O. Res. Soc.*, vol. i (1915), pp. 159–71, with plates).

B. THE DASARATHA DEDICATIONS

1. THE VAHIYAKÂ CAVE

'The Vahiyakâ Cave was assigned by Dasaratha, His Sacred Majesty (*Devânaṁ piyenâ*), immediately after his consecration, to the venerable Âjîvikas, for as long as sun and moon endure.'

2. THE GOPIKÂ CAVE

The text and translation agree with No. 1, except for the name of the cave.

3. THE VAḌATHIKÂ CAVE

The text and translation agree with No. 1, except for the name of the cave.

Comment

Dasaratha, a grandson of Asoka, succeeded his grandfather in the eastern provinces about 232 B.C. It would seem that the empire was divided, another grandson, Samprati, obtaining the western provinces. The position of the title *Devânaṁpiyena* after the proper name is so unusual that Fleet suggested as a grammatically possible rendering, 'Dasaratha, immediately after his consecration by His Sacred Majesty,' which would imply the accession of the grandson during his grandfather's lifetime. In the Maski inscription we find *Devânaṁpiyasa Asokasa*. The script is more cursive than that of most of the Asoka records. The facsimile of inscription No. 1 is reproduced in the *Oxford History of India*, p. 117. The text of that document is almost perfect; the others are more or less blurred, but all are legible.

BIBLIOGRAPHICAL NOTE

Of the principal modern references to the inscriptions.

N.B.—Old and obsolete references omitted; for full list to 1902 see R. Otto Franke, *Pāli und Sanskrit* (Strassburg, 1902).

A. *General.*

CUNNINGHAM, SIR A., *Inscriptions of Asoka* (Calcutta, 1877), chiefly useful now for topographical details: SENART, ÉMILE, *Les Inscriptions de Piyadasi* (Paris, 1881, 1888); still indispensable, although based upon faulty texts: V. A. SMITH, *Early History of India*, 3rd ed., 1914; and 'Asoka Notes' (12) in *Ind. Ant.*, 1903, 1905, 1908, 1909, 1910, 1918: F. W. THOMAS, 'Notes on the Edicts of Asoka.' in *J. R. A. S.*, 1914, 1915, 1919. Publication of the revised official edition of the inscriptions by PROF. E. HULTZSCH has been suspended and indefinitely delayed by the war.

B. *Minor Rock Edicts.*

(1) The three Siddâpura (Mysore) texts. BÜHLER, *Ep. Ind.*, iii, pp. 135–42, with facs., transcript, and ed.: RICE, Facs. and transcripts of all three in *Ep. Carnatica* (Bangalore, 1909), vol. xi; and facs. of Brahmagiri text only in *Mysore and Coorg from the Inscriptions* (London, 1909).

(2) The three northern texts, Rûpnâth, Sahasrâm, Bairât. Revised facs. and ed. by BÜHLER, *Ind. Ant.*, vol. xxii (1893), pp. 299–306: SENART AND GRIERSON, transcripts and discussion, *Ind. Ant.*, vol. xx (1891), p. 154: D. R. BHANDARKAR, *Ind. Ant.*, vol. xli (1912), p. 170: numerous papers by FLEET, HULTZSCH, and F. W. THOMAS in *J. R. A. S.*, 1903, 1904, 1908, 1909, 1910, 1911, 1912, 1913, 1916: THOMAS, *J. As.*, Mai-Juin, 1910: S. LÉVI, ibid., Jan.-Fév., 1911. The discussion is connected on some points with that of the Minor P. E.

(3) Maski text. Ed. with plates by YAZDANI in *Hyderabad Archaeol. Series*, No. 1, Calcutta, 1915: commented on by RICE, *J. R. A. S.*, 1916, p. 838.

C. *The Bhâbrû (Bhâbrâ) Edict.*

BURGESS, Facs. in *J. As.*, 1887: SENART and GRIERSON, Revised ed. and version, *Ind. Ant.*, vol. xx (1891), p. 165: various authors—5 notes in *J. R. A. S.*, 1901: S. LÉVI, 'Notes,' *J. As.*, Mai-Juin, 1896: HULTZSCH, *J. R. A. S.*, 1909, p. 727; 1911, pp. 1113-17: B. M. BARNA, ibid.. 1915, p. 805: PROF. DHARMANANDA KOSAMBI and LANMAN, *Ind. Ant.*, vol. xli (1912), p. 37: SAILENDRANATH MITRA, ibid., vol. xlviii (1919), p. 8.

D. *The Fourteen Rock Edicts.*

The standard edition is that by BÜHLER in *Ep. Ind.*, ii, pp. 447-72, with facs. of Girnâr and Kâlsî texts; transcripts of Girnâr, Kâlsî, Shâhbâzgarhi, and Mansahra texts, and version of Shâhbâzgarhi. Facs. of Sh. text by same, ibid., i. 16. Dhauli and Jaugada texts, ed. and transcribed by same, with facs. in BURGESS, *Amarâvatî* (*A. S. S. I.*, 1887). Another facs. of Girnâr text, collotype, in Burgess, *Kâthiawâd and Kachh* (*A. S. W. I.*, 1876), with obsolete version.

Many special points are discussed in various papers, including: **R. E. I.** *Ind. Ant.*, vol. xlii (1913), pp. 253-8; and vol. xlvii, 1918, pp. 221-3; *J. R. A. S.*, 1914, p. 393. **R. E. II.** *Ind. Ant.*, vol. xlvii (1918), p. 48. **R. E. III.** *J. B. O. Res. Soc.*, iv, 37. **R. E. IV.** *J. R. A. S.*, 1911, p. 485 note; *Ind. Ant.*, vol. xliv (1915), p. 208. **R. E. V.** *J. B. O. Res. Soc.*, iv, 144-6. **R. E. VI.** *Ind. Ant.*, vol. xlvii (1918), p. 51. **R. E. VIII.** *Ind. Ant.*, vol. xlii (1913), p. 159; Rhys Davies, *Dialogues*, 1st ser., p. 190. **R. E. IX.** *J. R. A. S.*, 1913, p. 654. **R. E. XIII.** *J. R. A. S.*, 1913, p. 655. Many of the papers under other headings touch on the Fourteen R. E. An important essay is that by R. O. FRANKE, 'Zu Asoka's Felsen-Edicten' in *Nachr. der Königl. Gesellsch. d. Wissenschaften zu Göttingen*, 1895.

The disquisitions by DR. MICHELSON in *J. A. O. S.*, 1911; *Amer. J. of Philology*, 1909, 1910; and *Indo-Germ. Forschungen*, 1910, 1911, while mainly concerned with questions of phonetics, throw light occasionally upon the interpretation of both R. E. and P. E.

E. *The Kalinga Edicts.*

Facs. and version by BÜHLER in BURGESS, *Amarâvati* (*A.S.S.I.*, 1887), revised ed. by SENART and GRIERSON in *Ind. Ant.*, vol. xix (1890). See also KERN, *Manual of Indian Buddhism* (Strassburg, 1896), p. 61.

F. *The Seven Pillar Edicts.*

Standard ed. by BÜHLER in *Ep. Ind.*, ii (1894), pp. 245–74, with facs. of Lauriyâ-Ararâj or Râdhiâ, Lauriyâ Nandangarh or Mathiâ, and Râmpurwâ texts. Facs. of Delhi Topra, or Sivalik, and Allahabad texts by FLEET and BÜHLER in *Ind. Ant.*, vol. xiii (1884), p. 306. Revised ed. by SENART and GRIERSON, ibid., vol. xvii (1888) and xviii (1889).

MICHELSON, 'Notes on the Pillar Edicts of Asoka,' *Indogerm. Forschungen*, 1908.

P.E. IV.—THOMAS, *J.R.A.S.*, 1916, pp. 120–3.

P.E. V.—MONMOHAN CHAKRAVARTI, 'Animals in the Inscriptions of Piyadasi' (*Memoirs A.S.B.*, 1906). **P.E. VII.**—D. R. BHANDARKAR, *Ind. Ant.*, vol. xiii (1884), p. 310. THOMAS, *J.R.A.S.*, 1915, p. 97; and 1916, p. 122.

G. *The Four Minor Pillar Edicts.*

(1) Sârnâth.—Facs. by VOGEL, *Ep. Ind.*, viii. 168. Discussed by SENART, *Comptes rendus de l'Académie des Inscriptions*, 1907, p. 25; VENIS, *J. & Proc. A. S. B.*, 1907; NORMAN, ibid., 1908; and BOYER, *J. As.*, tome x (1907), p. 119. See also THOMAS, *J.R.A.S.*, 1915, p. 112.

(2) Kauśâmbî.—Facs. and transcript by BÜHLER, *Ind. Ant.*, vol. xix (1890), p. 126; SENART, ibid., vol. xviii (1889), p. 309.

(3) Sânchî.—Facs. and transcript by BÜHLER, *Ep. Ind.*, ii, 367, 369; corrected ed. by HULTZSCH, *J. R. A. S.*, 1911, p. 167.

(4) Queen's.—Facs. and transcript by BÜHLER, *Ind. Ant.*, vol. xix (1890), p. 125. Emendation by HULTZSCH, *J.R.A.S.*, 1911, p. 1113.

The interpretation is connected with that of the Minor R. E.

H. *The Two Commemorative Tarâi Inscriptions.*

Both were ed. with facs. by BÜHLER, *Ep. Ind.*, v, 4. Discussion by V. A. SMITH, Introd. to MUKHURJI, *Report on Antiquities in the Tarâi, Nepâl*, Calcutta, 1901; and in *Ind. Ant.*, vol. xxxiv (1905), p. 1: PISCHEL, *Sitzungsber. d. kön. preuss. Akad. d. Wissenschaften*, 1903: FLEET, *J. R. A. S.*, 1908, pp. 471–98, 823: CHARPENTIER, *Ind. Ant.*, vol. xliii (1914), pp. 17–20.

I. *The Cave Dedications of Asoka and Dasaratha.*

All ed. and translated with facs. by BÜHLER, *Ind. Ant.*, vol. xx (1891), p. 361. The Gorathagiri inscriptions are published by JACKSON in *J. B. O. Res. Soc.* i (1915), pp. 159–71, with plates.

CHAPTER VI

The Ceylonese Legend of Asoka

The legends related in this chapter and in that following are related simply as legends, without criticism, or discussion of their historical value [1].

THE CONVERSION OF ASOKA

Kâlâsoka, king of Magadha, had ten sons, who after his death ruled the kingdom righteously for twenty-two years. They were succeeded by other nine brothers, the Nandas, who likewise, in order of seniority, ruled the kingdom for twenty-two years [2].

[1] The legends have been compiled by combining the narratives of the Dîpavaṁsa and the Mahâvaṁsa, both of which are derived from the traditions preserved at the Mahâvihâra monastery. Wijesinha's revision of Turnour's translation of the Mahâvaṁsa (Colombo, Government Record Office, 1889), and Geiger's version (1912) have been used. Their corrections of Turnour are material. For the Dîpavaṁsa, Oldenberg's edition and translation have been used. The indexes to Turnour's Mahâvaṁsa and Oldenberg's Dîpavaṁsa, and Still's *Index to the Mahawansa* (Colombo, 1907), make easy the verification of particular statements. For another summary of the legends see Hardy's *Eastern Monachism.*

[2] Turnour omits the words 'the Nandas.' The Dîpavaṁsa substitutes Susunâga for Kâlâsoka, makes Asoka to be the son of Susunâga, and omits all mention of the nine Nanda brothers, and their reign of twenty-two years (*Dîp.* v. 25, 97-99). These discrepancies prove the untrustworthiness of the chronicles.

A Brahman named Chânakya, who had conceived an implacable hatred against Dhana Nanda, the last survivor of the nine brothers, put that king to death, and placed upon the throne Chandra Gupta, a member of the princely Maurya clan, who assumed the sovereignty of all India, and reigned gloriously for twenty-four years[1]. He was succeeded by his son Bindusâra, who ruled the land for twenty-eight years.

The sons of Bindusâra, the offspring of sixteen mothers, numbered one hundred and one, of whom the eldest was named Sumana, and the youngest Tishya (Tissa). A third son, Asoka, uterine brother of Tishya, had been appointed Viceroy of Western India by his father. On receiving news of King Bindusâra's mortal illness, Asoka quitted Ujjain, the seat of his government, and hastened to Pâtaliputra (Patna), the capital of the empire. On his arrival at the capital, he slew his eldest brother Sumana, and ninety-eight other brothers, saving alive but one, Tishya, the youngest of all. Having thus secured his throne, Asoka became lord of all India, but by reason of the massacre of his brothers he was known as Asoka the Wicked.

Now it so happened that when Prince Sumana was slain, his wife was with child. She fled from the slaughter, and was obliged to seek shelter in a village

[1] Not 'thirty-four years,' as given both by Turnour and Wijesinha. The figure 34 is a copyist's blunder; see commentary quoted by Turnour, p. lii (Rhys Davids, *Ancient Coins and Measures of Ceylon*, p. 41, note).

of outcastes beyond the eastern gate. The headman of the outcastes, pitying her misery, entreated her kindly, and, doing her reverence, served her faithfully for seven years. On that very day on which she was driven forth from the palace she gave birth to a boy, on whom the name Nigrodha was bestowed. The child was born with the marks of sanctity, and when he attained the age of seven was already an ordained monk.

The holy child, whose royal origin was not known, happened one day to pass by the palace, and attracted the attention of the king, who was struck by his grave and reverend deportment. King Asoka, highly delighted, sent for the boy, who drew near with decorum and self-possession.

The king said, 'My child, take any seat which thou thinkest befitting.' Nigrodha, seeing that no priest other than himself was present, advanced towards the royal throne as the befitting seat. Whereupon King Asoka, understanding that this monk was destined to become lord of the palace, gave the boy his arm, and seating him upon the throne, refreshed him with meat and drink prepared for his own royal use.

Having thus shown his respect, the king questioned the boy monk concerning the doctrines of Buddha, and received from him an exposition of the doctrine of earnestness, to the effect that 'earnestness is the way to immortality, indifference is the way to death.' This teaching so wrought upon the heart of the king, that he at once accepted the religion of Buddha, and gave gifts to the priesthood. The next day Nigrodha returned to the palace with thirty-two priests, and by preaching the law, established king and people in the faith and the practice of piety. In this manner was King Asoka constrained to abandon the Brahmanical faith of his father, and to accept as a lay disciple the sacred law of Buddha.

These things happened in the fourth year after the accession of King Asoka, who in the same year celebrated his solemn coronation, and appointed his younger brother Tishya to be his deputy or vicegerent.

The sixty thousand Brahmans, who for three years had daily enjoyed the bounty of Asoka, as they had enjoyed that of his predecessors on the throne, were dismissed, and in their place Buddhist monks in equal numbers were constantly entertained at the palace, and treated with such lavish generosity that four lakhs of treasure were each day expended. One day, the king, having feasted the monks at the palace, inquired the number of the sections of the law, and having learned that the sections of the law were eighty-four thousand in number, he resolved to dedicate a sacred edifice to each. Wherefore, the king commanded the local rulers to erect eighty-four thousand sacred edifices in as many towns of India, and himself constructed the Asokârâma at the capital. All the edifices were completed within three years, and in a single day the news of their completion reached the Court. By means of the supernatural powers with which he was gifted, King Asoka was enabled to behold at one glance all these works throughout the empire.

From the time of his consecration as emperor of India, two hundred and eighteen years after the death of the perfect Buddha, the miraculous faculties of royal majesty entered into King Asoka, and the glory which he obtained by his merit extended a league above and a league below the earth.

The denizens of heaven were his servants, and daily brought for his use water from the holy lake, luscious, fragrant fruits, and other good things beyond measure and without stint.

The king, lamenting that he had been born too late to behold the Buddha in the flesh, besought the aid of the Snake-King, who caused to appear a most enchanting image of Buddha, in the full perfection of beauty, surrounded by a halo of glory, and surmounted by the lambent flame of sanctity, in honour of which glorious vision a magnificent festival was held for the space of seven days.

THE STORY OF MAHENDRA AND SANGHAMITRÂ, AND THE CONVERSION OF CEYLON

While Asoka during his royal father's lifetime was stationed at Ujjain as viceroy of the Avanti country, he formed a connexion with a lady of the Setthî caste, named Devî, who resided at Vedisagiri (Besnagar near Bhilsâ)[1]. She accompanied the prince to Ujjain,

[1] Turnour's text reads 'Chetiyagiri.'

and there bore to him a son named Mahendra, two hundred and four years after the death of Buddha[1]. Two years later a daughter named Sanghamitrâ was born. Devî continued to reside at Vedisagiri after Asoka seized the throne; but the children accompanied their father to the capital, where Sanghamitrâ was given in marriage to Agni Brahmâ, nephew of the king, to whom she bore a son named Sumana.

In the fourth year after King Asoka's coronation, his brother Tishya, the vicegerent, his nephew Agni Brahmâ, and his grandson Sumana were all ordained. The king, who had received the news of the completion of the eighty-four thousand sacred edifices, held a solemn assembly of millions of monks and nuns, and, coming in full state in person, took up his station in the midst of the priesthood. The king's piety had by this time washed away the stain of fratricide, and he who had been known as Asoka the Wicked, was henceforth celebrated as Asoka the Pious.

After his brother Tishya had devoted himself to religion, Asoka proposed to replace him in the office of vicegerent by Prince Mahendra, but at the urgent entreaty of his spiritual director, Tishya son of Moggali (Mudgâlya), the king was persuaded to permit of the ordination both of Mahendra and his sister Sanghamitrâ. The young prince had then attained the canonical age of twenty, and was therefore at once ordained. The princess assumed the yellow robe, but was obliged to defer her admission to the Order

[1] This date is given by the Dîpavaṁsa, vi. 20, 21.

for two years, until she should attain full age. Mahendra was ordained in the sixth year of the king's reign, dating from his coronation.

In the eighth year of the reign, two saints, named respectively Sumitra and Tishya, died. Their death was attended with such portents that the world at large became greatly devoted to the Buddhist religion, and the liberality of the people to the priests was multiplied. The profits so obtained attracted to the Order many unworthy members, who set up their own doctrines as the doctrines of Buddha, and performed unlawful rites and ceremonies, even sacrifices after the manner of the Brahmans, as seemed good unto them. Hence was wrought confusion both in the doctrine and ritual of the Church.

The disorders waxed so great that the heretics outnumbered the true believers, the regular rites of the church were in abeyance for seven years, and the king's spiritual director, Tishya son of Moggali, was obliged to commit his disciples to the care of Prince Mahendra, and himself to retire into solitude among the mountains at the source of the Ganges.

Tishya, the son of Moggali, having been persuaded to quit his retreat, expelled the heretics, produced the Kathâvatthu treatise, and held the Third Council of the Church at the Asokârâma in Pâtaliputra. These events happened in the year 236 after the death of Buddha, and seventeen and a half years after the coronation of King Asoka.

In the same year King Devânampiya Tissa (Tishya)

ascended the throne of Ceylon, and became the firm friend and ally of King Asoka, although the two sovereigns never met. The King of Ceylon, in order to show his friendship and respect, dispatched a mission to India, headed by his nephew, Mahâ Arittha. In seven days the envoys reached the port of Tâmalipti (Tamlûk in Bengal), and in seven days more arrived at the Imperial Court. They were royally entertained by King Asoka, who was graciously pleased to accept the rich and rare presents sent by his ally, in return for which he sent gifts of equal value. The envoys remained at the capital for five months, and then returned to the island by the way they had come, bearing to their sovereign this message from King Asoka: 'I have taken refuge in the Buddha, the Law, and the Order; I have avowed myself a lay disciple of the doctrine of the son of the Sâkyas. Imbue your mind also with faith in this Triad, in the highest religion of the Jina; take refuge in the Teacher.'

After the close of the Third Council, which remained in session for nine months, Tishya the son of Moggali resolved that the law of Buddha should be communicated to foreign countries, and dispatched missionaries to Kashmîr and Gandhâra; to Mahîshamandala (Mysore); to Vanavâsi (North Kanara); to Aparântaka (coast north of Bombay); to Mahârâshtra; to the Yavana country (on the north-western frontier); to the mountain regions of the Himâlaya; to Suvaṇṇabhûmi (? Pegu); and to Ceylon.

The mission to Ceylon consisted of Prince Mahendra and five colleagues, of whom one was Sumana, his sister's son.

Mahendra resolved, with the king's permission, to visit his mother and her relations on his way to Ceylon, and devoted six months to this purpose.

He found his mother at her home in Vedisagiri, and, having been received with great joy, was accommodated in the splendid monastery at that place which she had erected [1]. The preaching of Mahendra converted Bhandu, a grandnephew of his mother. After this event Mahendra lingered for another month, and then with his companions, to whom Bhandu attached himself, rose aloft into the air, and flying, 'as flies the king of swans,' arrived in Ceylon, and alighted upon the Missa mountain.

The first discourse pronounced by the leader of the mission converted the king, with forty thousand of his followers. The princess Anulâ, with five hundred of her attendants, desired to enter the Order, but was told that the male missionaries had no power to ordain females, who, however, might be ordained by the princess Sanghamitrâ.

The king of Ceylon, after due deliberation, again dispatched his nephew to King Asoka, with instructions to bring back Sanghamitrâ and a branch of the sacred *bo*-tree. King Asoka, although grieving sorely at the separation from his beloved daughter, gave his

[1] The allusion seems to be to the splendid buildings at Sânchî, about five miles south-west from Besnagar.

consent to her deputation to Ceylon, and proceeded with much ceremony to sever a branch of the holy tree.

The severance was effected, signalized by many miracles, and the envoys, accompanied by Sanghamitrâ, were dispatched to the port of Tâmalipti, escorted by an army commanded by King Asoka in person.

'The vessel in which the *bo*-tree was embarked briskly dashed through the water; and in the great ocean, through the circumference of a league, the waves were stilled; flowers of the five different colours blossomed around it, and various melodies of music rang in the air.' The holy branch, thus miraculously wafted to the shore of the island, was received with due honour, and was planted in the Mahâmegha garden, which the king had dedicated to the use of the Order. The branch threw off eight vigorous shoots, which were distributed and planted in as many localities.

In those days also the king of Ceylon built for Mahendra the Mahâvihâra, the first monastery of the island, and the construction of the Chetiyagiri (Mihintalé) monastery followed soon after.

The princess Anulâ, in company with five hundred virgins and five hundred women of the palace, was duly ordained as a nun by Sanghamitrâ, and straightway attained the rank of *Arahat*. The king erected a nunnery for Sanghamitrâ, who there abode in peace, until she died in the fifty-ninth year after her ordination, that being the ninth year of the reign of the Ceylonese King Uttiya. Her brother Mahendra had passed away in the previous year, while observing the sixtieth 'retreat' since his ordination.

While King Asoka was engaged in the festivals connected with the dispatch of the branch of the *bo*-tree, another mission, headed by his grandson Sumana, arrived from Ceylon to beg for relics to be enshrined in the great *stûpa* by the island king. The request of this second mission also was granted by King Asoka, who bestowed upon his ally a dishful of holy relics, to which Sakra, lord of the Devas, added the right collar-bone of Buddha, extracted from the Chulâmani *stûpa*. The relics were received with extreme honour, and enshrined with due ceremony in the Thûpârâma *stûpa*, the moment being marked by a terrific earthquake. Witnessing this miracle, the people were converted in crowds, and the king's younger brother joined the Order, which in those days received an accession of thirty thousand monks.

THE LEGEND OF THE THIRD CHURCH COUNCIL[1]

When, as has been related, the heretics waxed great in numbers and wrought confusion in the Church, so that for seven years the rite of confession and other solemn rites remained in abeyance, King

[1] See especially Dîpavaṁsa, i. 25; v. 55; vii. 37, 41, 56–59. The dates do not seem all to agree, but the intention evidently is to place the Third Council in 236, and the Second Council in 118 *Anno Buddhae*, the two intervals of 118 years being exactly equal. One of the Chinese dates for Asoka is 118 A. B. (I-tsing, ed. Takakusu, p. 14).

Asoka determined that the disorder should cease, and sent a minister to the Asokârâma to compel the monks to resume the services. The minister, having gone there, assembled the monks and proclaimed the royal commands. The holy men replied that they could not perform the services while the heretics remained. Thereupon the minister, exceeding his instructions, with his own hand smote off the heads of several of the contumacious ecclesiastics as they sat in convocation. The king's brother Tishya interfered, and prevented further violence.

The king was profoundly horrified and greatly alarmed at the rash act of his minister, and sought absolution. In accordance with the advice of the clergy, the aged Tishya, son of Moggali, was summoned from his distant retreat, and conveyed by boat down the Ganges to the capital, where he was received by the king with extraordinary honour and reverence.

Asoka, desiring to test the supernatural powers of the saint, begged that a miracle might be performed, and specially requested that an earthquake confined to a limited space might be produced. The saint placed a chariot, a horse, a man, and a vessel filled with water, one on each side of a square space, exactly on the boundary lines, and produced an earthquake which caused the half of each object within the boundary line to quake, while the other half of each remained unshaken. Satisfied by this display of power, Asoka inquired if the sacrilegious murder of the priests by the minister must be accounted as the king's sin. The saint ruled that where there is no wilful intention, there is no sin, and, accordingly, absolved Asoka, whom he instructed fully in the truth.

The king commanded that all the priests in India, without exception, should be assembled, and taking his seat by the side of his spiritual director, examined each priest individually as to his faith. The saint decided that the doctrine of the Vaibâdyavâdin school was the true primitive teaching of the master, and all dissenters were expelled, to the number of sixty thousand[1]. A thousand orthodox priests of holy character were then selected to form a convocation or Council. To these assembled priests, Tishya, son of Moggali, recited the treatise called Kathâvatthu in order to dissipate doubts on points of faith[2]. The Council, following the procedure of the First Council at Râjagriha and the Second Council at Vaisâli, recited

[1] Mahâvaṁsa, ch. v. The classifications of the Buddhist schools vary much. I-tsing (pp. xxiii, 7) says that all Ceylon belonged to the *Ârya-sthavira nikâya*, which had three subdivisions. Tibetan authorities (Rockhill, pp. 187 *seqq.*) make two main divisions of Buddhists, (i) *Sthavira*, (ii) *Mahâsanghika*. The *Sarvâstivâdin* school was a subdivision of the *Sthavira*, and the *Vaibâdyavâdin* was a sect of the *Sarvâstivâdin*. The *Vaibâdyavâdin* sect again was subdivided into four sections, *Mahîśâsaka*, *Dharmaguptaka*, *Tamraśatiya*, and *Kâśyapiya*. This explains how Fa-hien was able to obtain in Ceylon a copy of the Vinaya according to the *Mahîśâsaka* school (ch. xl).

The legends have probably been much influenced by sectarian bias.

[2] Turnour's translation is corrected by Wijesinha.

and verified the whole body of the scriptures, and, after a session lasting nine months, dispersed. At the conclusion of the Council the earth quaked, as if to say 'Well done,' beholding the re-establishment of religion. Tishya, the son of Moggali, was then seventy-two years of age.

THE STORY OF TISHYA, THE VICEGERENT

One day, Tishya, the younger brother of Asoka, and Vicegerent of the empire, happened to be in a forest, and watched a herd of elk at play. The thought occurred to him that when elks browsing in the forest divert themselves, there seems to be no good reason why monks well lodged and well fed in monasteries should not amuse themselves. Coming home, the vicegerent told his thoughts to the king, who, in order to make him understand the reason why, conferred upon him the sovereignty for the space of seven days, saying, 'Prince, govern the empire for seven days, at the end of which I shall put thee to death.' At the close of the seventh day the king asked the prince:—'Why art thou grown so wasted?' He replied, 'By reason of the horror of death.' The king rejoined, 'Child, thou hast ceased to amuse thyself, because thou thinkest that in seven days thou wilt be put to death. These monks are meditating without ceasing on death; how then can they engage in frivolous diversions?'[1]

[1] Compare the legend of Mahendra in chapter vii, *post*.

The prince understood, and became a convert. Some time afterwards he was on a hunting expedition in the forest, when he saw the saint Mahâdharmarakshita, a man of perfect piety and freed from the bonds of sin, sitting under a tree, and being fanned with a branch by an elephant. The prince, beholding this sight, longed for the time when he might become even as that saint and dwell at peace in the forest. The saint, in order to incline the heart of the prince unto the faith, soared into the air and alighted on the surface of the water of the Asokârâma tank, wherein he bathed, while his robes remained poised in the air. The prince was so delighted with this miracle that he at once resolved to become a monk, and begged the king for permission to receive ordination.

The king, being unwilling to thwart his pious desire, himself led the prince to the monastery, where ordination was conferred by the saint Mahâdharmarakshita. At the same time one hundred thousand other persons were ordained, and no man can tell the number of those who became monks by reason of the example set by the prince.

THE LAST DAYS OF ASOKA

The branch of the holy *bo*-tree, brought to Ceylon in the manner above related, was dispatched in the eighteenth year of the reign of Asoka the Pious, and planted in the Mahâmeghavana garden in Ceylon.

In the twelfth year after that event, Asandhimitrâ,

the beloved queen of Asoka, who had shared his devotion to Buddhism, died. In the fourth year after her decease, the king, prompted by sensual passion, raised the princess Tishyarakshitâ to the dignity of queen-consort. She was young and vain, and very sensible of her personal charms. The king's devotion to the *bo*-tree seemed to her to be a slight to her attractions, and in the fourth year after her elevation her jealousy induced her to make an attempt to destroy the holy tree by art magic. The attempt failed. In the fourth year after that event, King Asoka the Pious fulfilled the lot of mortality, having reigned thirty-seven years[1].

[1] Compare the legend of the 'Dotage of Asoka' in chapter vii, *post*. According to the Tibetan tradition, Asoka reigned for fifty-four years (Rockhill, p. 233).

CHAPTER VII

The Indian Legends of Asoka

THE LINEAGE AND FAMILY OF ASOKA

(1) King Bimbisâra reigned at Râjagriha. His son was (2) Ajâtasatru, whose son was (3) Udayibhadra, whose son was (4) Munda, whose son was (5) Kâkavarnin, whose son was (6) Sahâlin, whose son was (7) Tulakuchi, whose son was (8) Mahâmandala, whose son was (9) Prasenajit, whose son was (10) Nanda, whose son was (11) Bindusâra.

King Bindusâra reigned at Pâtaliputra, and had a son named Susîma.

A certain Brahman of Champâ had a lovely daughter. A prophecy declared that she was destined to be the mother of two sons, of whom one would become universal monarch, and the other would attain the goal of the life of a recluse. The Brahman, seeking the fulfilment of the prophecy, succeeded in introducing his daughter into the palace, but the jealousy of the queens debarred her from the royal embraces, and assigned to

[1] The genealogy as given in the text is from the prose *Asokâvadâna* in the *Divyâvadâna* (Burnouf, *Introduction*, 2nd ed., pp. 319 *seqq.*). The reader will observe that Chandragupta is omitted, and that Bindusâra, the father of Asoka, is represented as being the son of Nanda. The metrical *Asokâvadâna* (Râjendralâla Mitra, *Nepalese Buddhist Literature*, pp. 6–17) substitutes Mahîpâla for Ajâtasatru, and exhibits other minor variations.

her the menial duties of a barber. After some time the girl managed to explain to the king that she was no barber, but the daughter of a Brahman. When the king understood that she belonged to a caste with a member of which he could honourably consort, he at once took her into favour and made her chief queen. In due course, the Brahman's daughter, whose name was Subhadrângî, bore to the king two sons, the elder named Asoka, and the younger named Vigatâsoka.

The ascetic Pingala Vatsâjiva, when consulted by King Bindusâra concerning the destiny of the two boys, feared to tell his sovereign the truth, because Asoka was rough-looking and displeasing in the sight of his father; but he frankly told Queen Subhadrângî that her son Asoka was destined for the throne.

It came to pass that King Bindusâra desired to besiege Taxila, which was in rebellion. The king ordered his despised son Asoka to undertake the siege, and yet would not supply him with chariots or the needful munitions of war. Ill-supplied as he was, the prince obediently started to carry out the king's orders, whereupon the earth opened, and from her bosom supplied all his wants. When Asoka with his army approached Taxila, the citizens came forth to meet him, protesting that their quarrel was only with oppressive ministers, not with the king or the king's son. Taxila and the kingdom of the Svasas made their submission to the prince, who in due course returned to the capital.

It came to pass that one day Prince Susîma, the king's eldest son, was coming into the palace from the garden when he playfully threw his glove at the head of the prime minister Khallâtaka. The minister was deeply offended, and from that day engaged in a conspiracy with five hundred privy councillors to exclude Susîma, and to place Asoka on the throne.

The people of Taxila again revolted, and Prince Susîma, who was deputed to reduce them to obedience, failed in his task. King Bindusâra, who was then old and ill, desired to send Asoka to Taxila, and to recall Susîma, that he might take up the succession.

The ministers, however, contrived to exclude the elder prince, and to secure the throne for Asoka, on whose head the gods themselves placed the crown, at the moment when his father expired. Susîma marched against Pâtaliputra, to assert his rights and expel the usurper; but Asoka and his minister Râdhagupta obtained the services of naked giants, who successfully guarded the gates, and by stratagem Susîma was inveigled, so that he fell into a ditch full of burning fuel, and there miserably perished.

THE TYRANNY AND CONVERSION OF ASOKA

One day, when five hundred of his ministers ventured to resist the royal will, Asoka, transported with rage, drew his sword, and with his own hand cut off the heads of all the offenders.

Another day, the women of the palace, whom Asoka's rough features failed to please, mocked him by breaking off the leaves of an *asoka* tree in the garden. The king, when he heard of the incident, caused five hundred women to be burnt alive.

The ministers, horrified at these acts of cruelty, entreated the king not to defile his royal hands with blood, but to appoint an executioner to carry out sentences.

The king accepted this advice, and a man named Chandagirika—a wretch of unexampled cruelty, who loved to torture animals, and had slain his father and mother—was sought out and appointed Chief Executioner. For his use the king caused to be built a prison, which had a most attractive exterior, so that men might be tempted to enter it, and thus suffer all the tortures of hell which awaited them within; for the king had commanded that no man who entered this prison should leave it alive.

One day, a holy ascetic named Bâlapandita[1] unwittingly entered the gate, and was instantly seized by the jailer. The holy man, though given seven days' respite, was at the end of the term of grace ruthlessly cast into a seething cauldron of filth, beneath which a great fire was kindled. The cruel jailer, looking in, beheld the saint, seated on a lotus, and unscathed by fire. The miracle having been reported to the palace, the king himself came to see it, and being converted by the sight and the preaching

[1] Samudra in the metrical version.

of the holy man, embraced the true religion and forsook the paths of wickedness.

The prison was demolished, and the jailer was burnt alive.

The above legend from the *Asokâvadâna*, which is given with further details by Hiuen Tsang (Beal, ii. 86), places the 'prison' or 'hell' at Pâtaliputra the capital.

Another form of the legend, which is merely referred to by Hiuen Tsang without comment, places the 'hell' at Ujjain in Mâlwa (Beal, ii. 271).

The conversion of the king, according to Hiuen Tsang, was due to the great saint Upagupta, whom he met after the destruction of the 'hell.' With the aid of Upagupta, King Asoka summoned the genii and commanded them to build *stûpas* throughout the land for the reception of the relics of Buddha's body, which had been taken out of the eight *stûpas* where they had originally been enshrined after the cremation of the Sâkya sage. At the moment of a solar eclipse the genii, in obedience to the commands of the king and the saint, simultaneously deposited the relics in all the *stûpas*.

The *Avadâna* story is that when King Asoka desired to distribute the sacred relics of the body of Buddha among the eighty-four thousand *stûpas* erected by himself, he opened the *Stûpa* of the Urn, wherein King Ajâtasatru had enshrined the cremation relics collected from seven of the eight original *stûpas*. The eighth, that at Râmagrâma, was defended by the guardian Nâgas, who would not allow it to be opened. The relics thus withdrawn from the *Stûpa* of the Urn were distributed among eighty-four thousand *stûpas*, 'resplendent as the autumn clouds,' which were erected in a single day by the descendant of the Mauryas. 'The worshipful, the fortunate Maurya caused the erection of all these *stûpas* for the benefit of created beings; formerly he was called on earth Asoka the Wicked, but this good work has earned for him the name of Asoka the Pious[1].'

The metrical *Avadâna* is still more extravagant than the prose form of the tale, and alleges that 3,510 millions of *stûpas* were erected at the request of the people of Taxila, and that ten millions were erected by the Yakshas on the shores of the sea.

THE PILGRIMAGE OF ASOKA

Having erected the eighty-four thousand *stûpas*, King Asoka expressed a desire to visit the holy places of his religion. By the advice of his counsellors he sent for the saint Upagupta, son of Gupta the perfumer. Upagupta had been in accordance with prophecy born a century after the death of Buddha, and, when summoned by the king, was dwelling on Mount Urumunda in the Natabhatika forest near Mathurâ.

The saint accepted the royal invitation, and, accom-

[1] This passage proves that the hero of the *Asokâvadâna* is Asoka Maurya.

panied by eighteen thousand holy men, travelled in state by boat down the Jumna and Ganges to Pâtaliputra, where he was received with the utmost reverence and honour [1].

The king said: 'I desire to visit all the places where the Venerable Buddha stayed, to do honour unto them, and to mark each with an enduring memorial for the instruction of the most remote posterity.' The saint approved of the project, and undertook to act as guide. Escorted by a mighty army the monarch visited all the holy places in order.

The first place visited was the Lumbini Garden. Here Upagupta said: 'In this spot, great king, the Venerable One was born [2]'; and added: 'Here is the first monument consecrated in honour of the Buddha, the sight of whom is excellent. Here, the moment after his birth, the recluse took seven steps upon the ground.'

The king bestowed a hundred thousand gold pieces on the people of the place, and built a *stûpa.* He then passed on to Kapilavastu.

The royal pilgrim next visited the Bodhi-tree at Bodh Gayâ, and there also gave a largess of a hundred thousand gold pieces, and built a *chaitya.* Rishipatana (Sârnâth) near Benares, where Gautama had 'turned the wheel of the law,' and Kusinagara, where the Teacher had passed away, were also visited

[1] Compare the story of Tishya, son of Moggali, in the 'Legend of the Third Church Council' in chapter vi, p. 215, above.

[2] Compare the Rummindeî pillar inscription in chapter v.

with similar observances. At Srâvastî the pilgrims did reverence to the Jetavana monastery, where Gautama had so long dwelt and taught, and to the *stûpas* of his disciples, Sâriputra, Maudgalâyana, and Mahâ Kâsyapa. But when the king visited the *stûpa* of Vakkula, he gave only one copper coin, inasmuch as Vakkula had met with few obstacles in the path of holiness, and had done little good to his fellow creatures. At the *stûpa* of Ânanda, the faithful attendant of Gautama, the royal gift amounted to six million gold pieces.

THE STORY OF VÎTÂSOKA.

Vîtâsoka, the king's brother[1], was an adherent of the Tîrthyas, who reproached the Buddhist monks as being men who loved pleasure and feared pain. Asoka's efforts to convert his brother were met by the retort that the king was merely a tool in the hands of the monks. The king therefore resolved to effect his brother's conversion by stratagem.

At his instigation the ministers tricked Vîtâsoka into the assumption of the insignia of royalty. The king when informed of what had happened feigned great anger, and threatened his brother with instant death. Ultimately he was persuaded to grant the offender seven days' respite, and to permit him to exercise sovereign power during those seven days. During this period the fear of death so wrought upon

[1] Vîtâsoka = Vigatâsoka.

the mind of Vîtâsoka that he embraced the doctrine of Buddha, in which he was instructed by the holy Sthavira Yasas. With difficulty the king was persuaded by the Sthavira Yasas[1] to grant to his brother permission to become a monk. In order to initiate the novice gradually into the habits of the life of a mendicant friar, Asoka prepared a hermitage for him within the palace grounds. From this hermitage Vîtâsoka withdrew, first to the Kukkutârâma monastery, and afterwards to Videha (Tirhût), where he attained to the rank of a saint (*arahat*). When Vîtâsoka, clad in rags, returned to the palace, he was received with great honour, and was induced to exhibit his supernatural powers. He then again withdrew to a distant retreat beyond the frontier, where he fell ill. Asoka sent him medicine, and he recovered.

In those days it happened that a devoted adherent of the Brahman ascetics threw down and broke a statue of Buddha at Pundra Vardhana in Bengal. As a penalty for the sacrilege eighteen thousand inhabitants of that city were massacred in one day by order of Asoka. Some time after another fanatic at Pâtaliputra similarly overthrew a statue of Buddha. The persons concerned, with all their relatives and friends, were

[1] The Ceylonese Mahâvaṁsa (ch. iv) represents the Sthavira Yasas (Yaso) as a leading personage at the Second or Vaisâli Council in the reign of Kâlâsoka, or Asoka I. This fact is one of the many indications that Kâlâsoka probably is a fiction, and that certainly no reliance can be placed on the accounts of any of the three church councils.

burned alive, and the king placed the price of a *dînâra* on the head of every Brahmanical ascetic.

Now, when the proclamation was published Vîtâsoka, clad in his beggar's garb, happened to be lodging for the night in the hut of a cowherd. The good wife, seeing the unkempt and dishevelled appearance of her guest, was convinced that he must be one of the proclaimed ascetics, and persuaded her husband to slay him in order to earn the reward. The cowherd carried his victim's head to the king, who was horrified at the sight, and was persuaded by his ministers to revoke the proclamation. Not only did he revoke the cruel proclamation, but he gave the world peace by ordaining that henceforth no one should be put to death [1].

In Fa-hien's version of the legend the brother of the king is anonymous. The pilgrim tells us that the younger brother of King Asoka lived the life of a recluse on the Vulture's Peak hill near Râjagriha, where he had attained to the rank of a saint (*arhat*). The king invited the recluse to the palace, but the invitation was declined. The king then promised that if his brother would accept the invitation, he would make a hill for him inside the city. 'Then the king, providing all sorts of meat and drink, invited the genii, and addressed them thus: "I beg you to accept my invitation for to-morrow; but as there are no seats, I must request you each to bring

[1] The inscriptions prove that Asoka did not abolish capital punishment.

his own." On the morrow the genii guests came, each one bringing with him a huge stone, four or five paces square. After the feast, he deputed the genii to pile up their seats, and make a great stone mountain; and at the base of the mountain with five massive square stones to make a rock chamber, in length about 35 feet, and in breadth 22 feet, and in height 71 feet or so.'

The same story is told by Hiuen Tsang in order to explain the origin of the stone dwelling which was still to be seen at Pâtaliputra in the seventh century A.D.[1] The name of Mahendra is given to the hermit-prince by Hiuen Tsang, who relates of him a legend, which may be compared with that of Vitâsoka. The two stories have some points in common.

THE STORY OF MAHENDRA, AND THE CONVERSION OF CEYLON

King Asoka early in his reign had a half-brother, the son of his mother, who was younger than the king, and belonged to a noble family. The young man was extravagant, wasteful, and cruel in disposition. In his dress also he aped the royal costume.

The indignation of the people became so great that the ministers ventured to remonstrate with the king,

[1] Beal, ii. 91. Major Waddell identifies Mahendra's Hill with the Bhikhna Pahârî at Patna, on which the Nawâb's palace stands, and states that the neighbouring *muhalla*, or ward, is called Mahendru. But the matter is doubtful.

and to say: 'Your majesty's brother in his pride assumes a dignity beyond his due. When the government is impartial, the subjects are contented; when the subjects are content, the sovereign is at peace. We desire that you should preserve the principles of government handed down to us by our fathers, and that you should deliver to justice the men who seek to change those principles.'

Then King Asoka, weeping, addressed his brother and said: 'I have inherited from my ancestors the duty of protecting my people; how is it that you, my own brother, have forgotten my affection and kindness? It is impossible for me at the very beginning of my reign to disregard the laws. If I punish you, I dread the resentment of my ancestors; if I pass over your transgressions, I dread the ill opinion of my people.'

The prince, bowing his head, admitted his error, and begged for nothing more than a respite of seven days[1]. The king granted this request, and threw his brother into a dark dungeon, though he provided him with exquisite food and all other luxuries. At the end of the first day the guard cried out to the prisoner: 'One day has gone; six days are left.' By the time the sixth day had expired, the prisoner's repentance and discipline were complete. He attained at once to the rank of a saint (*arahat*), and feeling conscious of miraculous powers, ascended into the air.

[1] Compare the Ceylonese 'Story of Tishya, the Vicegerent' in chapter vi, p. 244, above.

Asoka went in person to the dungeon, and told his brother that having now, contrary to expectation, attained the highest degree of holiness he might return to his place. Mahendra replied that he had lost all taste for the pleasures of the world, and desired to live in solitude. Asoka consented, but pointed out that it was unnecessary for the prince to retire to the mountains, as a hermitage could be constructed at the capital. The king then caused the genii to build a stone house, as already related.

Mahendra, after his conversion, journeyed to the south of India, and built a monastery in the delta of the Kâverî (Cauvery), of which the ruins were still visible nine hundred years later [1].

He is also related to have made use of his supernatural powers to pass through the air to Ceylon, in which island he spread the knowledge of the true law, and widely diffused the doctrine bequeathed to his disciples by the Master. From the time of Mahendra, the people of Ceylon, who had been addicted to a corrupt form of religion, forsook their ancient errors and heartily accepted the truth. The conversion of Ceylon, according to Hiuen Tsang, took place one hundred years after the death of Buddha [2].

[1] Beal, ii. 231.

[2] Beal, ii. 246. Compare the legends of the Mahâvaṁsa and Dîpavaṁsa. Hiuen Tsang, like the *Asokâvadâna*, placed Asoka Maurya a century after Buddha, the date assigned by the Ceylonese legend to Kâlâsoka.

THE STORY OF KUNÂLA

In the seventh century A.D. pilgrims were shown a *stûpa* at Taxila, which was said to have been built by Asoka to mark the spot where the eyes of his beloved son Kunâla were torn out. The story of Kunâla is to the following effect.

After the death of his faithful consort Asandhimitrâ, King Asoka, late in life, married Tishyarakshitâ, a dissolute and unprincipled young woman. She cast amorous glances on her stepson Kunâla, her worthy predecessor's son, who was famous for the beauty of his eyes. The virtuous prince rejected with horror the advances made by his stepmother, who then became filled with 'the spite of contemned beauty [1],' and changed her hot love into bitter hate. In pursuance of a deep-laid scheme for the destruction of him who by his virtue had put her vice to shame, the queen with honied words persuaded the king to depute Kunâla to the government of distant Taxila.

The prince obediently accepted the honourable commission, and when departing was warned by his father to verify orders received, which, if genuine, would be sealed with an impression of the king's teeth [2]. The queen bided her time, with ever-growing

[1] *Spretae iniuria formae* (Virgil).

[2] Mr. Beal has cited an exact English parallel in the verses describing the gift of lands to the Rawdon family, as quoted in Burke's *Peerage*, s. v. Hastings:

hatred. After the lapse of some months she wrote a dispatch, addressed to the viceroy's ministers at Taxila, directing them immediately on receipt of the orders to put out the eyes of the viceroy, Prince Kunâla, to lead him and his wife into the mountains, and to there leave them to perish.

She sealed the dispatch with royal red wax, and, when the king was asleep, furtively stamped the wax with the impression of his teeth, and sent off the orders with all speed to Taxila. The ministers who received the orders knew not what to do. The prince, noticing their confusion, compelled them to explain. The ministers wished to compromise by detaining the prince in custody, pending a reference to the capital. But the prince would not permit of any delay, and said: 'My father, if he has ordered my death, must be obeyed; and the seal of his teeth is a sure sign of the correctness of the orders. No mistake is possible.' He then commanded an outcaste wretch to pluck out his eyes. The order was obeyed, and the prince, accompanied by his faithful wife, wandered forth in sightless misery to beg his bread.

In the course of their weary wanderings they arrived at Pâtaliputra. 'Alas,' cried the blind man, 'what

'I, William, king, the third of my reign,
Give to Paulyn Rawdon, Hope and Hopetowne,
. . . .
And in token that this thing is sooth,
I bit the whyt wax with my tooth.
Before Meg, Mawd, and Margery,
And my third son Henry.' (*Ind. Ant.* ix. 86.)

pain I suffer from cold and hunger. I was a prince; I am a beggar. Would that I could make myself known, and get redress for the false accusations brought against me.' He managed to penetrate into an inner court of the palace, where he lifted up his voice and wept, and, to the sound of a lute, sang a song full of sadness.

The king in an upper chamber heard the strains, and thinking that he recognized the voice and touch as those of his son, sent for the minstrel. The king, when he beheld his sightless son, was overwhelmed with grief, and inquired by whose contrivance all this misery had come about. The prince humbly replied: 'In truth, for lack of filial piety I have thus been punished by Heaven. On such and such a day suddenly came a loving order, and I, having no means of excusing myself, dared not shrink from the punishment.'

The king, knowing in his heart that Queen Tishyarakshitâ was guilty of the crime, without further inquiry caused her to be burnt alive, and visited with condign punishment every person, high or low, who had any share in the outrage. The officials were some dismissed, some banished, some executed. The common people were, according to one account, massacred, and, according to another, transported across the Himâlayas to the deserts of Khotan[1].

[1] Beal, i. 143, ii. 310; Burnouf, p. 360. Compare the wild Tibetan legends about the introduction of Buddhism into Khotan in Rockhill, *The Life of the Buddha*, pp. 232 *seqq.*; and Stein,

In those days a great saint named Ghosha dwelt in the monastery by the holy tree of Mahâbodhi. To him the king brought Kunâla, and prayed that his son might receive his sight. The saint commanded that on the morrow a great congregation should assemble to hear his preaching of the Law, and that each person should bring a vessel to receive his tears. A vast multitude of men and women assembled, and there was not one of those who heard the sermon but was moved to tears, which fell into the vessels provided.

The saint collected the tears in a golden vase, and said these words: 'The doctrine which I have expounded is the most mysterious of Buddha's teaching; if that exposition is not true, if there is error in what I have said, then let things remain as they are; but, if what I have said is true and free from error, let this man, after washing his eyes with these tears, receive his sight.'

Whereupon Kunâla washed in the tears and received his sight.

A STORY OF TISHYARAKSHITÂ

Tishyarakshitâ, queen of King Asoka, in pursuance of her incestuous passion for her stepson, Prince Kunâla, who repulsed her advances, resolved to avenge herself, and, in order to accomplish her purpose, took advan-

Ancient Khotan, 1907, pp. 158–164. These legends mention the saint Yaśas. The story of Kunâla is folklore. Compare the legend of Phaedra and Hippolytus, and Jâtaka No. 472 (*Mahâpaduma*) in the translation by Mr. Rouse, who cites other Indian parallels (vol. iv, p. 117).

tage of the king's sufferings from a dangerous and apparently incurable disease, to acquire complete control over his mind, and for some days she was granted unrestrained use of the sovereign power.

Asoka, believing his malady to be incurable, gave the order: 'Send for Kunâla; I wish to place him on the throne. What use is life to me?' Tishyarakshitâ hearing these words, thought to herself: 'If Kunâla ascends the throne, I am lost.' Accordingly she said to King Asoka: 'I undertake to restore you to health, but a necessary condition is that you forbid all physicians to have access to the palace.' The king complied with her request, and she enjoined everybody to bring to her any person, man or woman, who might be suffering from the same malady as the king.

Now it happened that a man of the shepherd caste was suffering from the same malady. His wife explained his case to a physician, who promised to prescribe a suitable remedy after examining the patient. The man then consulted the physician, who brought him to Queen Tishyarakshitâ. She had him conveyed to a secret place, where he was put to death. When his body was opened she perceived in his stomach a huge worm, which had deranged the bodily functions. She applied pounded pepper and ginger without effect, but when the worm was touched with an onion, he died immediately, and passed out of the intestines. The queen then begged the king to eat an onion and so recover his health. The king replied: 'Queen, I am a Kshatriya; how can I eat an onion?'

'My lord,' answered the queen, 'you should swallow it merely as physic in order to save your life.' The king then ate the onion, and the worm died, passing out of the intestines[1].

THE DOTAGE OF KING ASOKA

The king resolved to give a thousand millions of gold pieces to the Master's service, and when far advanced in years had actually given nine hundred and sixty millions. In the hope that the vow would be completed before he died he daily sent great treasures of silver and gold to the Kukkutârâma monastery at the capital. In those days Sampadî, the son of Kunâla[2], was heir-apparent. To him the ministers pointed out that the king was ruining himself by his extravagance, and would, if permitted to continue it, be unable to resist the attacks of other monarchs or to protect the kingdom.

The prince, therefore, forbade the treasurer to comply with the king's demands. Asoka, unable to obtain

[1] Fa-hien (ch. xvi) notes that the inhabitants of Gangetic India did not 'eat garlic or onions, with the exception of Chaṇḍâlas (outcastes) only.' The prejudice exists to this day. The high-caste people perceive in onions a fanciful resemblance to flesh meat. This story is from the Kunâla section of the *Divyâvadâna* in Burnouf, 'Introduction,' p. 133.

[2] The Jain legends represent Sampadi (Samprati) as a great patron of the Jain church. Nothing authentic is known about him. The legend of Asoka's dotage is given by Burnouf, 2nd ed., pp. 381 *seqq.* Compare the Ceylonese story of 'The Last Days of Asoka' in chapter vi, *ante*, p. 245.

supplies from the treasury, began to give away the plate which furnished the royal table, first the gold, next the silver, and finally the iron. When all the metallic ware had been exhausted, the ministers furnished the king's table with earthenware. Then Asoka demanded of them, 'Who is king of this country?' The ministers did obeisance and respectfully replied: 'Your majesty is king.' Asoka burst into tears, and cried: 'Why do you say from kindness what is not true? I am fallen from my royal state. Save this half-apple[1] there is nought of which I can dispose as sovereign.' Then the king sent the half-apple to the Kukkutârâma monastery, to be divided among the monks, who should be addressed in this wise: 'Behold, this is my last gift; to this pass have come the riches of the emperor of India. My royalty and my power have departed; deprived of health, of physic, and of physicians, to me no support is left save that of the Assembly of the saints. Eat this fruit, which is offered with the intent that the whole Assembly may partake of it, my last gift.'

Once more King Asoka asked his minister Râdhagupta: 'Who is sovereign of this country?' The minister did obeisance and respectfully replied: 'Sire, your majesty is sovereign of this country.'

King Asoka, recovering his composure, responded in verse, and said:—

This earth, encinctured by its sapphire zone,
This earth, bedecked with gleaming jewels rare,

[1] *Amalaka* fruit, *Emblica officinalis*.

This earth, of hills the everlasting throne,
This earth, of all creation mother fair,
I give to the Assembly.

The blessing which attends such gift be mine;
Not Indra's halls nor Brahmâ's courts I crave,
Nor yet the splendours which round monarchs shine,
And pass away, like rushing Gangâ's wave,
Abiding not a moment.

With faith unchangeable, which nought can shake,
This gift of Earth's immeasurable sphere
I to the Saints' Assembly freely make;
And self-control I crave, of boons most dear,
A good which changeth never[1].

King Asoka, having thus spoken, sealed the deed of gift, and presently fulfilled the law of mortality.

The forty millions of gold pieces which yet remained to complete King Asoka's vow for the gift of a thousand

[1] According to Fa-hien (chapter xxvii), this gift of the empire was recorded in an inscription on a stone pillar to the south of Pâṭaliputra. The site of the pillar has not been identified with certainty. The speech of Asoka in prose is as follows:—

'This earth, which ocean enwraps in a glorious garment of sapphire, this earth whereof the face is adorned with mines of diverse jewels, this earth, which supports all creatures and Mount Madara, I give to the Assembly.

'As the reward of this good deed I desire not to dwell in the palace of Indra, nor yet in that of Brahmâ, nor do I in any wise desire the felicity of kingship, which, quicker even than running water, passes away and is gone.

'The reward which I crave for the perfect faith whereby I make this gift is that self-control which the saints honour, and which is a good exempt from change.'

millions, were expended by the ministers in the redemption of the earth, and Sampadî was placed upon the vacant throne. He was succeeded by his son Vrihaspati, who was succeeded in order by Vrishasena, Pushyadharma, and Pushpamitra.

APPENDIX

By the kindness of Dr. Bloch and of Major Alcock, I. M.S., Superintendent of the Indian Museum, Calcutta, I am able to give the following list of casts of the Asoka inscriptions in the Indian Museum:—

I. The Fourteen Rock Edicts and Kalinga Edicts:—Girnâr, Dhauli, Jaugaḍa, Kâlsî, Shâhbâzgaṛhi, Mânsahra (except the fourth portion, containing Edict XIII).

II. Minor Rock Edicts:—Sahasrâm and Siddâpura (except version No. III, from Jaṭinga-Râmeśvara).

III. Cave Inscriptions:—The three Barâbar Hill records of Asoka and the three Nâgârjuni Hill records of Daśaratha.

IV. The Tarâi Pillars: — Niglîva and Rummindêi (Paḍariâ).

V. Pillar Edicts and Minor Pillar Edicts:—Allahabad (including the Queen's and Kauśâmbî Edicts), Lauṛiyâ-Ararâj, Lauṛiyâ-Nandangaṛh (Navandgaṛh).

The original Bhâbrû Inscription was preserved in the rooms of the Asiatic Society of Bengal, and is now in the Indian Museum.

Casts of some of the inscriptions also exist in the Provincial Museum, Lucknow.

INDEX

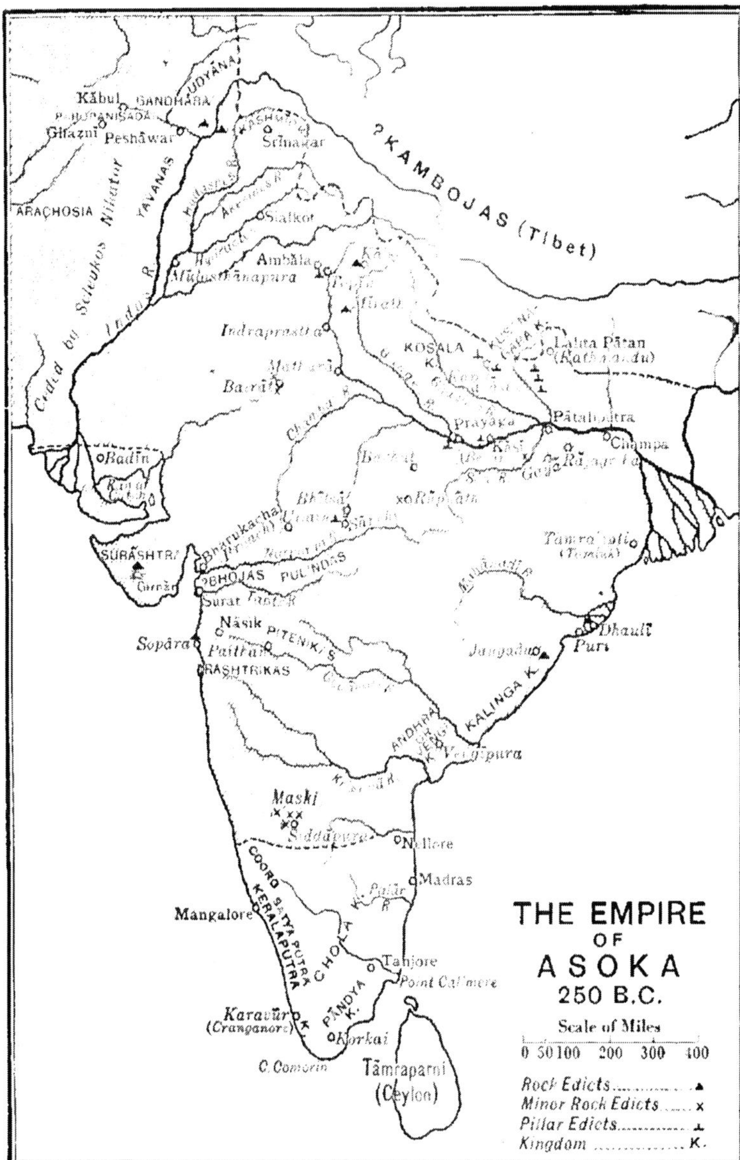

WAXTYPE

GEORGE PHILIP & SON, LTD.